THE NOTTINGHAM
LABOUR MOVEMENT
1880-1939

PETER WYNCOLL

LAWRENCE AND WISHART

London

Lawrence and Wishart Limited
39 Museum Street
London WC1A 1LQ

First published 1985

Photoset in North Wales by
Derek Doyle & Associates, Mold, Clwyd
Printed and bound in Great Britain by
Oxford University Press

Contents

Part Three: Struggles and Setbacks: The Inter-War Years
1918 to 1939

Illustrations

Foreword

The author of this book died on 22 September 1982. He was forty-three years old.

Peter Wyncoll was born in Nottingham on 24 May 1939, and Nottingham remained the focus of his political and intellectual interests throughout his life. His father came originally from Banbury in Oxfordshire and was by training an engineer. During the Second World War he worked in an armaments factory in Nottingham and it was there that after the war was over he set up his own photographic business. He had married a young woman who was working as a secretary in Boots, the great firm of pharmaceutical retailers and they had three children: Peter was the eldest, and there were two daughters. Peter went to state schools; he failed the eleven plus, in those early post-war years the great divide which children had to cross before they could then climb onto a higher level of educational opportunity, and he left school at fifteen: one of the very many examples of the victims of the tyranny of wrong-headed ideas about intellectual potential and development. At this time it was firmly believed by the great majority of educationalists that intelligence really could be measured, and predicted, at the age of eleven or twelve.

On leaving school Peter went to work in his father's business. He was obviously interested in politics from an early age since he joined a union and also the Young Socialists, later becoming the Nottingham Area Secretary. At some point he became secretary of one of the Labour Party wards, and he twice stood, unsuccessfully, for the local council. But in addition to his political work in the town he developed a growing interest in the history of the labour movement, and in general the picture we have of Peter in the late 1950s and early 1960s is of a young man who was rapidly extending and expanding his intellectual and political horizons, full of ideas and bustling with energy. He was awarded a Labour Party scholarship in 1964 to study at Ruskin College, Oxford and he passed the Diploma in Politics and Economics, awarded by the University of Oxford, two years later. Ruskin was a good place for a young socialist in the mid-1960s. It was attracting an interesting range of working-class ability and it was intellectually lively. In the same year that Peter completed his Diploma course, he was awarded a Mature State Scholarship for a study of Chartism in Nottingham which was later published by the Nottingham Trades Council. The scholarship, which gave him entry to a number of universities, Peter took to the University of Hull which at this time had a close connection with Ruskin. He read for a joint degree in Politics and American Studies and graduated in 1969. During his years as a student he continued to be active in politics and was chairman of the University Socialist Society.

In the same summer as he graduated he was appointed to the full time staff of the National Union of Public Employees (NUPE). He first lived in Northampton, and was responsible for union work in Northamptonshire, Leicestershire and Rutland and in the towns of Peterborough and Derby: a heavy responsibility for someone just thirty years old. In 1974 he moved to Coalville, in Leicestershire and three years later he was promoted within the Union to an Assistant Divisional Officer, responsible for Northamptonshire, Derbyshire and Leicestershire. He was in charge of the divisional educational programme which he especially enjoyed and at which he worked with great enthusiasm. Education, whether his own or adult education in general, was always a central interest. His own book collecting was on a very considerable scale and he read what he collected. His continued interest in the history of the labour movement in general and in his own region above all remained central to his socialist ideals. He taught WEA classes for many years, mainly on subjects that related to the labour movement in the East Midlands; and to improve his teaching methods he took a two year evening course at Coalville Technical College which gave him an Adult Teaching certificate – with distinctions in all papers – in 1978.

Union organisers do not expect to work straight office hours. There are branch meetings to attend, executive committees to prepare for, industrial negotiations to be undertaken, members to be supported and encouraged: a good union organiser, as Peter was, always works in other people's time. The work demands stamina, commitment and an ever-present recognition that working men and women without their union will fall back in personal dignity and suffer material deprivation. Peter knew these things above all because so many of his members were in low-paid jobs. Large numbers belonged to ethnic minorities who were constantly encountering racial prejudice, to be added to their lowly position in the wages league; and Peter, who fought steadily for all his members, experienced abuse and vilification from too many of his own colour. He had ideas in his union work; it was his suggestion that encouraged an interest in banners for NUPE branches, and the first was made in 1973 for the Northamptonshire branches; and it was Peter who was the main initiative behind the launching in 1978 of an East Midlands divisional newspaper, which still continues.

Exactly when he decided to work for a doctorate is not quite clear, but he had been collecting material since his undergraduate days: both oral testimony and printed materials. He applied to the Open University to register for a Ph.D. and it was arranged that the present writer would act as supervisor. Peter came over to Hull every few months and there was correspondence and telephone conversations in between the visits. Only those who have worked for doctorates or undertaken research for a book can really appreciate the dedication involved in preparing a thesis at the same time as carrying on a job with hours that were both irregular and often long drawn out. It could not have been done without the devoted and selfless support of his wife whom he had married in 1974; but done it was, and he received his formal award some three months before he died.

Peter Wyncoll was an ordinary man with remarkable qualities. He impressed those who knew him with his love of history, his deep feeling for the working people, his own people, and their struggles and his abiding commitment for the ideas and ideals of a socialist society. All these things were natural and ordinary, to be taken for granted in the normal workaday world, except, of course, that they demand an integrity that must be continuously renewed in the workaday world. Peter Wyncoll enhanced his own life, and those who met with him. He liked the theatre, and greatly enjoyed music, especially the English music of Elgar and Vaughan Williams. He took pleasure in gardening and kept bees. He was a man of many seasons, and when he died his friends and colleagues knew that a light and an energy had gone from their own lives.

***

The city and region that are discussed at length in this book have their own peculiarities within the national pattern of social life and politics. Nottingham was a long-established hosiery town to which was added lace in the nineteenth century, and it was surrounded by hosiery villages as well as by a growing coalfield. It had a radical tradition with Fergus O'Connor as its MP for a few years from 1847, and there were always small groups of militant radicals and later socialists in the second half of the nineteenth century. But the working class politics of Nottingham offer a good example of the social and political conservatism of the skilled trades in the closing decades of the century and of the ways in which the emerging labour movement of the twentieth century have been shaped and moulded by the traditions of the past. The history of labour in Nottingham also provides interesting examples of the powerful influence of individual personalities and of the continuing effect of their ideas into later periods. No one can read this book without reflecting on the tenacity of past ideas and past traditions and of their continued importance in conditions of economic and social life which have moved away from the original structures. The social and political philosophy of A.J. Mundella which looked towards a working partnership between capital and labour exercised lasting effects upon the social consciousness of (mostly) the skilled workers in the town, and continued to exercise an influence, in general terms, when the privileged positions of the lace workers, for example, were being seriously undermined. Labour history cannot always be written in terms that generalise in broad trends, and it is not seldom that the importance of personality is underplayed in favour of more 'objective' and impersonal forces.

The miners of Nottingham and of the country provide an illuminating case study of the inter-action between the movement of social forces and the role of the individual. Nottinghamshire is a coalfield with good geological conditions. Workable seams of good quality coal lie quite close to the surface and for over a century the Nottingham coalfield has been one of high productivity, higher than average wages and a mining community with markedly conservative characteristics. The miners' leaders, and the led, were staunchly Liberal in their political affiliations in the half century before 1914; and they joined with the similarly Liberal leaderships of the lace and hosiery workers in Nottingham itself. In the lock-out of 1893 some of the mineowners broke away from the national dispute and re-opened their pits at the old rate of wages, and had the Miners' Federation not been agreeable to the Nottinghamshire miners returning to work, it is possible that the county union would have sought an industrial independence of the kind that George Spencer initiated after the General Strike of 1926. The political and industrial stance of the Nottinghamshire miners in the national strike of 1984-85 has a very long history, and very powerful roots in their past.

It is the intimate, indeed integral, relationships between economic structures and social consciousness that makes this study of Nottingham so very interesting, and among the many generalisations it provokes is the way in which the different parts of the industrial labour force were and are affected by the dominant climate of opinion in the town and the region. The prevalence of Lib-Lab ideas which so powerfully restricted the growth of a labour-socialist consciousness among the skilled workers, or those who had at some stage enjoyed a privileged position, would also seem to have affected the thinking and the practice of other, often newer, industrial groups. Engineering is one example. Militant consciousness, either industrial or political, is not wholly a product of the work-place; and the influence of community is a subject that those concerned with the delineation of social consciousness cannot afford to deny. It is, for example, reasonable to argue that the mixing of miners within the boundaries of Nottingham town itself has some influence upon their political attitudes, although this is not to argue that it was of major significance. But no analysis is mono-causal; it must always be assumed to be complex. It would, for instance, be interesting to compare the mixed Lib-Lab community of Nottingham miners with the Lib-Lab villages of many parts of the Durham coalfield to illustrate the general point being made here.

The labour history of one town is always a helpful addition to our understanding of the many strands which have gone to the moulding of the British working class in the last hundred years, and this study of Nottingham offers both confirmation of old generalisations and material for new thinking and new departures. The publishers and myself are greatly indebted to Ms Sandra Taylor for the considerable work she undertook in preparing Peter Wyncoll's thesis for publication; and we are equally indebted to the permanent officials of the National Union of Public Employees for their generous and continuous support. Above all, on behalf of all Peter Wyncoll's friends and colleagues, I must offer our grateful thanks for her help to Peter's widow, Wendy. To her we present this volume as an indication of the respect and affection that we all had for a very fine comrade and friend.

March 1985   JOHN SAVILLE

Acknowledgements

In the course of writing this book many debts have been incurred. Foremost amongst these is that to Professor John Saville of the University of Hull, whose thoughtful comments and kind encouragement have done a great deal to ensure that the task was completed. I am also indebted for assistance to the staffs of many libraries and institutions but particularly to the staff of the Nottingham Public Library and of the Nottingham University Library. I would also like to thank the local Studies Library of the Nottinghamshire County Library for permission to reproduce photographs, including that on the front cover.

I also wish to place on record my thanks to the many veterans of the Nottingham labour movement, who were prepared to allow me into their homes in order to share their memories of the labour movement between the two World Wars.

The general secretary and the national executive of the National Union of Public Employees also deserve thanks for their kindness in allowing a period of leave of absence without which the book could never have been completed. Particular thanks are due to my fellow full-time officers of NUPE in the East Midlands Division whose willingness to cover my normal work load during my sabbatical leave was such a very great help.

Finally, I must place on record the debt which I owe my wife, both for her assistance in preparing and typing the manuscript and for her patience and understanding throughout the project.

Peter Wyncoll,
May 1981

Abbreviations

AEU	Amalgamated Engineering Union
ASE	Amalgamated Society of Engineers
ASLEF	Associated Society of Locomotive Engineers and Firemen
BSP	British Socialist Party
CP	Communist Party
ILP	Independent Labour PARTY
LNER	London and North Eastern Railway
LRC	Labour Representation Committee
MFGB	Miners' Federation of Great Britain
NAC	National Administrative Council
NCLC	National Council of Labour Colleges
NMA	Nottinghamshire Miners' Association
NUDAW	National Union of Distributive and Allied Workers
NUGMW	National Union of General and Municipal Workers
NUPE	National Union of Public Employees
NUR	National Union of Railwaymen
NUWM	National Unemployed Workers' Movement
OMS	Organisation for Maintenance of Supplies
PAC	Public Assistance Committee
SDF	Social Democratic Federation
SDP	Social Democratic Party
SLP	Socialist Labour Party
UAB	Unemployed Assistance Board
UDC	Urban District Council
WSPU	Womens Social and Political Union

Introduction

This study of the labour movement in Nottingham, from 1880 to 1939, sets out to examine, at the local level, the development of working-class political struggle in a period when socialism in all its varied forms was becoming a major influence. The main concern is to attempt to understand why it was that in 1873 Nottingham was referred to as a 'Banner town, always at or near the front of Reform Movements',[1] whilst by 1918 it was considered by many to be the 'Despair of Labour Politicians'.[2] Nottingham was a great city of commerce and industry which developed a labour movement that in the early years of the nineteenth century gave the word 'Luddite' to the language and in 1847 elected England's only Chartist MP. In the 1870s the secretary of the town's branch of the First International wrote a remarkable pamphlet about the Paris Commune which drew the attention of Karl Marx.[3] Despite this early radicalism, by the early twentieth century Nottingham's labour movement lagged behind that of other towns.

Part of the explanation of this apparent paradox may be found in an analysis of the organisation of labour within Nottingham's major industries, lace and hosiery. The sophisticated division of labour gave rise to an 'aristocratic' Lib-Lab stratum which for forty years controlled institutions like the local Trades Council. Less certainly, it seems possible that the geological conditions of the Nottinghamshire coalfield, and the political dominance of Liberal coal-owners, may have dampened the potential militancy of the mining community. Certainly the role played by the Nottinghamshire Miners' Association (NMA) was one which cramped and retarded the local labour movement.

In 1880 very few members of the Nottingham labour movement could remember the election of Fergus O'Connor as the town's Chartist Member of Parliament in 1847, and fewer still the burning of the castle in the Reform Bill riots of 1831. It must have seemed to many that socialism in Britain was almost extinct, suffocated by the development of reformist policies, and weakened by the abandonment of an independent class outlook by leading sections of the trade union movement.

After the failure of the final Chartist petition in 1848 and despite the efforts of a brave group of Nottingham supporters of the First International in the late 1860s and early 1870s, many of the ideas and ambitions of the first socialists had virtually disappeared. Large sections of the organised workers became the left wing of the Liberal Party and the loss of socialist aims, perspectives and organisation slowed the independent political advance of the working class for a long period.[4]

This check to labour's political advance led Frederick Engels in 1881 to describe the working-class movement as 'the tail of the Great Liberal Party'.[5] Certainly, only a close inspection of the Nottingham political scene affords any indication of socialist activity in 1880. During the course of the year a general election made clear that the hold of the Liberal Party on the town's working-class vote was as strong as ever:

Seely	(Liberal)	8,499
Wright	(Liberal)	8,055
Isaac	(Conservative)	5,575
Gill	(Conservative)	5,052

This result was mirrored in many other towns and it is significant that in the whole country only three working men were returned as Members of Parliament, all of them Liberals.

The basis for results like these was, of course, the strength and resilience of British capitalism. By the 1880s underlying economic trends were beginning to threaten the stability of British society. As these trends began to force political and social change the first signs of a socialist revival among scattered groups of middle-class idealists and thoughtful working men could be seen. Britain's world supremacy was being seriously challenged by about 1875. The years which followed were marked by a long series of economic crises. Prices fell, markets became saturated and profit margins were squeezed. All of these developments were seriously to affect Nottingham's traditional industries of lace and hosiery.

Coinciding with this depression, British capitalism began to develop to the stage of monopoly. In Nottingham the employers in both the lace and hosiery industries responded to the threat of increasing competition by moving their machines out of town into country areas where labour was cheaper. In 1886 William Mansell, secretary of the Nottingham Stonemasons, told the Royal Commission on the Depression of Trade and Industry that both the lace and hosiery trade were 'going away from

the town (abroad) and to small villages adjacent to the town'.[6] William
Flint, who gave evidence to the Commission on behalf of the Nottingham
branch of the Amalgamated Society of Engineers, described his industry
as being 'very much depressed' and advanced the view that 'great
over-production of late years in the lace machines',[7] was its major cause.
In the lace trade the depression was ascribed to the demands of the trade
unions, but the president of the Lace Manufacturers' Association told the
Royal Commission in 1886 that the Nottingham twist-hands were
co-operative and had within the last year agreed to a reduction of
between 15 and 20 percent in their rates.

The real reasons for the slump in this period were much more
complicated. Many factors were involved in generating the crisis of
British capitalism in the 1880s, including over-production and the impact
of foreign competition. These, however, were the most important agents
making for important new developments within the British labour
movement, which, as the crisis deepened, led to a growing questioning of
the existing social order by increasing numbers of workers. It was this
questioning which led to the revival of socialist thought and its
development in the twentieth century. The latter part of this study
assesses the culmination of this spirit, for despite earlier retardation, the
containment of Nottingham's labour movement within bourgeois
concepts of respectability and self-advancement was by 1939 shattered
by a thriving (if fragmented) movement of conscious opposition to the
existing order.

By 1901 Nottingham was established as a major industrial centre.
During the sixty years with which this study deals Nottingham continued
to expand at a great rate. In 1891 the population stood at 186,575; by
the outbreak of the Second World War it was 283,003. In 1881 most of
Nottingham's population was employed in the staple industries of hosiery
and lace. There were over 500 firms engaged in various branches of the
lace trade, whilst another 150 were involved in the manufacture of
hosiery fabrics. Throughout the next sixty years, however, the lace and
hosiery trades declined in importance in the local economy as
Nottingham industry was forced to respond to the pressures of
international and national economic change through long drawn-out
processes of diversification.

The stimulation of much of the structural economic change at the end
of the nineteenth century was the expansion of the Nottinghamshire
coalfield; indeed the coal industry expanded at a rate unimaginable
before the railway age throughout the East Midlands. Most of the
Nottinghamshire pits in this period were to the north of the city, but some

were within the boundaries or just beyond them. As a result the collier was an important member of the local community; between the years 1881 and 1891 the number of coal miners living in Nottingham rose from 3,035 to 5,027,[8] whilst by 1930 there were over 50,000 living in the county.

Once the mining industry had expanded to provide the raw material from which came the energy needed for industry, engineering and other industries were able to develop. These years were the early days of Boots, Players and Raleigh, three firms which in the years that followed became increasingly vital to the Nottingham economy. By 1930 the Raleigh Cycle Company employed 4,300, Boots over 5,000 making pharmaceutical products and the tobacco factories of John Player many thousands more.[9] Industrial developments of this size ensured that Nottingham's fame, which at the beginning of this study rested firmly on the conjunction in every Victorian window of the aspidistra and the lace curtain, had by 1939 come to rely at least in part on the major commodity needed to sustain what some have called the 'aspirin age'.[10]

The years of economic change which saw the emergence of new industries and the rationalisation of old ones also saw a transformation in the representative institutions of the working class to meet new industrial needs. Many of these new institutions retained a heritage which restricted their political identity. Like many other groups of workers, the Nottingham lace workers had built 'New Model' trade unions for their industry, in the period following the Great Exhibition of 1851. Levying high weekly subscriptions, preferring conciliation and arbitration to industrial action, and carefully monitoring the supply of skilled labour allowed entry into the industry, these trade unionists were riddled with the superior attitudes which in later years were to provide the bedrock of Lib-Labism.

During the early 1870s the lace industry started to suffer from depression, and the machinery of conciliation and arbitration began to break down. Wage rates soon came under attack and the surrender of the Levers Lace Society to employer pressure for abatements led first to its collapse and then to the formation of a breakaway organisation committed to ignoring the Arbitration Board. During the course of 1873 the situation continued to deteriorate and a strike soon followed. This dispute developed into the greatest the trade had yet seen and a great deal of bitterness was generated. Although during the strike old wounds were healed and solidarity amongst the workers restored, the strike had to be called off and defeat admitted after a struggle which had lasted several months.

The failure of this strike, further pressure on wage rates, lower profit margins and the growth of the trade outside Nottingham all helped to convince the twist-hands that only greater trade union strength and efficiency could restore their bargaining position. Accordingly, in August 1874 a new Amalgamated Society of Lace Operatives (Lace Makers' Society) was formed from the three New Model unions which had preceded it. Although numerically much stronger, the Lace Makers' Society was thoroughly infected with all the weaknesses of superior craft attitudes displayed by the old organisations. These attitudes were a major stumbling block to any attempt to build any kind of working-class consciousness beyond the simple, narrow sectional interest of the skilled twist-hands, and such views were destined never to be completely purged from the organisation.

In the hosiery industry, technical developments from the 1850s onwards led to a gradual erosion of hand-frame production and the introduction of factory based mechanisation. This was an uneven process for whilst there were 1,000 power rotary-frames, 1,200 sets of circular power machines and 400 warp hosiery power-frames in Nottingham in 1865, there were also 11,000 narrow hand-frames and 4,250 wide hand frames.[11] Competition between hosiery producers was notorious, bankruptcies frequent and thrusts for increased productivity the order of the day. The result was a tendency for the larger undertaking to survive and flourish. One such company was the Nottingham Manufacturing Company, whose directors were the Liberal philanthropists Hine and Mundella.

The series of technological and organisational changes undergone by the hosiery industry during the years after 1850 had important ripple effects in the field of industrial relations and trade union organisation. Initially at least, the relatively high wages paid by employers like Mundella earned the loyalty of the workforce so that he could boast:

> Why do all the trade unions stand by me so firmly? Because I have helped to double and quadruple their wages. I don't want to dwell upon this, but since I became an employer I have carried my feelings for the work-people to the verge of Quixotism. Had I been less considerate for the good of others I should now have been a very rich man.[12]

Liberal paternalism was a key aspect in Mundella's attitude to the local working class and to this end he used his position as Liberal councillor for the elegant middle-class Park Ward on the City Council.

Mundella's influence in the town was very significant and it seems likely that he played a key role in persuading important elements in

Nottingham's ruling group that the time had come to seek an accommodation with the leading trade union personalities. In 1872, for instance, whilst a special Trades Union Congress was being held in Nottingham, Mundella persuaded the town authorities, including the Mayor, to attend the opening and to extend a hearty welcome. Later, at an official banquet at the town hall, the trade union leaders were entertained by leading citizens, including Mundella. Special excursions, 'at homes', and other 'honours' were also arranged. It seems that during the official banquet a toast to 'The Queen' brought forth a cry of 'flunkeyism', whilst half a dozen trade unionists remained seated. The majority of the trade union leadership soon acquired a taste for this kind of treatment, considering it a proof of their power and a symbol of their equality. Mundella's major role was, however, as an advocate of arbitration and conciliation. Theodore Rothstein has accused Mundella of being partly responsible for helping to smother the 'last spark of class dignity and class consciousness', and although this is something of an exaggeration there is little doubt that his ideas in the field of class collaboration did help to retard the development of a truly independent labour movement.

As the growth of mass production techniques increased the wages of the factory work-force, the obsolete outwork industry faced a deepening crisis. Resentful of the new inventions and jealous of those who worked them, the framework knitters eventually came out on strike towards the end of 1860. Other disputes quickly flared and many of the employers began to argue for a general lock-out to teach the workers a lesson. Mundella fought against this plan, insisting that it would mean 'throwing the whole population on the streets. We should have a dreadful state of commotion. We were sick of it.'[13] Instead, Mundella suggested that both sides of the industry should attend a round table conference and this eventually took place on 17 September 1860. The settlement which finally emerged conceded the wage demands of the workers whilst at the same time establishing a board of arbitration to prevent a recurrence of industrial trouble. The impact of these developments on the hosiery trade was extremely significant. One aged worker remarked: 'I have been in the hosiery trade since I was 10 years of age and I have never been at such a meeting before.'[14] Undoubtedly, Mundella's flair and intelligence was primarily responsible for the establishment of the Board of Arbitration. Its existence helped to shape the hosiery industry and its trade unions for many years to come. Equally significant was the effect of this agreement on the hearts and minds of other groups of workers. The principle of conciliation, arbitration and cooperation advocated by

Mundella struck deep roots into the Nottingham labour movement. For many years hardly a voice was raised against them whilst Mundella's own popularity was well demonstrated in 1868 when, on returning to the town after winning a Sheffield parliamentary seat, he was welcomed by a huge crowd of 20,000 at the Midland Station. Later, at his warehouse, he was presented with an Address by one of the hosiery workers. A broadsheet circulated in the town celebrated his triumph thus:

> Mundella is the poor man's friend
> And Sheffield people may rejoice
> There's none more able to defend
> Them, than the man they've made their choice.
>
> His interest is the poor man's cause,
> And all their rights he will maintain;
> His aim will be to make good laws
> Success and honour to his name.[15]

Entering his carriage, with a sax-tuba band playing, Mundella was escorted by a tremendous crowd to his residence in the Park. 'Never', wrote the *Nottingham Daily Express*, 'was a reception more hearty and generous. Everybody seemed anxious to excel everybody else in shouting out congratulations.'[16]

Numbered amongst those shouting loudest in 1868 were probably the leaders of the Rotary Framework Knitters' Society which was established in 1865. This organisation had been established in order to be officially represented on the Board of Arbitration, the success of which was already helping to produce a new respect and recognition for the workers' organisation. This recognition had the effect, initially at least, of helping the union to increase its membership, although in the long run it also helped to delay the creation of a firmly established, financially sound organisation. This dichotomy came about because confidence in the Board of Arbitration also had the effect of keeping subscriptions low, the workers relying on levies to meet any emergency.

> 'They maintain their union just as well and better with the Board as without it,' remarked Mundella. 'Their union now costs them only a shilling per year instead of a shilling per week.'[17]

It will be seen from this just how vulnerable the men's organisation really was. Completely reliant on the success of the Board, they had in the long run presented themselves as hostages to the employers.

The flaw in the arbitration machinery began to develop in the early 1870s. The workers were fundamentally split over sectional interests and petty jealousies weakened their bargaining position. Delegates from the Hand Framework Knitters were always at odds with the Circular Union (which had been formed in 1857) and with the Rotary Power Union, with the result that the workmen were consistently outvoted by the employer representatives. A number of strikes during the 1870s put the Board under increasing strain and although it continued to meet into the 1880s it was finally dissolved in 1884. It is, of course, significant that the major faults in the system of arbitration began to show themselves in the late 1870s. In this period an economic downturn meant that hosiery workers were forced to accept reductions in wages. Subsequently, several strikes for higher wages helped to accelerate the developing trend of moving machinery out of the towns into the nearby villages where labour was cheaper. By the mid 1880s this dispersion to the areas outside the town led union officials to claim that Nottingham was merely becoming a sales centre for hosiery made outside in the country districts.

The influence of Nottingham's Liberal employers on the character of working-class organisation and institutions was not only felt in hosiery, but also in the Nottinghamshire coal industry. John Edward Ellis, the Quaker proprietor of Hucknall Collieries was to become a Liberal Member of Parliament, whilst Colonel Seely of the Babbington Coal Company recognised the value of working-class votes by campaigning ardently during the 1880 general election for Liberal policies of pension reform and wage increases.[18] Men such as these were to have a crucial role in the 'liberal' stance of the miners' unions.

During the 1880s the output of the Nottinghamshire miners averaged slightly more than $5\frac{1}{4}$ million tons per annum. During the 1890s this rose to nearly 7 million tons and by 1900 the Nottinghamshire pits produced about 3 per cent of the total output of the United Kingdom.[19] Between 1881 and 1891 the mines absorbed labour at a greater rate than any other industry. Beyond the periphery of the town the opening of new pits encouraged a drift into those areas, and small mining communities began to appear as at Cinderhill, about three miles from Nottingham. Many more miners and their families congregated in the working-class areas in the Western division of the town, whilst others, after the opening of the Clifton pit between 1868 and 1869, began to live in the back-to-back housing in the Meadows area in the south of Nottingham. Unlike the workers in the Nottingham lace and hosiery industry, whose trade unions owed a great deal to the virtues advocated by Samuel Smiles, with elaborate benefits as one of the main objectives, the miners' organisation during its early period had the single aim of redressing their grievances by direct action. The contribution the miner was able to pay for his trade union membership made it impossible for the colliers' organisation to provide benefits, with the result that they were forced to concentrate on attempts to improve pay and conditions by industrial action.

Before the 1880s mining trade unionism often took on the characteristics of a mere ephemeral strike organisation, hastily thrown together in the midst of revolt. Clegg, Fox and Thompson have pointed out in their *History of British Trade Unions since 1889*, that the mining unions were in a very different position from the craft societies which were able, by a mixture of unilateral action and localised bargaining, to avoid major disputes with their employers.[20] Miners' unions, on the other hand, had to face organised groups of employers, some of whom were already setting wages and conditions over wide sections of the industry.

The 1870s witnessed a collapse in miners' unions throughout the country, largely due to an overall fall in the price of coal and the concerted demand by employers for wage cuts and the introduction of sliding scales. The Webbs, in their *History of Trade Unionism*, interpret the colliers' acceptance of a sliding scale in ideological terms, and argue that it involved

> the sturdy leaders of many trade union battles gradually and insensibly accepting the capitalists' axiom that wages must necessarily fluctuate according to the capitalists' profits.[21]

Clegg, Fox and Thompson, however, have argued that a recognition of the need for wage reductions was a condition for union survival in this period. These agreements, they claimed, demonstrate that automatic adjustments through a formal machinery were to be preferred to frontal clashes.[22] In the case of the Nottinghamshire miners both views were probably true. Compromise on wage levels possibly did help to keep some kind of rudimentary organisation together before 1881, but an examination of the political record of the leadership also indicates that key individuals in the union had been conditioned into the basic acceptance of the capitalist system.

Dr Alan Griffin, the historian of the Nottinghamshire Miners' Association, has pointed out that it was an improvement in demand which eventually ushered in the NMA in 1881. In July of that year, at a meeting held in Kimberley, a Nottinghamshire miners' union, with branches throughout the county, was formed. Amongst these branches, those at Clifton, Arnold, Bestwood and Wollaton are of particular relevance to this study since they all employed colliers who living in or close to Nottingham formed part of the local labour movement. In other parts of the country and indeed, in the northern part of Nottinghamshire, the miners' organisation was characterised by the strong corporate spirit which was generated amongst miners not only by the sharing of common danger, but from the fierce sense of community which derived from settlement in pithead mining villages. Both factors played an important part in the development of a strong mining militancy, which was, in the immediate vicinity of the town of Nottingham, seriously weakened by the intermingling of colliers with workers employed in the textile and other industries.

The last twenty years of the nineteenth century were ones in which the British economy was beginning to be restructured to meet the requirements of a rapidly changing world. The response of the working class was to reorganise in the traditional industries, and to form new organisations to represent those semi and unskilled workers who were to become a major component of the labour force. The extent to which this happened was largely dependent on the growth and adoption of socialist political perspectives. This was inevitably a protracted process, and the limitations imposed by the traditions of skilled craft unionism were to retard the emergence of new organisations, and the effectiveness of many which did. This restraint was especially felt in Nottingham, where the skilled workers of the lace and hosiery industries had preserved their status and wage bargaining power well into the 1870s.

The intention of this study is to examine the process in which new working-class organisations emerged, committed to challenging the political ideology of Lib-Labism; to detail the shifts and splits in the labour movement; and to identify the role played by the local leadership in directing the development of the movement. Overall the intention is to reveal how the character and political identity of the labour movement on the eve of the Second World War was the product of the tensions and conflicts expressed in its history.

REFERENCES

[1] *International Herald*, 15 March 1873.

[2] *Labour Leader*, 18 March 1918.

[3] Thomas Smith, 'Letters on the Commune. The Law of the Revolution: or the Logical Development of Human Society', *Nottingham Daily Express*, March 1872.

[4] There had been a strong branch of the First International in Nottingham which, under the leadership of Thomas Smith, had tried hard to keep the ideas of socialism alive. See, Henry Collins and Chimen Abramsky, *Karl Marx and the British Labour Movement*, 1965, pp. 248, 255, 269 and 275. See also Royden Harrison (ed.), *The English Defence of the Commune*, 1971, pp. 239-77.

[5] *Labour Standard*, 23 July 1881.

[6] Evidence of William Mansell, *Second Report of the Royal Commission on the Depression of Trade and Industry*, 1886, Appendix II.

[7] Evidence of William Flint, *Royal Commission on Trade and Industry*, 1886.

[8] Mineral Statistics 1869 to 1901, quoted in R.A. Church, *Economic and Social Change in a Midland Town*, 1966, p. 232.

[9] *Souvenir Programme*, Nottingham TUC, 1930.

[10] This phrase is used by Isabel Leighton, *The Aspirin Age*, 1949.

[11] Nottingham Chamber of Commerce, *Annual Report*, 1860.

[12] *Leicester Chronicle*, 6 September 1868. Quoted in W.H.G. Armytage, *The Liberal Background to the Labour Movement*, 1951, p. 23.

[13] Ibid., p. 32.

[14] Ibid., p. 33.

[15] Broadsheet in Nottingham Public Library.

[16] *Nottingham Daily Express*, 20 November 1868.

[17] *Nottingham Review*, 20 March 1968.

[18] *Nottingham Journal*, 15 March 1880.

[19] Mineral Statistics 1869 to 1901, see reference 8.

[20] H.A. Clegg, A. Fox, and A.F. Thompson, *The History of British Trade Unions since 1889*, Vol.I, 1961, p. 43.

[21] Sidney and Beatrice Webb, *The History of Trade Unionism*, 1920 edn., p. 339.

[22] Clegg, Fox, and Thompson, op. cit., p. 23.

PART ONE

The Old Order Begins
To Disintegrate
1880 to 1895

CHAPTER ONE

The Trade Union Mood

The mood and attitudes of most trade union members when this study begins were deeply conservative. They were well summed up at the 1883 Trades Union Congress which took place in Nottingham. Thomas Smith, a member of the local branch of the Lithographic Printers, was elected president and during his opening address he told the Congress:

> We have seen our local industries grow to prodigious proportions and I believe the reason for our recent period of exceptionally good trade has been mainly due to the strength and moderation of our local trade unions ... the laws of trade unions elevated the character of the workmen by cultivating habits of industry, sobriety and providence.[1]

Although most of Smith's address was full of the kind of labourist rhetoric which claimed that 'the twin elements of England's greatness were the unity and better understanding between capital and labour,' it did contain one brief but significant note of dissatisfaction with the economic system when he expressed the view that although the nation had nearly perfected the means of producing wealth, it had 'yet to learn how it is to be equitably distributed'.

This comment was almost a lone straw in the wind, for in the same year the Nottingham Association of Organised Trades boasted that its annual dinner had been attended by Henry Broadhurst, a Lib-Lab MP, and supported by 'several gentlemen of position in the town'.[2] The desire for recognition and status was a central feature of the psyche of many trade unionists and was often an important factor in hampering political progress. In November 1885, for instance, at a specially convened meeting of the Trades Council, a major disagreement ensued on the question of support for John Burns, the Social Democratic Federation (SDF) candidate for West Nottingham in the general election. Aaron Stewart, of the Nottinghamshire Miners' Association, complained that Burns, in addressing his constituents, had stated that he had the support of the trade unionists of the district. In the row which followed, Mr Samson, a delegate, emphatically denied that Burns had ever said he had the support of trade unionists in any of his addresses. Osborne of the Hosiery Workers then claimed that Burns had announced that he was backed by the trade unionists of the country, 'which very much appeared to include the Nottingham trade unionists ... in his opinion they should in no way interfere in the present election.'[3] Subsequently, as if to underline the anti-political nature of many union members, the Trades Council passed a resolution 'that this body is not in any way supporting Mr Burns or any other candidate.' In fact Robinson, the Trades Council president and several others amongst the Trades Council leadership, were active Liberal Party members.

The 'no politics' arguments which they used on this and other occasions need to be seen as part of the tactics employed by 'respectable' trade unionists who sensed that they were about to be seriously challenged by a generation of young, socialistic members. Underpinning the 'no politics' argument of the leading trade unionists in the town was the labourist philosophy which, it has been suggested, was

> the theory and practice of class collaboration; it was a tradition which in theory (always) and in practice (mostly) emphasised the unity of capital and labour, and the importance of conciliation and arbitration in industrial disputes.[4]

The truth of this judgement was often well demonstrated in Nottingham. In February 1886, for instance, the Trades Council wrote to Gladstone, the Prime Minister, in order to thank him for the appointment of Henry Broadhurst as an Under-Secretary of State, and in the same year it was reported that the Nottingham hosiery workers were attempting to reorganise their trade union, 'with a view to a more friendly relationship with the employers'.[5] This is a reference to the habit of arbitration which, under the influence of A.J. Mundella, the Nottingham hosiery manufacturer, had been such a feature of the town's lace and hosiery trades during the late 1860s and 1870s.[6]

The majority of the older generation of skilled trade unionists who dominated the Trades Council in the 1880s, had an outlook of respectable labourism. This was demonstrated at the 1889 Trade Union Congress when Corbett, a Nottingham representative of the Brickmakers' Society, attacked a group of militants who were complaining about the activities of Henry Broadhurst. According to Corbett an attempt had been made to mislead the working men of the country:

> into thinking that the trade unionists of Nottingham were directly opposed to

Mr Broadhurst. That, however, he could assure the Congress was not according to fact ... the Parliamentary Committee, its president and its secretary had the full confidence of all trade unionists in Nottingham.[7]

This spirited defence of Broadhurst could have been made by any one of a dozen of the older generation of Nottingham trade unionists. Not surprisingly, the local Liberal Party wrote to tell him that they had passed a resolution:

congratulating our member Henry Broadhurst MP upon his signal refutation of the scandalous charges that have been made against his honour and integrity as a trade unionist ... [8]

Another Nottingham correspondent wrote to say that he had:

watched with much interest the course of matters which culminated at the Trade Union Congress yesterday and am delighted that you were so triumphantly vindicated ... [9]

In fact, Corbett was wrong to suggest that Broadhurst had the 'full confidence of all trade unionists in Nottingham'. There were some amongst the most progressive elements who saw through his technique of spicing his speeches with fulsome praise for his audience.[10] Amongst the town's mining population were those who could not forgive his opposition to the Eight Hour Bill, whilst many resented his taste for the company of influential Liberals.

The desire to emulate successful men like Broadhurst was an undoubted influence on many local trade unionists. Through organised bodies many saw the opportunity of individual social mobility, status and prestige in a society which provided very limited openings for social advancement. It is in this light that Trades Council attempts to achieve official recognition should be viewed. In April 1887 the Trades Council wrote to the Lord Chancellor urging the appointment of working men on the Bench of Magistrates. In November of the same year a Trades Council deputation visited the Town Clerk in an attempt to get a share of seats on the University College Committee. In March 1889 the delegates were involved in a long discussion on the 'fitness' of a group of trade unionists who, it was proposed, should visit the Paris Exhibition at the expense of Morley, one of the Town's Liberal MPs. In December 1892 they joined in fulsome praise of Hardstaffe, the Trades Council president, who had just been appointed a Justice of the Peace.[11] In March 1891 the Mayor of Nottingham wrote to the Trades Council to request a meeting at his private residence, 'in order that he might have a chat with them on labour subjects'. Later the Trades Council's *Annual Report* boasted of the fact that the Mayor had 'honoured a section of the Trades Council with invitations to a banquet.'[12]

There can be little doubt that the strength and power of labourist ideas was deeply embedded in the local movement. Not surprisingly, however, the labourist philosophy found itself under increasing challenge as economic and social change began to make its impact on late Victorian society. In 1890, for instance, a new organisation in opposition to the Lace Operative Society which dominated the Trades Council at this time, set out its aims as being 'to correct many abuses of the past and regain for the workmen some of the ground lost to them by the present inefficient and costly Executive.' According to this group their officials had formed 'a sort of ring, who wriggle and twist and argue and expostulate before the members to such an extent that they virtually "rule the roost" '.[13] These complaints suggest some kind of aversion for the bourgeois ideology which through the medium of a range of cultural institutions had done so much to mould the generation of trade union leaders in control of the Nottingham Trades Council – bodies like the Mechanics' Institute, the Temperance Societies and the Nonconformist church which had played a vital role in dispensing the respectable wisdom and virtues so characteristic of labourism.

Opposition to the prevailing mood of conciliation was strengthened by economic transformations which increased the numbers of semi and unskilled workers. Whilst the old guard dismissed this section as unworthy of the attention of skilled trade unionists, the new, more socialist-minded unionists saw them as the key to the development of a new future. The old guard was well represented by George Allcroft, the secretary of the Nottingham No.2 branch of the ASE. When interviewed by an investigator working with the Webbs on their *History of Trade Unionism* he explained his lack of concern over the siting of the Midland Railway workshops in Derby: 'any town is better off without the crowd of wretched ill paid labour that a railway works would bring with it.' Later the Webbs researcher characterised Allcroft and his colleague Conery as 'the most old fashioned conservative engineers I have met.'[14]

The first attempts at organising a united labour movement in the form of a Trades Council had been made in 1861, very much in response to the establishment of the Nottingham Chamber of Commerce. The aim was to attain a 'peaceful settlement of labour disputes' and to avoid 'those social disasters called strikes'.[15] Dependent on protecting the status of the skilled craftsmen, this early organisation was necessarily representative of only a small section of Nottingham's working class, and as such was a weak organisation. It was not until January 1884 that the

United Trades Council of Nottingham was formed out of previous trade union alliances, and it is significant that this was the year which saw the start of a long period of heavy unemployment in Nottingham. The aims of this new organisation were:

> To afford moral assistance and sympathy to the whole of the trades in Nottingham in times of trouble, to organise trade societies for protective and friendly purposes, to bring about an amicable adjustment in cases of dispute, to petition Parliament upon questions affecting the rights of the working classes and to co-operate with similar associations.[16]

Throughout 1884 the task of consolidation was undertaken. During the early months various trades were invited to participate and as the year advanced the United Council intervened in several industrial disputes. In April support was given to striking bricklayers, and in August deputations were sent to Sir James Oldknow, owner of the Wollaton Colliery, where it was believed union activists were being victimised.[17] The unemployment statistics were a major factor in persuading the United Council of the need to extend their organisation and develop effective defences against the employers' attempts to force down wage levels. According to Harry Collier, the Secretary of the Nottingham branch of the Amalgamated Society of Carpenters and Joiners, the most prominent symptom of the depression was the employers 'taking a mean advantage of those who were employed to reduce wages, alleging that others would work for less'.[18] The annual report of the Organised Trades for 1886 emphasised this point by stating that throughout the year 'encroachments upon the wages and privileges of the working men have been continuous and severe.'

The depression of the 1880s had two effects on the working class: the erosion of status and wage rates in the skilled sector and massive unemployment and poverty amongst all other sections. The winter months of 1886-87 saw severe distress, with crowds of unemployed demonstrating in the streets, and in January the Mayor appealed for funds to provide a soup kitchen. Predictably, the United Council was divided between two courses of action, with vigorous resistance of encroachments on the status of the skilled workers on the one hand and attempts to organise the unemployed on the other. Throughout 1887 the energies of the Council were spent in resisting wage reductions: in February a threatened 11 per cent reduction for brickmakers; in August the reduction of wages of engineers and firemen employed by the Midland Railway Company; and in the same month a further attempt to reduce the wages of bricklayers.[19]

As the depression of the 1880s continued, the challenges faced by the Council became more serious and the organisation found itself increasingly involved in trying to better the lot of the poorer-paid and sweated workers. This was the period in which the movement to organise the unskilled was beginning to gather momentum and the Council did a great deal of work to help this development. A United Council enquiry into the extent of sweating in the area produced evidence of extensive sweating in the clipping and scalloping departments of the lace industry. Sweating in the hosiery trade was a feature of the seaming operation and the Boot and Shoe workers reported sweating as a feature of work in the country areas surrounding the town. On occasion the United Council publicised the names of employers who were known as sweaters, and in December 1888, after hearing a deputation from the Tailors' Society they agreed to join a protest at a Town Council decision to place a police clothing contract with a sweating employer.[20] In the same period the engineers were busy trying to organise the unskilled workers in their trade. Evidence collected by the Webbs suggests that although it was true to say that 'the engineering trades in Nottingham are well organised and far above the average of other trades', it was also the case that the sinker makers, the drillers and the labourers were unorganised. The labourers, according to the Webbs, were 'at present entirely unorganised, although several attempts have been made to get them into the Gas Workers' Union'.[21]

In 1892 Nottinghamshire had a total population of 503,311. According to the Webbs, 31,050 were members of trade unions, only 6.14 per cent of the total population. This was slightly lower than the surrounding region, Leicestershire having 7.34 per cent unionised and Derbyshire 6.82 per cent. Compared with the northern parts of England it was very low — Northumberland had 11.23 per cent of its total in trade unions.[22] In March 1889 it was reported that only 200 of the 1,500 tailors in Nottingham were organised. The same kind of figures were true of many other trades, and it was the realisation of this position which drove the trade union movement to see the need to transform its representative bodies. A significant series of negotiations from December 1889 to June 1890 led to the formation of the Association of Organised Trades and the Federated Trades Council. The first meeting of this body, the modern Trades Council, was held in the Lace Operatives union offices on 19 June 1890 and was attended by 41 delegates representing 21 trade union branches.

The earliest organising work of the new Trades Council took place in October 1890 when it mounted a special meeting with Lady Dilke around a campaign to unionise women workers. Lady Dilke spoke about the plight of the match girls and matchbox makers and the conditions of white lead girl workers before appealing to the Nottingham women workers to 'follow the example of their downtrodden sisters in other parts of the country and form themselves into protective organisations'.[23] This meeting may well have had some success since shortly afterwards it was reported that women working in the local hosiery trade had formed a union which claimed to have 400 members.

Other Nottingham trade unionists were also heavily involved in organising workers who at this stage were outside the official trade unions. In August 1890, for instance, the Gas and General Workers' Union, which had formed a Nottingham branch in December 1889, held an outdoor recruiting meeting which was very well attended:

> First to hold forth was Jebbett the chairman, a man of few words, robust and earnest nevertheless ... then the rapid ejaculations of the immaculate Proctor pouring upon us with relentless grievances of Labour from the Antipodes to Great Britain, from the continent of America across the Pacific to darkest Africa, on through Arabia's burning sands, with a final peroration upon the conditions of those he was addressing. Then, like a breath of wind upon a hot scorching day the quiet, persuasive tone of the ever youthful Reuben Davis who, in a few words, delivered a speech fit for the occasion. This brought up the apostle from London, Mark Hutchins, impulsive and fiery, with flashing eye, he recited the tyranny which brought forth the union.[24]

As this rhetoric shows, the mood of the trade union movement in Nottingham was beginning to move sharply away from the old philosophy of respectability and conciliatory industrial relations. A Nottingham contributor to the *Workmen's Times* felt that the Trades Council

> bids fair to become one of the strongest in the Kingdom, at the present time something like thirty societies are connected with the Council with a promise of two more joining at the next meeting ... a list of sixteen societies is made out for visitation by the deputations appointed for the purpose and no doubt these societies will be prevailed on to join.[25]

In the months which followed this prediction looked very near the mark. In September the Gas Workers' No.1 branch and the Cabinet Makers affiliated. Early in October the Gas Workers' No.2, the Steam Engine Makers, the Hucknall Framework Knitters, the Lithographic Artists and the Blastfurnacemen all joined. On 17 October four delegates from the Nottinghamshire Miners' Association attended for the first time and Bailey, their full-time agent, gave notice of his intention to move a resolution at the next meeting calling on the Trades Council to organise the tram and bus men. A few weeks earlier four new trade union branches had affiliated, leading the *Workman's Times* to remark 'on every side we see a desire to federate and consolidate the whole interest of the working class.'[26] The same report went on to rejoice that

> one very appropriate and interesting feature of the Trades Council meeting was the presence of a lady delegate representing the Female Cigar Workers ... and another large shop has joined the Women's Hosiery Union.

In November the *Workman's Times* was able to report further success for the growing numbers of Nottingham trade unionists when it claimed that 'the shoe has pinched very severely those firms not on the fair shops list operated by the building trades and Typographical Association.'[27] All of the available evidence indicates that the few months at the end of 1890 saw unparalleled expansion of the Nottingham trade unions. The Typographical Association was reported to be growing in strength both by an accession of new members and the recruitment of new workshops to the list. The Basford Bleachers Association which in March 1890 had 40 members reported more than 450 on its books by November.

The established unions in the 1880s (for instance the Engineers and Lacemakers) did not absorb on a permanent basis the mass of the lower paid. The 'closed' unions deliberately restricted entry to the trades they organised and their bargaining power hinged upon this restriction.[28] Many of those most active in the explosion of trade union activity which occurred in 1889 and 1890 were younger men and many of them were attracted by the ideas of socialism. Bailey, Hardstaffe and the rest of the Nottingham older generation of trade unionists tended to cling to the old labourist ideology, demonstrating as Asa Briggs has pointed out, that 'there is real value in labour history, as in other branches of history, in thinking in terms of generations.'[29] The very dramatic growth in trade union organisation which young men like Samuel Bowers or Ernest Gutteridge in Nottingham and similar individuals all over the country helped to establish, was described by G.D.H. Cole as 'the child of socialism out of unemployment'.[30] Equally important in Nottingham was the general discontent of the unskilled and the return of a temporary prosperity. During the years 1889 to 1891 union membership doubled. Growth of this kind brought with it many changes, the most important of which was, as E.J. Hobsbawm has pointed out, a sharp turn to the left and with it 'the creation of a new cadre of leaders and policy makers ... mostly inspired by various forms of socialism.'[31] All of this was certainly true of Nottingham where the rapid expansion of unskilled unionism did much to challenge the sectional and aristocratic unionism of the lacemakers and other craft organisations.

REFERENCES

[1] Trades Union Congress, *Annual Report*, 1883.

[2] Nottingham Association of Organised Trades, *Annual Report*, 1883.

[3] Minutes, Organised Trades, 16 November 1885.

[4] John Saville, 'The Ideology of Labourism', in R. Benewick, R.N. and B. Parekh (eds), *Knowledge and Belief in Politics*, 1973.

[5] Minutes, Organised Trades, 17 February 1886.

[6] See W.H.G. Armytage, *The Liberal Background to the Labour Movement*, 1951, pp. 32-3.

[7] Trades Union Congress, *Annual Report*, 1889.

[8] Letter, Wollaton Ward Liberal Association to Henry Broadhurst, 5 September 1889.

[9] Letter, Edward Medley to Henry Broadhurst, 3 September 1889.

[10] See, for instance, notes for a speech at Market Harborough in the Broadhurst Papers.

[11] Minutes, Nottingham Trades Council, 6 December 1892.

[12] Nottingham Trades Council, *Annual Report*, 1892.

[13] Nottingham Lace Trade Protection Society, *Webb Trade Union Collection*, Section B, Vol. XCII.

[14] Evidence of George Allcroft, *Webb Trade Union Collection*, Section A. Vol. XVI.

[15] Quoted in, *Souvenir Programme*, Nottingham TUC, 1930, p. 25.

[16] Minutes, Joint Committee of the United Trades Councils in Nottingham, 10 July 1884.

[17] Minutes, Organised Trades, 29 August 1884.

[18] Evidence of Harry Collier, *Royal Commission on the Depression of Trade and Industry*, 1886, Appendix II.

[19] For details of each of these disputes see, Minutes, Organised Trades, 10 February 1887 and 11 August 1887.

[20] Minutes, Organised Trades, 9 February 1888.

[21] *Webb Trade Union Collection*, Section A, Vol. XVI, Engineering and Metal Trades.

[22] Sidney and Beatrice Webb, *The History of Trade Unionism*, 1920 edn., Appendix V, pp. 741-743.

[23] *Workman's Times*, 24 October 1890. For Lady Dilke, see *Dictionary of Labour Biography* (ed. J.M. Bellamy and J. Saville) Vol. III, 1976.

[24] Ibid.

[25] *Workman's Times*, 29 August 1890.

[26] Ibid., 19 September 1890.

[27] Ibid., 14 November 1890.

[28] See, for instance, H.A. Turner, *Trade Union Growth, Structure and Policy*, 1962. This is primarily a study of the cotton unions although the analysis is of relevance to unionism in general.

[29] Asa Briggs, 'Introduction', in Briggs and Saville (eds), *Essays in Labour History 1886-1923*, 1971, p. 3.

[30] G.D.H. Cole, *The Second International, A History of Socialist Thought*, Vol. III, 1956, part I, p. 133.

[31] E.J. Hobsbawm, 'Trade Union History', *Economic History Review*, August 1967, p. 358.

CHAPTER TWO

Trades Council Politics

The conflict and growing tensions between the old guard labourist trade unionists, and the new socialist-inclined leaders, can be seen clearly in the discussions surrounding the need for independent labour representation. As early as 1884, Nottingham's town councillors were criticised for failing to respond positively to the plight of the unemployed, and this led the United Council to investigate the feasibility of having working-men as representatives on the City Council. This move appears to have been an isolated incident, for nothing further is mentioned in the records until 1886. The annual report of the Organised Trades for 1886 makes the point that although an effort to promote a labour representation committee was 'well supported at first, the question is not making such progress as its promoters would wish'.[1] Predictably perhaps, progress when it did arrive followed a trade dispute with a local Liberal employer.

In August 1887 a United Trades committee visited Mr Vickers who, it was alleged, had provoked bricklayers to strike by reducing their rate of pay. In February 1888 after a long correspondence with Vickers had produced no progress, it was resolved to lay the matter before the Wollaton Ward Liberal Association. In the unsympathetic answer which they received lay the seeds of real political change, for by October 1888 the United Committee was discussing seriously the names of candidates for the municipal elections, producing an 'approved list' and agreeing to oppose strongly any attempt to nominate Vickers.[2] Within a year the United Committee were to find themselves in the thick of a political debate which was to occupy them for the next three decades. At their meeting on 8 August 1889, after hearing accusations from the Nottingham tailors that Mr Baggaley, a local Liberal candidate, was an employer of sweated labour, it was agreed that the Council should seek an interview with the Bridge Ward Liberal Association to oppose his candidature. At the same meeting it was agreed to oppose the nomination of Mr Elsey for Sherwood Ward. Two months later, after a long and animated discussion in which Samuel Bowers, the leader of the Rotary

Power Hosiery Workers figured large in the demands for active trade union involvement, it was agreed to send the names of Baggaley, Wooton, Elsey and Pyatt to the press as bad employers, unworthy of trade union support.[3]

It was one thing to elect a working man to represent labour interests, and quite another to elect a working man who intended to refrain from becoming integrated into Liberal Party ideology. This tension was very much at the forefront when working men in Nottingham stood for election, and was of especial concern to the younger generation of trade unionists like Samuel Bowers. Following on from the opposition to Baggaley's candidature, the Tailors approached the Hosiery Workers with the suggestion that Bowers should stand as a trade union candidate. The local Liberal Party were not slow in recognising the need to absorb the leadership of local trade unions, and Bowers was duly adopted. Nevertheless it seems clear that this forthright defender of workers' rights was not the type of working man usually preferred. The differences between the traditional working-class candidate, and the new radicals can be seen clearly in a comparison of the two Nottingham candidates, Samuel Bowers and William Bailey.

William Bailey, the Nottinghamshire Miners' Agent, was nominated to stand as Liberal candidate for the St Alban Ward in 1889. This ward housed many of Nottingham's resident miners, and was thus a good seat for Bailey, and he easily defeated two Conservative candidates.[4] From the point of view of the Liberal leadership Bailey was a far safer candidate than Samuel Bowers. Whilst Bailey was at pains to stress his adherence to the Liberal Party stating that he came forward 'not merely as an earnest Liberal but as a working-man candidate', Bowers placed his primary allegiance with the working class, claiming that:

> the trade unions on the town had this time been unanimous in the selection of a candidate for their representative on the Council ... he was not, therefore, the representative of any clique or section of the labour party. He came forward purely on labour lines, but at the same time he would not hide the fact that he had political opinions of his own.[5]

Just before the poll Bowers told an open air meeting in Red Lion Square that

> they had no one on the Council to represent them; the present members were there to represent their own interests and they would be fools if they did not represent themselves first ... if they wanted men to look after their own interests they must send men like himself to the Council Chamber.[6]

The views which Bowers expressed were like those of similar activists all over the country, capable of developing in favour of independent labour representation and it appears that this is what Bowers really believed in. Unfortunately, despite a meeting of the unemployed at the Lace Makers' office which passed a resolution calling on, 'the working class at St Mary's Ward to give their vote and support to Mr Sam Bowers, the labour candidate',[7] Bowers lost the election although his vote was respectable:

A.T. Wooton	Conservative	569
S. Bowers	Liberal	398

Bowers' defeat did not deflect the determination of those who believed in independent working-class representation and they promptly redoubled their efforts to try and commit the Trades Council to this principle.

The first meeting of the new Trades Council took place on 19 June 1890. At its second meeting on 10 July, Bowers gave notice that at the next meeting he would call attention to the question of labour representation and move a resolution. News of this development must have spurred the local Liberals into action, for at the Trades Council meeting on 30 July the president announced that he had received a letter from the president of the Liberal Union, Alderman Gripper. It was explained that Mr Davis, a member of the Liberal executive, would 'inform' the Trades Council of the opinion of the Liberal Party on this question. It appears that Robinson, the Trades Council president, had met Davis and the Liberals had expressed themselves willing to meet a Trades Council deputation. It was suggested that the Liberal Party was prepared to adopt trade union candidates for several wards if the Trades Council would select men to be brought forward. Bowers spoke in favour of the deputation but predictably his proposition was opposed by an amendment that 'the Trades Council should have nothing to do with political questions'.[8] In the event a deputation did meet the local Liberals, but it was decided to take no action on their proposals until funds were available.

By October, however, arrangements were being made to decide what steps to take to secure the return of a labour candidate. The most progressive elements were determined to remove 'some of the fine glib-tongued gentlemen who will promise anything at election time on purpose to secure a seat on the Council'.[9] In the event John Skerritt, a Nottingham joiner, was nominated as a Trades Council candidate without Liberal support for Wollaton Ward. By late October Skerritt's campaign, which was based on a programme advocating 'clean streams, clean streets and healthy habitations; fair wages, shorter days and pleasant recreation',[10] was well under way with Wollaton Ward reportedly being vigorously worked by the 'Labour Party'. As far as canvassing returns could be relied on it was claimed that Skerritt stood a good chance of winning the seat. Although it was reported that Skerritt was being supported by the Pleasant Sunday Afternoon Class as well as Mr Peacock, the Temperance candidate for Market Ward, the realists amongst his supporters were aware that

> the elements against which the labour party has to fight are very formidable and it will need cute and careful watching on the part of the vigilance committees to circumvent the political sharks who are ever on the alert to trap a voter by a liberal portion of that commodity known in Nottingham vernacular as 'grease' or 'golden ointment'.[11]

This prediction proved accurate and enough palms were greased and thirsts slaked to ensure that Skerritt did not win. Naturally enough his defeat was deeply regretted by the progressives, particularly as they could point to 'a section of the labour party who have not hesitated to oppose Mr Skerritt'.[12] Despite this disappointment those active in the cause of independent labour could claim that they had succeeded in ensuring that labour questions had come well to the fore:

> nowhere has this been more displayed than in Nottingham during the municipal elections just decided. Every one of the candidates who has been successful at the poll is pledged to support the giving of Corporation contracts to those who pay the standard rate of wages ... [13]

That this group knew that they had a long way to go before they achieved their objective is demonstrated by the following argument:

> not much reliance can be placed upon the promises of politicians if we take past experience as our guide. Hence we are strongly of the opinion that the most strenuous efforts should be made by organised labour to secure direct representation on the Council.[14]

There were fundamental splits in the local trade union movement in relation to the question of independent labour representation, and feelings were to become very bitter. During the 1889 election four Building Trades Council delegates to the United Council had signed the manifesto of a Conservative candidate. So intense were the emotions aroused that the Building Trades Council withdrew from the United Council in protest. Similarly in the 1890 elections when John Skerritt stood as Trades Council candidate, the General Railway Workers' Union publically supported the opposing Liberal candidate, an action which earned them sharp rebuke from the more progressive elements on the Trades Council. Attitudes to labour representation were extremely mixed and contradictions abounded.

Shortly after the 1890 municipal elections the Building Trades Council was reported to have decided to 'persevere in their desire to secure direct labour representation'.[15] In December the Trades Council heard a delegate from the Engineers make a 'capital speech' in moving a resolution which called in a very early reference for the setting up of a 'Labour Representation Committee'. This resolution was carried unanimously and this might be considered to indicate that a growing number of trade unionists in the town wanted to see early progress made. But there were also those who were becoming disenchanted with the political process. One of these wrote to the *Workman's Times* after Broadhurst had failed to turn up to a demonstration in support of Scottish railway workers:

> I wonder how long the masses will continue to be gulled by politicians and expect any good from them, or for that matter, from Parliament.[16]

Those who hoped that the Trades Council would 'put on one side their little jealousies and party politics' seem to have had some success and, in March 1891 representatives of the Trades Council, the Building Trades Council and a group of socialists who had set up an organisation called the Workers' Electoral Federation all met at the offices of the Lace Makers to try and form 'one solid labour party'.[17]

The culmination of the determination to obtain labour representation came in May 1891, when the *Workman's Times* reported that the Nottingham Trades Council

> mean business. They have long talked about labour representation and municipal elections and they are now crystallising their thoughts into deeds. One of the first steps is to draw up a programme, the acceptance of which they will urge on all ... [18]

Later in the month at the Labour Electoral Congress in Westminster Town Hall, Bailey, the Miners' Agent and Liberal councillor, concluded a long speech by saying that:

> he would like to see at the next election some 40 or 50 men running and if they progressed as the influence they were able to wield deserved, within the next ten years they ought to have at least 100 labour representatives in the House ... [19]

In June it was reported that the Trades Council had elected a Labour Representation Committee, the progressives hoping that it would 'do something besides talk this next November.'[20] In August this Trades Council committee announced that they would run four labour candidates in the November municipal elections. This announcement apparently caused

> quite a flutter amongst the Liberal Party. They have in five or six wards within the last week or so, selected their candidates ... I should like to know if this is a fair specimen of the liberalism and labour we heard so much about last November ... we are only asking for four seats out of sixteen ... but it appears that if we are to get them, we shall have to make a few three-cornered fights. We have taken a back seat long enough.[21]

The exasperation expressed here by an individual who was probably a member of the Workers' Electoral Federation was well justified, for of the four 'labour' candidates named by the Trades Council three were to run with Liberal support, and one with Conservative backing. Not surprisingly, therefore, the *Workman's Times*, after reporting that an 'energetic' movement was under way in the town, carried a letter from a Nottingham worker signing himself 'Demos' which made the point that

> Of all the silly and ridiculous programmes I have ever come across this one beats all ... if they mean business why are they not already in the field advocating measures which will induce the unemployed, the overworked, the cab and busmen, the women workers and workers of all kinds to take an interest in, make common cause and work to secure the return of genuine labour representatives independent of *either* party.[22]

Obviously with feelings running so high, a split was inevitable between the socialists and those who were still the psychological captives of the old political parties. As the tension increased it was reported that

> The labour representation committee are just now having their patience tried. Several of the so-called trade union leaders in the town seem determined that it shall be a party affair. Some have gone so far as to say that if it is not a party affair they will do their best to make it burst like a balloon. It is rather consoling to know that the parties who talk in this manner have more audacity than intelligence.[23]

Subsequently, however, at a Trades Council sub-committee meeting between Bailey, the president, Trusell, the vice-president and Richards, the secretary, it was agreed that a deputation should visit various trade union branches in order to appeal for funds towards the expenses of fighting four wards. This appeal was aimed at financing contests in St

Ann's, Trent, Forest and Meadows Wards. Because of the shortness of time the genuine socialists in the town now had no alternative but to stand on the sidelines while a campaign developed which demonstrated the depth of the rifts in the organisation of the Trades Council.

Of the Trades Council sponsored candidates, Harry Collier looked the most incongruous. Standing as a Conservative-Labour candidate, Collier was only 36 years of age. He had been secretary of his branch of the Amalgamated Society of Carpenters and Joiners since 1881 and also served on its national committee. Standing in the heavily working-class Meadows Ward, Collier was supported by A.H. Jones, the president of the Nottingham branch of the Typographical Society and W. Mansell, the president of the Builders' Society.

The Lib-Lab Candidate in Forest Ward was Thomas Cheetham, a 41 year-old compositor. During his campaign Cheetham boasted that whilst he was branch secretary of the Typographical Society its membership had increased from 37 in June 1881 to 252 in June 1891. Certainly, Cheetham seems to have been rather a smug and self-satisfied individual. From the platform of one of his meetings he proudly told the audience that

> if evidence was wanted to prove the estimation in which he was held by the Society of which he was the Secretary he might mention that 12 months ago he was presented with a marble clock, a purse of £10 and a brooch for his wife, in recognition of his 'untiring service as Branch Secretary'.[24]

Skerritt, the candidate in St Ann's, was another joiner. 36 years of age, in 1890 he stood against the Liberal in Wollaton Ward. Now he had their full backing, as well as the support of Richards, the Trades Council secretary. Sam Bowers, the Lib-Lab candidate for Trent Ward comes across as the most progressive of the four candidates. Born in Kirkby-in-Ashfield he was 39 years old. As a boy he had worked on the land before beginning, at the age of 12, to work up to fourteen hours a day in the neighbouring colliery. Bowers had come to Nottingham in 1878 to work in a hosiery factory. Two years later he was the Hosiery Workers' representative on the forerunner of the Trades Council and later whilst out of work, having been victimised, he was elected full-time secretary of the Rotary Power Frame Workers by a majority of some 400 votes.

During the campaign in which these four candidates were involved the strain inside the Trades Council built up very considerably. The disappointing results added further fuel to the fire and strengthened the cynicism of those who believed that only truly independent working men could represent the interests of labour. Analysing the result 'Rotary Hand', who before the poll had been in favour of the Liberal alliance, made the following points:

> The bulk of the Liberal Party like the Conservative Party have not much love for Labour. The following facts speak for themselves:
>> In Trent Ward where Sam Bowers ran as a Liberal-Labour candidate he polled 464, last year the Liberal polled 605 or 141 more than Sam Bowers. In Forest Ward, T. Cheetham ran as Lib-Lab and polled 619, last year's Liberal polled 905 or 286 more than T. Cheetham. In the Meadows Ward a Conservative is run in the person of H. Collier who polled 471, last years Tory polled 601 or 130 more than H. Collier. I think one year's trial of the political parties is enough for the bulk of honest trade unionists ... never mind – we know how to pay them for it.[25]

As the year drew to a close the discontent which had been simmering for so long finally boiled over. On 12 December at a meeting attended by over one hundred people in the Dove and Rainbow public house, a resolution was passed which decided to form an Independent Labour Union. The officers elected to run this embryonic Independent Labour Party included: Mansell (Stonemasons), Camm (Joiners), Goldsmith (Cabinetmakers), Stratton (Tailors), Jones (Miners), Elvin (Tailors), Potter (Hosiery Workers), Yeld (Painters), Nolan (Plumbers), Thundercliffe (Bakers), and Mansell (Printers).[26]

During the spring and summer of 1892 many of the old political certainties began to break down. Nationally, the influence of socialist ideology lent a new solidarity to the labour movement. In Nottingham this was reflected by an increased number of socialist lecture programmes and the formation of a Fabian Society. In January 1891 Herbert Bland lectured on 'The Future of English Politics' and 'The New Reform Bill'. By 1892, Cunninghame Graham had persuaded the miners of the West Nottingham constituency to pass a resolution pledging that they would not vote for any candidate who would not support the miners' Eight Hour Bill.[27] The shift in political opinion which this move represented was reflected in several of the most important trade union branches. On April 23rd the *Workman's Times* reported that

> the gasworkers have passed a resolution to support no Parliamentary candidate who will not support the Miners' Eight Hour Bill. With the miners, the gasworkers and the hosiery workers nearly unanimous on the eight-hour day, besides many belonging to other trades, I don't see the security of Henry Broadhurst's seat in the same light as the wire-pullers of the Liberal Party, we are working men first, politicians afterwards.[28]

In May 1892, at a special meeting of the Trades Council, a resolution from the Labour Representation Committee was discussed which called for a meeting with certain members of the Town Council, 'to confer on the immediate desires of the Labour Party'.[29] Whilst this motion was deflected by manipulations of the right wing, the general trend towards an independent labour party could not be denied. Already in April the *Workman's Times* had published an article calling for supporters of the idea to send in their names and addresses, and at a meeting held that month Sam Bowers was elected secretary of what was now called the Independent Labour Party.

The proximity of the 1892 election caused the Lib-Lab protagonists to give the issue one more try at a full meeting of the Trades Council. At a meeting on 29 June they managed to get 24 votes for a resolution which stated that:

> In the opinion of this Council, in consideration of the general circumstances, it will be unwise to continue the existence of a direct Labour Representation Committee.[30]

Opposition to this resolution was led by Jones of the Miners' Association and their resolution argued that:

> Direct labour representation can best be served and maintained by the formation of an independent labour organisation under the patronage of the Trades Council, with provision for individual membership and the affiliation of trade societies as a whole.[31]

This motion received 22 votes in its favour. It is clear from the support for these two resolutions just how evenly divided opinion was amongst Trades Council delegates. It seems that when the Jones resolution was about to be put to the vote, the Trades Council president, Hardstaffe of the Lace Workers, left the chair whilst 'inviting the meeting to nail the resolution to the table'. Certainly there seems to have been a good deal of bitterness generated by this disagreement. The socialist delegates to the Trades Council claimed that half the Council was

> so enamoured with the Liberal Party that sooner than sever themselves from them they will prostitute their labour principles to the Liberal Party.[32]

But the group was not discouraged, since they went on to say that the decision of the Trades Council had 'cleared the ground for the Independent Labour Party which already had over 100 members'.[33]

Henry Broadhurst, the Lib-Lab MP for Nottingham West, was defeated in the 1892 election, losing the seat he had won easily in 1886 because of his opposition to the miners' Eight Hour Bill.[34] This was not the only reason for his defeat, for the principles which Broadhurst represented were under furious attack from the radical sections of the labour movement. Sam Bowers had determinedly worked against him and in July it was reported that:

> Amongst the old trade unionists a very bitter spirit has been shown to Mr Sam Bowers for his action in opposing Henry Broadhurst. They have been indulging in the idea that he should be dismissed from his secretaryship (of the hosiery workers) at the General Meeting. The meeting has come and gone but, instead of Sam getting dismissed, a unanimous vote of confidence was passed in him. What a smack in the face for those fossilised old trade unionists who are content to be the hacks of a political party.[35]

Although Bowers easily maintained his position inside his own trade union the bitterness remained and in the wider movement the struggle between right and left seems to have intensified.

The struggle between left and right in Nottingham was to colour local politics for many years. Nevertheless the period 1887 to 1893 had seen the emergence of a strong body of committed working men determined to fight for independent labour representation. The split in political ideology closely reflected the industrial traditions of Nottingham: the main opposition to the socialists being led by the officials of the Lace Operatives and the Miners' Association. The ability of the new young radicals to challenge this craft dominance depended not only on the development of a strong socialist tradition, but also on the politicisation of semi and unskilled workers. The following two chapters will show how the Lib-Lab faction maintained a modicum of control through struggles to preserve craft exclusiveness in industry, and also how this strategy was doomed by wider industrial changes.

REFERENCES

[1] Nottingham Association of Organised Trades, *Annual Report*, 1886.
[2] Minutes, Organised Trades, 9 February 1889.
[3] Ibid., 21 October 1889.
[4] *Nottingham Daily Express*, 30 October 1889 and 2 November 1889:

W. Bailey	Liberal	1,063
W. Falconbridge	Conservative	746
T. Brailsford	Conservative	746

Majority 317

[5] *Nottingham Daily Express*, 24 October 1889.

6 Ibid., 29 October 1889.
7 Ibid., 1 November 1889.
8 Minutes, Nottingham Trades Council, 10 July 1890.
9 *Workman's Times*, 29 August, 1890.
10 Ibid., 7 November 1890.
11 Ibid., 31 October 1890.
12 Ibid., 7 November 1890.
13 Ibid.
14 Ibid.
15 *Workman's Times*, 14 November 1890.
16 Ibid., 6 February 1891.
17 Ibid., 20 March 1891.
18 Ibid., 15 May 1891.
19 Ibid., 22 May 1891.
20 Ibid., 26 June 1891.
21 Ibid., 7 August 1891.
22 Ibid.
23 *Workman's Times*, 14 August 1891.
24 *Nottingham Daily Express*, 27 October 1891.
25 *Workman's Times* , 5 December 1891.
26 Ibid., 12 December 1891.
27 Ibid., 5 March 1892.
28 Ibid., 23 April 1892.
29 Minutes, Nottingham Trades Council, 5 May 1892.
30 Ibid., 29 June 1892.
31 Ibid.
32 *Workman's Times*, 9 July 1892.
33 Ibid.
34 *West Nottingham Division Result*

C. Seely	Liberal Unionist	5,601
H. Broadhurst	Lib-Lab	5,309
	Majority 292.	

35 *Workman's Times*, 16 July 1892.

CHAPTER THREE

Organisation of the Workforce

The persistence of labourist politics amongst the Nottingham working class can be attributed in part to an industrial structure which deeply divided and fragmented any potential solidarity. Each of the two major industries, hosiery and lace, was organised in such a way that a small exclusive section of the work-force dominated, and this feature was reflected both in union structure and in political expression. Eric Hobsbawm, in a pioneering study of the labour aristocracy, has pointed out that in the 1860s leading hands in the Nottingham lace trade were earning three times the wages of dressers and menders, sometimes more.[1] This exclusiveness persisted into the twentieth century, for in 1906 lace makers in the Levers branch of the industry were fourth in a table of fifteen occupations in which 40 per cent or more of the workers earned more than £2 each week.

Wage levels were only one form of marking the divisions in the workplace. Far more subtle were the social relations which sustained the aspirations and ambitions of the labour aristocracy. Robert Gray has suggested that the nature of an industry's technology, the division of labour and the deployment of managerial authority are all factors which contribute to an understanding of the position of the labour aristocracy.[2] Certainly the wider structure of the industry and employers' strategies in expanding profit potential engulfed lace makers in a capitalist framework: there is little doubt that the practice of sweating outworkers helped to involve some lace makers in the phenomenon characterised by Eric Hobsbawm as 'co-exploitation'. Whilst it is important not to over-exaggerate this technique as a contribution to labourist political ideology, it seems clear that the relationship of the skilled with the unskilled helped the Lace Makers' Society to maintain its exclusiveness whilst at the same time reinforcing the feeling of superiority and élitism which the twist-hands demonstrated.

By 1883, when the Trades Union Congress was held in the Mechanics Hall, Nottingham, the Lace Makers' Society was claiming 4,040 members. It must be remembered, however, that the 3,000 to 4,000 operatives who actually controlled the lace making machinery (twist-hands) were only a small proportion of the people who got their living from the lace industry. Every lace maker had two or three auxiliary workers to help him, whilst the number of workers engaged in other processes through which the lace had to pass before it could be placed on the market was considerable. Additionally, the localisation of lace manufacturing in Nottingham led to the establishment of a number of allied industries usually termed the 'making up' trades, of which blouse making was by far the most important. Undoubtedly the twist-hands' organisation was the most important trade union in Nottingham during the 1880s. One of its members, John Jepson, was the secretary of the Federated Trades Council and the lace makers were deeply involved in efforts to establish a united trades council. In 1886 the lace makers sent three delegates to the Trades Council, Bowring representing the Plain Net section, Jepson the Curtain branch and Sansom the workers in the Levers section. As the 1880s continued, however, the 'golden years' began to fade and an acute slump developed.

Perhaps as a consequence of the worsening slump, the Lace Makers' Society found itself having to mount a recruiting campaign by arranging for national speakers to visit the town. Joseph Arch was amongst those invited in 1884 but his meeting was countered with a lock-out by the employers. The aristocrats of the industry were undoubtedly worried at the deepening depression, but this concern does not seem to have fully recognised the need to organise the auxiliary workers, or those employed in the sweated trades. The union was also weakened because the twist-hands, although anxious to control entry into the industry, were prepared to allow members to remain in the union even if they became owners or shareholders in a lace machine.[3] Twist-hands were sometimes loaned as much as £200 for this purpose. Arrangements like this facilitated both the fragmentation of the industry and the growth of the trade in outside centres like nearby Long Eaton. The Lace Makers' Society also allowed its members to go to Long Eaton and other centres outside the town for rates of pay lower than those laid down in the agreed price list.

This movement out of the town accelerated from 1886, and in 1888 several Nottingham firms removed and established themselves on the Continent. These developments placed the union under serious stress. In 1884 £9,500 was paid out in unemployment benefits; in 1885 2,500 members received a further £10,537. The weekly excess expenditure during this period averaged £100. In 1885 a Long Eaton lock-out forced the Society to declare all Long Eaton shops 'open' where employers did not victimise Society members. This retreat demonstrated that the union was on the defensive and the Long Eaton employers capitalised on this weakness by refusing to pay the Nottingham rate. By August 1886 the union's funds were reduced to about £3,000 with the consequence that unemployment benefit had to be cut from seven to five shillings a week. In 1886, after a town meeting called by the Mayor to discuss the developing crisis, the Nottingham manufacturers were successful in forcing a reduction in wages of about 15 per cent in both the Levers and Curtain branches.

This continually deteriorating situation put the union under a tremendous strain. In 1888 over 2,000 lace workers were out of work, and many union members applied to the Society for grants towards the cost of emigration to Canada, America and Australia.[4] The maintenance of union rates became increasingly difficult and in practice this was only possible in large factories which were fully unionised. In May 1889 the Lace Manufacturers' Association gave notice of wage reductions of 40 per cent on Curtain goods, 25 per cent on Levers goods and 15 per cent on all other goods. The lace unions refused to accept the appointment of an arbitrator and the employers responded by demanding an immediate reduction of 25 per cent or the removal of their industries to Long Eaton. One manufacturer did this, bringing the total number of machines in Long Eaton to 207, with a further 120 at Ilkeston. Subsequently, the union called a mass meeting at the Nottingham Mechanics' Hall and more than 2,000 men attended. The strike which followed began in July 1889. Some 1,800 Levers and 700 Curtain operatives came out, and over 3,000 warehouse workers were also involved.[5] Finally, after agreement between the two sides, the strike was settled by Alderman Renals as an independent mediator. It was agreed that the new price list would be suspended on the return of the men, pending the formation of a new Board of Conciliation.

By the time it was settled in September, the strike had cost the union a huge amount of money. Over £1,200 had been paid out weekly and there is no doubt that the union desperately needed a settlement. When the new price list emerged from the conciliation process it allowed an average $12\frac{1}{2}$ per cent reduction in both the Levers and Curtain branches; it came into operation in November 1889 and became the norm for the industry until the close of the century. Despite the relative industrial peace which the new Board was able to achieve, a trickle of machines continued to leave the town. In 1889, 38 were removed to Sandiacre, Ilkeston, and Long Eaton and the continual erosion of the number of machines in

Nottingham remained a major problem. The natural consequence of these developments came late in 1889 when the Long Eaton and District Association of Operative Lace Makers was formed. The Nottingham union was outraged at this development, but in many ways they had only themselves to blame for the successful breakaway. The policies which the union had pursued throughout the 1880s had to some extent encouraged the removal of machinery from the town and although the potential of Long Eaton had existed since the Midland Railway linked it with Nottingham in 1839, its potential as a haven for non-unionist lace makers was largely due to the mistakes of the Nottingham Lace Makers' Society.

The twist-hands' union was also primarily to blame for the failure to organise the auxiliary workers effectively. After 1886 unions did develop to some extent in the auxiliary and finishing sections but this was really despite the twist-hands rather than through any positive programme of organisational work on their part. The most important of these 'New Unions' were the Auxiliary Society of Male Lace Workers and the Bleachers and Dressers' Association; but many thousands of lace workers remained outside any organisation and the exclusive and aristocratic nature of the Lace Makers' Society can only have weakened the bargaining position of the vast majority of those who earned a living in the trade. Working from their homes in dank and insanitary areas like Sneinton Bottoms or the back-to-back houses of the Meadows, the women and young children were never able to scratch more than a miserable existence and there is little evidence that their plight really concerned the craftsmen of the Lace Makers' Society.

The craft orientation of the lace workers was repeated in Nottingham's hosiery industry. There were two main sections in the trade, circular frame and rotary frame, and although the workers were employed alongside one another in the factories, they saw themselves as having quite distinct identities and interests, and their collective strength was inevitably weakened. They had separate unions and although co-operation was attempted no joint fund was established. A Federation was formed in 1874, but this had little success and in 1877 the Circular Society accused the Rotary Union of having failed to support them during an important strike. In May 1882 the Circular Society voted to wind up the alliance as 'the Circular Society had not been benefited by the alliance.'[6] The lack of good will and solidarity evidenced here was, like many other aspects of the hosiery trade in this period, exacerbated by the very difficult trading situation. In 1880 the *Annual Report* of the Nottingham Association of Organised Trades had earnestly wished for a revival of the trade, pointing out that 'much capital has been thrown into the hosiery manufacture, which suffers now from over production as much as any branch of trade could do.'[7]

Towards the end of the 1880s the hosiery workers, like many other groups, seem to have been influenced by the wave of new unionism. In November 1889 it was reported that the Handframe Knitters who had only 60 members, and the Shirt, Pants and Drawers Union who had approximately 70 members, were both experiencing an expansion of membership and that at Hucknall, '100 knitters joined last month'.[8] This spurt of interest amongst outworkers can be seen as a last desperate effort to safeguard a deteriorating position, for in December 1890 the *Workman's Times* reported that the Handframe Workers' Society was reduced to 17 members and had decided to disband.[9] Amongst the factory workers however, the unions seem to have been making steady progress. By 1891 Robinson of the Basford Trimmers was president of the Trades Council, and in June of the same year a recruiting campaign in the out-districts was under way. Prior to the commencement of the meeting at Arnold the local prize band paraded the streets to attract attention. Sam Bowers of the Rotary Union told his audience that 'it depended on the men of Arnold whether they would support their fellow workmen and be thoroughly organised, or continue to be the "black spot" in the hosiery trade.' This meeting seems to have been a great success and Bowers caused a great deal of laughter and merriment by vividly portraying the

> ideal son of the luxurious indolent aristocracy. He made him live before our eyes, cigarette in mouth, walking stick in hand, linen round the wrists and a 'stick up' under the chin.[10]

The problems faced by the hosiery unions in this period were legion. The working of overtime particularly worried the mens' organisations. The *Workman's Times* reported in July 1891:

> The Union was in a position some 10 years ago to regulate it; but as we are all aware, things went from bad to worse and now a manufacturer has only to say 'I want you to work from 6 o'clock in the morning 'till 8 or 9 at night' and woe to a union man who kicks his heels against it. It is Hobson's choice – do it or go.[11]

At the same time as overtime demands were being introduced many workers were being laid-off. In April 1892 the officials of the Leicester Hosiery Workers called attention to the numbers of penniless Nottingham operatives who had called at their offices, having walked from

Nottingham in search of work. The situation of the handframe knitters was even worse. Arthur Bonser and Samuel Oscroft told the 1892 Royal Commission on Labour that 5,000 people were still employed in the outwork industry in the Midlands. Many of these, according to Bonser and Oscroft, were victims of sweating. The middleman, it was claimed, 'is what is commonly called a sweater ... if there is any man working under him whom he can take advantage of he will do so.' Later it was alleged that the secretary of the Handframe Knitters had been 'out of work now for over 20 weeks merely through the spite of the sub-contractor on account of his being an official of the union'.[12]

Samuel Bowers of the Rotary Frameworkers gave evidence to the 1892 Royal Commission on Labour, estimating that about 1,500 men and 400 women were members of the hosiery unions, whilst between 400 and 500 men and between 600 and 700 women were totally unrepresented. In Bowers's opinion there was no easy way to estimate what average earnings were on account of the totally iniquitous system of organising the workforce:

> We have such a bad system of working in Nottingham that you really could not say what a man could do. Some are working one frame, some two, and some three.

Bowers went on to claim that there was a good deal of discontent in the trade 'on account of the irregularity of the prices that are paid', Reminded by Mundella that for 20 years the price had been maintained by the Board of Arbitration, Bowers said that the Board had been broken down by the employers 'who will not have it'. Later he spoke strongly against the middlemen 'who buy a few machines or get them on credit, and fetch the work from the manufacturers, and do it at sweating prices'. Asked by Mundella how it was that the union allowed this, he replied that they had only just organised so could not yet enforce equality of payment. Bowers went on to complain that hours of work were still between fifty-four and fifty-six a week as a consequence of the Factory Acts being 'in abeyance practically' because of the unwillingness of the Inspector to enforce them. In any event Bowers claimed that when the union tried to reduce the hours of work the employers 'shifted half the machinery nearly out of the town into the country places to defeat us.' Like his colleagues in the outwork trade Bowers claimed that 'a lot of cruel sweating was going on, particularly in the sewing of shirt buttons.' Bowers's assertion that an attempt was being made to supplant men's labour with that of women was challenged by Mundella who argued that women could not handle some machines. To this Bowers replied 'She can manage for the manufacturer's purpose and that is to run down wages.'[13]

The employment of very large numbers of women in the hosiery and lace trades was a factor in Nottingham's demographic history. At each census between 1811 and 1841 women outnumbered men by more than 3,000. Between 1851 and 1861 the excess of female labour rose to more than 7,000 as the factories and warehouses being built attracted migrants from the surrounding counties. Employment in the lace and hosiery trades rapidly increased and these jobs were subsequently added to by the engineering trades, printing and paper box manufacture. By the end of the century the lace trade employed 14,701 women (compared with 6,925 men). Over 30 per cent of all working women were connected with the industry, which included large numbers in the making-up trade. Similarly, by 1901 women greatly outnumbered men in the hosiery industry. Technological change in both industries simplified the machinery and the unions were gradually persuaded to allow women to work some of the smaller machinery. By 1897 the number of women in the hosiery factories formed 75 per cent of the total labour force.[14]

This female proletariat, even when not organised into trade unions, must obviously have played a significant role in helping to shape the emerging local labour movement. The attitudes of the husbands, brothers and fathers of this large group of working women, as one might expect of the Victorian male, left a good deal to be desired. Many agreed with Broadhurst, the prominent Lib-Lab, who argued that 'it was very natural for ladies to be impatient of restraint at any time', and the factory was therefore an unsuitable place for them. He concluded, 'Wives should be in their proper place at home.' Early efforts to organise women workers all seem to have foundered, but in 1887, following a strike which was the consequence of an employer's attempt to force a heavy reduction in wages, a Female Cigar Workers' Union was formed. According to the Webbs, taking evidence in the early 1890s, the union had a membership of about 420. Only one small shop which had been lost in a strike was outside the union, and the ten women in this work place were quickly blacked. Several other strikes had succeeded in raising wages considerably and as the Webbs pointed out, the union was the only one in England entirely controlled and governed by working women members. With Mrs Bryant as its secretary the union preferred to remain independent of their male colleagues although it seems that they kept closely in touch with them.[15]

The wave of new unionism which began at the end of the 1880s seems to have considerably affected Nottingham's women workers. As elsewhere, new unionism did much to challenge the sectional interests of aristocratic unionism and at last there were signs that the male unionists of the town were coming to realise how important it was to organise the female labour force. Many women were employed as sweated labour and it may have been the concern expressed by the Tailors' Society at a Trades Council meeting in 1888, when police clothing contracts were given to well-known sweating employers, which first made male unionists appreciate the importance of recruiting women workers.

By 1890 the *Workman's Times* was writing about the need to organise female labour in Nottingham. It reported that both the Women's Hosiery Union and the Female Cigar Makers were now 'firmly established'.[16] These unions had been established, it was noted, with the help of male union members, demonstrating a 'friendly attitude ... supporting and encouraging in every possible way those through whose instrumentality women's unions have been formed'.[17] Later in 1890, Bowers and other Nottingham delegates to the Trades Union Congress approached Lady Dilke in order to ask that she come to Nottingham to 'assist in the work of organising amongst the female workers'.[18] By November, however, the correspondent of the *Workman's Times* was expressing concern that recruitment amongst women workers was not so good as had been expected:

> As early as a quarter to eight in the morning anyone may notice that a stream of 'our girls' has begun and should the individuals who notice this care to see the same girls returning home at night they may do so by being in the Lace Market at 8 p.m. ... what are these large parcels that so many are carrying away? Night work which must be done by the morning, or the slave of labour to capital will have the consolation of paying for the same out of her poorly paid weeks work.[19]

The limited unionisation of women workers was not peculiar to Nottingham in this period, but given the extent of their involvement in local industries their marginality was a serious danger. Not only did women provide a source of cheap labour, but employers could benefit by using them to dilute the organised male labour force. The consequent weakening of working-class solidarity and fragmentation of interests had obvious repercussions on the advance of the local labour movement. Perhaps more subtly, the opposition to the use of women workers to undermine male wage rates became translated into an opposition to women working, and at an ideological level this reinforced the 'respectability' and liberalism of male craft élites. From this perspective women workers were not even considered worthy of unionisation.

The organisation of the hosiery and lace trades which gave rise to a divided working class and an élite 'aristocracy' can be seen as a factor influencing the labourist traditions of the local labour movement.

A further influence was that brought to bear by the Nottinghamshire mining industry. The traditional explanation for the strength of Liberalism in the Nottinghamshire field is that of particular geological conditions. Thick and unbroken seams, relatively easy working conditions and high output, are all advanced to explain the relative lack of industrial and political militancy. It also seems probable that the whole range of direct and indirect, overt and covert pressures used by the coal owners and other capitalists to seduce the local leadership, was equally important in producing a generation of leaders as thoroughly labourist as William Bailey, Miners' Agent, local preacher, Borough councillor and member of the Board of Guardians.

These last factors are doubly important because it is not really true to claim that working conditions in Nottinghamshire generated a great deal less industrial strife than other coalfields. In fact, the 1880s and 1890s contain a fair number of disputes which demonstrate that the constant colliery by colliery argument about rates and working conditions was, as in other parts of the country, playing an important role in establishing the mining solidarity which was such a feature of early twentieth-century disputes. This process, however, had been slowed in the Nottingham area partly by the initial lack of homogeneity which must have followed the necessary labour migration into the area as the industry expanded. The recruitment of men from other industries, like agriculture and handframe knitting, was also important and the settlement of colliers alongside other important working-class groups had the inevitable effect of retarding the growth of a particular mining militancy.

The butty, or small labour contractor method is another feature of the system of coal mining in Nottinghamshire which needs to be carefully analysed when seeking to explain the strength of Liberalism in the county. The newly-established NMA had most of its strength in the Leen Valley. The pits in this area employed a labour force about half of which, in the case of face workers, were butties. This group of workers played an important role in the leadership of the NMA, and it seems likely that many amongst them were also involved in the range of cultural institutions which played such a crucial role in helping to win the working class for middle-class ideas. At Hucknall in 1881, for instance, the Wesleyan, New Connexion and Primitive Methodists all had congregations. There were three sick clubs and a branch of the Oddfellows. The co-operative movement was well established and the advocates of temperance had branches of the Good Templars and Independent Order of Rechabites. By their involvement in the leadership of organisations like this, as well as their privileged position at work, the butties had a certain stake in the status quo, which must have impelled them towards support for Liberalism or the ideas which it represented. This basic predilection for safe, respectable, Gladstonian Liberalism was built on by the more intelligent elements amongst the coalowners and their success was well demonstrated in 1889 when, after the death of Ellis, a Liberal coalowner, the miners left work at twelve noon to 'show sympathy'.[20]

From the start the newly-formed NMA found it extremely difficult to build a viable organisation. Seriously weakened at the outset by a strike in 1882 at the Bestwood pit, which lasted five weeks and ended with the victimisation of the pit leadership, by 1884 the union's membership had fallen from 2,167 to about 1,000 in the course of a year. In this period the trade cycle had begun to dip and as the succeeding slump set in the price of coal fell from 5s 5d a ton in 1884, to 4s 10d in 1885. As the price of coal fell the collapse of the union might have been expected, but the colliers' subsequent loss of earnings was cushioned to some extent by an overall fall in the cost of living, and the union survived.

The survival of the miners' union in Nottinghamshire had much to do with its acceptance and recognition by the Liberal coalowners. John Edward Ellis, a local owner who stood and was elected as a Liberal MP, warmly supported the NMA and was proud of his record regarding wage reductions. Colonel Seely of the Babbington Coal Company campaigned vigorously for pensions for widows of men killed in pit accidents.[21] Such men had an important effect on the mentality of the NMA, and on the strength of Liberalism within the coalfield. Not all employers were sympathetic; the Wollaton Colliery Company victimised active members of the union in 1884, confiscated gathered coals (coal dropped from the trams onto the haulage roads), reduced wages and stopped supplying home coal. The attempt to break the men's organisation started when the Company gave notice of reduced wages to eleven stalls only. The union committee subsequently resolved:

> that if the men are permitted to submit to any reduction whatever, another section of the colliery will be attacked 'till the whole pit is reduced.'[22]

Later, some of the butties refused to pay their share of the checkweighman's wage and this was connived at by the owners, who hindered the checkweighman, John Hopkins, 'from doing his duty, he being a staunch society man'.[23] It seems that a sycophantic butty, John

Hutton, alleged that Hopkins had tried to coerce him into membership of the union, with the consequence that Hopkins, together with other active union members, was excluded from the employment of the company. Undoubtedly the men's organisation found it extremely difficult to resist this kind of pressure. The union was not yet really strong enough to win major disputes as was demonstrated in September 1885. A national conference held in Nottingham had decided to campaign for a 15 per cent increase in wages, but the campaign was a complete failure. Only 200 men in Nottinghamshire obeyed the union's instructions to hand in strike notices and they quickly withdrew them. Similarly, a national conference held in November 1886 decided to agitate for a seven hour day and increased wage rates. Reports given at this conference indicated that the Nottinghamshire miners had no heart for a fight, possibly because they were amongst the best paid in the country, earning between 4s 9d and 5s 3d a day.

In 1887 William Bailey, a well known Primitive Methodist preacher, became the full-time secretary-agent of the Nottinghamshire Miners. Due to the energy and enthusiasm of Bailey, and to the improving state of trade and the general upsurge of interest in trade unionism, the membership of the union rose rapidly from about 500 on his appointment to 18,835 in December 1893. At the Good Friday miners' demonstration on Bulwell Common in 1887 the signs of a new confidence could already be seen. About 5,000 are said to have attended. The Hucknall men had marched to the common behind a local temperance band. Others employed at Babbington pit had come from Cinderhill with their own band, whilst the Pleasley band had marched in front of the men from Sutton. Henry Broadhurst MP was the main speaker and it seems likely that it was after speaking on the same platform as Bailey that the doyen of the Lib-Lab movement decided to 'take up' the local miners' leader. Subsequently Bailey was to become a key figure in the politics of the Nottingham labour movement. An ardent Liberal, he had been a founder of the Labour Electoral Association in 1886 and with Broadhurst's help, as well as the local Liberal Association, he and his supporters were able to hold back the cause of those who believed in independent labour politics.

The early years of the NMA had been tremendously difficult. After the formation of the union its initial impetus helped it to reach a peak of only just over 2,000 members in 1883. With the fall in demand and prices the membership fell to its lowest level in 1886 with approximately 350 members. Yet a year later, under the stimulus of new and energetic leadership, coupled with signs of recovery in the coal trade, the organisation was able to recruit large numbers of additional members so that by the end of the 1880s its future was secure. This hard won security was based in large part on the pits of the Leen Valley. Most of the new branches opened by the NMA in the late 1880s were either in Nottingham or its immediate vicinity. The union's headquarters at Old Basford was only a couple of miles from the centre of the town and there is little doubt that the growing labour force in this area, as well as the increasing membership of the union, helped to give the organisation and particularly its leadership a growing political importance which neither the established Liberal hierarchy nor the growing number of socialist propagandists could afford to ignore.

In many respects the limited trade union organisation of Nottingham's labour force was typical of many other towns and cities in the 1880s and 1890s. Its uniqueness may be found in the particular conjuncture of features which enabled employers to undermine potential solidarity whilst at the same time harnessing the leadership to Liberal ideals. In the major industries of lace and hosiery the semi, unskilled, and women workers, were used to undermine the hard-won control over working conditions and wages, which had been exercised by skilled craftsmen from the mid-Victorian period. These men held tenaciously to their commitment to Liberalism whilst suffering the indignity of encroachments on the very ideals, such as craft exclusiveness, on which that Liberalism was founded. Yet despite this they failed to recognise the wisdom of wider union organisation, and campaigned against those who did.

Although entirely different from the lace and hosiery industries, the Nottinghamshire miners' union faced similar difficulties. When employers chose to recognise the 'worth' of the miners' demands, their union won support, but whenever they chose to stray beyond the acceptable Liberal limits dictated from above, the men faced intransigent opposition. In such circumstances the real weaknesses of the Nottinghamshire miners were revealed. The campaign for the Eight Hour Bill, the emergence of new leaders committed to independent labour representation, and the gradual development of organisations for the unskilled, provided the inspiration which was to break the stranglehold of labourist politics.

REFERENCES

[1] Eric Hobsbawm, *Labouring Men*, 1964, p. 292.

[2] R. Gray, *The Labour Aristocracy in Victorian Edinburgh*, 1976, pp. 91-120.

[3] Minutes, Amalgamated Society, 8 April 1876 and 21 July 1878.

[4] Accounts and Papers, Amalgamated Society 1869-1900, 22 November 1887, 12 December 1887 and 14 May 1887.

[5] *Nottingham Daily Express*, 29 July 1889.

[6] *Webb Trade Union Collection*, Section C, p. 63.

[7] Nottingham Association of Organised Trades, *Annual Report*, 1880.

[8] Eric Horriben, *Hucknall*, 1973, p. 119.

[9] *Workman's Times*, 26 December 1890.

[10] Ibid., 26 June 1891.

[11] Ibid., 10 July 1891

[12] Evidence of Arthur Bonser and Samuel Oscroft, *Royal Commission on Labour*, 1892.

[13] Ibid., evidence of Samuel Bowers.

[14] Quoted in R.A. Church, *Economic and Social Change in a Midland Town*, 1966, p. 278.

[15] *Webb Trade Union Collection*, Section C, Vol.21, Evidence of Samuel Bowers.

[16] *Workman's Times*, 29 August 1890.

[17] Ibid.

[18] *Workman's Times*, 12 September 1890.

[19] Ibid., 21 November 1890.

[20] Horriben, op. cit., p.122.

[21] *Nottingham Journal*, 15 March 1880.

[22] Minutes, *Nottinghamshire Miners' Association*, 28 April 1884.

[23] Minutes, *Nottingham Trades Council*, 29 August 1884.

CHAPTER FOUR
Industrial Struggles

The aristocratic Lib-Lab stratum of the working class maintained and defended their position by exercising control over the work process. This was done by restricting the entry of new workers through long apprenticeships, and also by limiting the introduction of technology which could be used by the semi-skilled. The trade unions which such workers built were crucial in enabling them to maintain their position. From the 1870s onwards both workers and unions faced serious attack from employers who recognised the need to defeat their control in order to increase profit margins. Most seriously affected were those engaged in trades suffering from the loss of demand and unfavourable trade conditions, such as the hosiery workers. Certainly lace workers experienced extremely bitter industrial relations; employers reduced rates, removing factories to areas where non-union labour could be taken on, and regularly locking out those who refused to accept encroachments on their skill; but they were buffered to a large degree by the boom in demand for lace goods especially in the years from 1879 to 1882.

The lace unions preserved the position of their members by exerting strict rules on membership and entitlement to union benefits. The rules of the Lace Makers' Society were hard and inflexible and the minutes show the executive administering them harshly. In November 1880, for instance, a group of members who could no longer afford the subscription owing to short-time working were allowed no sick or other benefits once they were six weeks in arrears.[1] Similarly, they were unwilling to alter membership regulations to include auxiliary workers except in an effort to secure a closed shop and to control the employers' use of 'black sheep'.

Hosiery workers were in an entirely different situation. Whilst their unions attempted to preserve the exclusiveness of skilled workers, they had become such a small minority by the 1880s that their bargaining position was fundamentally undermined. At the 1883 Trades Union Congress the Circular Society claimed a mere 200 members, the Rotary

67

Union a more respectable 700, and the Warpers' Association only 120.[2] Membership continued to decline year by year so that by 1887 the Webbs found that the Rotary Power Workers had only 500 members. This loss, caused the hosiery unions to be far more flexible in their rules. According to Sam Bowers the union never struck a member off the books: 'They used to, but found they lost many members entirely in bad times.' Organisation was weak and no shop committees existed, although Bowers told the Webbs that 'several times the union had tried to institute such shop committees but the men are too much afraid of the employers, the men were thoroughly cowed by the removal of the trade.' Clearly, whilst the lace employees were able to resist attacks on their status by stringent control, the hosiery workers were only too vulnerable.

The late Victorian years witnessed a developing counter-offensive by the employers against the trade unions.[3] The most militant manufacturers were prepared to use the law as a weapon with which to intimidate the unions, and this was the case in the Nottingham hosiery industry. In July 1891 eight workers who had been employed at W. Perry's No.4 factory were charged with conspiring to intimidate, and also with persistently following blacklegs. In the event this charge was struck out through lack of evidence, but similar charges continued to be made by other employers. One hosiery worker was brought to court on the allegation that he had told a blackleg 'he would get his head kicked in', whilst others were accused of 'baaring' at strike breakers. These charges were proved and the accused fined £2 each, leading the *Workman's Times* to describe the proceedings as 'a burlesque on justice'.[4] Onslaughts such as this provide some explanation for the development of political militancy, certainly by a section of hosiery workers. Not only did the union leaders play a major role in encouraging the organisation of the semi and unskilled workers, but they also avidly supported the arguments in favour of independent labour representation.

The conviction behind organisation of the unskilled came from a recognition of employer strategies throughout the 1880s. Bowers explained to the Royal Commission on Labour in 1892 that so severe was the attack on hosiery workers that at no time in the preceding 12 to 14 years had there not been at least one or two shops on strike. He explained that the employer always had enough non-union labour to break the strike:

> They can do it when we fetch one or two shops out. Then they have just enough surplus labour to fill them and that is when they have us beat. They generally schemed to have one or two shops strike instead of offering us a general reduction or letting us get a general strike.[5]

Of particular concern to hosiery workers was the large number of women workers employed in the industry. By 1906 67.7 per cent of the total female population of Nottingham was at work. 14,000 women were employed in the lace trade, whilst a further 11,000 were occupied in the manufacturing of hosiery, shirts and tobacco, as well as those engaged in dressmaking and millinery.[6]

Attempts to organise women workers were made in earnest from 1890 onwards. In 1890, due largely to Sam Bowers, a female hosiery workers' union was established with 400 members on its books.[7] In October 1892 Bowers arranged for Lady Dilke, together with Miss A.B. Marland and Miss A. Holyoake, to visit the town to help in the task of organising the female hosiery workers. This was successful and resulted in the establishment of a tailoresses' branch.[8] This attempt at organisation touched only a very small number of those employed. Moreover, precisely because the organisation of women workers was geared to the industrial concerns of male workers, the unions established were fragmentary. The Female Lace Workers' Society of Nottingham, the Nottingham Trade Union of Women Workers in the Lace Trade, the Nottingham branch of the National Federation of Women Workers, as well as the Female Cigar Workers and the Women's Hosiery Union all competed for membership with predictable debilitating effects.

There were particular difficulties in organising women workers. Wage rates were extremely low, and women's relationship to their employment was often governed by merciless middlemen. The large pool of unemployed women workers meant that employers could threaten reductions, loss of employment, or short-time working with impunity. For male hosiery workers the inability to organise women workers effectively further weakened their own position. By 1895, only two employers were still paying the wage rates agreed in the 1886 price-list. The Rotary Power Union, led by Bowers, seized on this opportunity to challenge employers collectively. The union demanded a return to the 1886 list, allowing a 10 per cent reduction to achieve uniformity. Strike action throughout 1895 and 1896 was necessary but the employers would only agree to a new list with reductions of 20 per cent.

Even this agreement was rejected by some employers who were able to use non-union labour in order to keep their undertakings going. In 1896 at least three hosiery firms moved machinery out of town rather than accept the prices agreed after the strike.[9] This removal, and others which followed it, caused the number of male and female hosiery workers to fall steadily. Opposition to the revival of joint regulation in the hosiery trade had been developing for some time and the factory owners told the Royal Commission on Labour in 1892 that 'even if they were to agree to a

Board tomorrow, the next day some of the members would run away from the arrangement.'[10] Difficulties of this kind were a factor in the increasing competition in the trade, not only between hand and power machinery, but between town and country. The advantage of the rural employer lay in lower wage costs, and the manufacturers of the country districts did everything possible to retain this advantage by stamping out incipient trade unionism wherever it showed itself.

These trends continued in the hosiery trade after the 1896 price-list had been agreed. In January 1897, for instance, Cope and Company was taken over by a new firm who immediately began trying to run it with the so-called 'free labour' organised by William Collison, prime mover in an organisation which offered to supply employers with blackleg labour.[11] The Trades Council immediately passed a resolution expressing the view that this attempt was 'degrading to the interests of manhood', but the use of non-union labour continued.[12] Five months later the hosiery firm of Eden and Southern began removing machinery to Mansfield, where they refused to employ members of the hosiery unions. Subsequently, the Nottingham Trades Council helped to organise a special meeting in Mansfield but these efforts were unable to stem what was part of a concerted attack by the employers on the living standards of workers in the industry.

The fortunes of the mining industry in this period were quite unlike those of Nottingham's other traditional industries. Late in 1887 a national conference of miners recommended a restriction of output in an attempt to clear surplus stocks and to secure a 10 per cent increase in pay. In Nottinghamshire the pits at Wollaton, Bestwood and Babbington refused to work more than an eight hour day. This led to a lock-out of the men at Bestwood and after a short struggle the policy was abandoned. This victory for the employers was quickly followed up. The men at Wollaton had won an increase of 2d a ton on soft coal and 1d a ton on the hard coal seam in November 1887. In May 1888, however, the company gave notice of a reduction to the old rate. 60 men who refused to accept the decrease were dismissed, with the result that the pit stopped work in sympathy. The 700 men involved received strike pay of 8s a week, plus 1s for each child under the age of 12. When funds began to run out after a month this had to be reduced until eventually the men were receiving only 2s a week. Predictably, the non-unionists began to return to work and eventually the strike was settled on the company's terms.

In the late summer of 1888 agitation for a 10 per cent increase resumed. The colliers were now making good time and the price of coal was beginning to move up. In these changed circumstances the advance was conceded within a fortnight. Undoubtedly the leadership drew important lessons from this series of events and in order to capitalise on the still rising price of coal a second campaign for a further 10 per cent increase was launched in the spring of 1889. In response the coal owners offered an immediate 5 per cent with 5 per cent to follow on 1 October. Throughout 1890 the demand for coal increased and the price of coal followed accordingly. Against this background the Nottinghamshire miners struck for yet another advance. 5,000 miners came out and the owners immediately responded by offering 5 per cent, with another increase of the same amount to follow on 1 July 1890. This easy victory marked the end of a successful period of wage agitation: in little more than two years the union had secured an increase of 40 per cent on the basic rate.

After the success of the wage campaign the Nottinghamshire Miners' Association began to concentrate on the need for an eight hour day. This campaign included mass meetings, conferences, and leaflet campaigns, and was generated not only by a desire for improved working conditions, but also by a need to maximise job opportunities by reducing working hours and by restricting entry into the industry. At a conference in 1890, William Bailey said:

> At a time like the present, when they were striving to get better wages, it was very important that they should try to prevent anyone who chose to apply from being allowed to go down the mine.[13]

This campaign, despite the support of other groups who had a vested interest in seeing the success of the eight hour agitation, failed to make much progress. A marked deterioration in trading conditions during 1892 saw a rapid fall in the pit-head price of coal. At 7s 3d a ton it was 9d lower than the previous year and 1s lower than in 1890. During the third week of March 1892 all pits in Nottinghamshire were at a standstill. According to Bailey the men were not on strike but 'taking their spring holiday'.[14] Subsequently the union decided that one day a week should be 'play day' with the consequence that every Nottinghamshire pit was idle on the Saturdays between 16 April and 27 August. Giving evidence to the Royal Commission on Labour in 1892 F.C. Corfield, representing the Nottinghamshire coal owners, listed their objections to the introduction of an eight hour day:

> Parliament ought not to be asked to legislate for adult labour. The effect of its introduction would be a reduction in output which would raise the price of coal and reduce earnings. The greater hurry consequent upon shorter hours

would increase danger in the mine. The system would lack elasticity, since neither masters nor men could take advantage of 'good times' by working longer hours.[15]

None of these objections carried much weight with the colliers.

In the early months of 1893 the employers attempted to cut the basic wage of mineworkers. The total wage paid was made up of a 'basic rate' and a percentage addition known as the 'current percentage'. In June 1893 the coal owners demanded a general cut of 25 per cent. Not surprisingly, the miners made their opposition plain. At least one employer (Seely) was opposed to the cut demanded but when the time came he issued lock-out notices with the rest of the coal owners. Alderman Thomas Bayley MP of the Digby Coal Company, was also sympathetic to the men and whilst speaking at their annual demonstration on Bulwell Forest he urged them to stand firm and implied he was prepared to re-open at the old rates. The lock-out notices had expired in the last week of July, and in September Bayley broke with the Coal Owners' Federation. This dispute created a great deal of bitterness. At one stage a man found working at Seely's Radford coal wharf was made to parade around the streets with his hands tied, a rope round his neck and bearing a black flag. Later the NMA received a £500 loan from the Lacemakers; a thousand loaves given by the Prudential Insurance Company were distributed at Bulwell, Basford and Clifton. The union's own fund allowed only 1s 6d per member over the ten weeks the lock-out lasted and although at the outbreak of the lock-out NMA funds stood at £17,000, by the end of the dispute the union was £30,000 in debt.

The attempt to reduce the wages of Nottinghamshire miners was met with militancy and anger. Percy Redfern, a Nottingham shopboy, recalled the passion with which the reduction was met:

> In the darkness, trucks of supposedly new won coal were overturned and burned; and next morning many of the younger men met ... each armed with some sort of club. Finally they marched out, along another road, to a more distant pit, and wild stories came back of mine officials hunted from the pit-bank and pit gear burned. Stemming the torrent, gathering their men together, the local trade union leaders, earnest Methodists, steadily preached patience and order.[16]

A company of dragoons was quartered in the district. Every morning the mounted, fully-armed soldiers, jangled past Redfern's shop and violence was repressed whilst the dispute went sullenly on. In September the Trades Council pledged its full support and set up an appeal for the miners. During the discussion which followed concern was expressed that the appeal might be frustrated by 'recent riotous proceedings'. All trade unionists were asked to 'assist the authorities in maintaining peace'. Gangs of roughs and youths, it was alleged, were, by their actions 'causing a revulsion of feeling on the part of local townspeople'. Rioting was certain, delegates were told, to alienate public sympathy.[17] By October the Trades Council had collected upwards of £40 for the miners' fund and later Bowers of the Hosiery Workers moved a Trades Council resolution which called for the 'public ownership of the mines and railways for the benefit of the nation and not, as at present, for the enrichment of individual capitalists'.[18]

One of these capitalists, Colonel Seely, was sympathetic to the union. He made loans available to the men and his wife provided meals for miners' children. Most owners had withdrawn the lock-out notices by 12 October, with the result that the miners were able to claim what they considered to be a famous victory. The men had received a good deal of public support. The union dispute fund was fuelled by collections organised by the *Nottingham Daily Express* and by money collected at churches, chapels, football matches and factories. The great lock-out of 1893 is an excellent example of the militant policies of the Miners' Federation. The settlement of the dispute, however, produced a situation which ultimately divorced union leaders like Bailey from the rank and file. The miners' leaders found themselves imprisoned by a form of conciliation agreement from which it was difficult to escape, partly because they themselves had hailed it as such a great advance at the end of the lock-out. Henceforth, militancy was to come from the rank and file.

From the conclusion of the 1893 lock-out the special character of the Leen Valley and the Nottingham pits became more clearly marked. The coal-owners together with the Digby, Wollaton, Clifton and Babbington Companies, formed an association of their own. The men employed in these mines enjoyed a five day week from 1892 whilst those in other parts of the county were sued by the owners for breach of contract when they tried to achieve the same advance. Ellis conceded the eight hour day in 1895 and it is plain that he, together with other enlightened employers like Bayley and Seely, was on friendly terms with the union leadership. Intelligent members of the English bourgeoisie, as Theodore Rothstein has pointed out, were not short of political acumen.[19] Coal-owners like Bayley, Seely and Ellis fully realised that the trade unions constituted a sort of safety valve for discontent, and there is no doubt that their support for the NMA had more than a touch of self-interest. Against this background it seems likely that this group of employers became, over a period, the political mentors not only of Bailey and the first generation of miners' leaders, but of Aaron Stewart, John George Hancock and George Spencer, who between them dominated the NMA for the next 25 years.

There is evidence to suggest that the new-found industrial militancy of Nottinghamshire's rank and file miners was reflected into a firmer stance on political matters. In 1892 Henry Broadhurst, an opponent of the eight hour day, was defeated in his bid to regain West Bridgford in the general election. William Bailey, the NMA leader refused to endorse Broadhurst because of his stance against the Eight Hour Bill.[20] Broadhurst felt a keen disappointment at his defeat which he explained by reference to the 'ingratitude of the miners', and in a later analysis of the election results his bitterness broke through:

> As the contest proceeded I missed from my meetings a number of influential people who had supported me in 1886 ... the election took place on the first Monday in July. On the Saturday a great open-air demonstration was held on the Forest. No speakers from the outside world were there to assist me, but I received great aid, as I had done at all my meetings, from the able and devoted labour leaders in Nottingham representing every branch of industry except miners ... when I contested Nottingham in 1886 no miners' organisation worthy of the name existed. Everything was practically in a state of chaos. When Mr Bailey, the newly appointed Miners' Agent, arrived on the scene I gave this gentleman every assistance in my power, introduced him to many of my political friends in the locality and requested all my supporters to aid him as far as was in their power in his task of organising the miners ... yet, when the contest came, Mr Bailey openly espoused the cause of Colonel Seely and exerted every effort to secure my defeat.[21]

Broadhurst's references to the help which he received from the 'able and devoted labour leaders' of Nottingham were certainly something of an exaggeration. Although there is no reason to doubt that in the late 1880s he had done a good deal to help the political and trade union career of William Bailey. The general election and the eight hour question did much to sour the relationship between the miners' leadership and the Liberal establishment; at rank and file level it opened the door to the socialist propagandists who were now beginning to appear with increasing regularity.

The economic conditions which underlay the sharpening of tensions between employers and workers in the late nineteenth century could not alone produce a shift to the left in working-class thinking. The fierceness of the antagonism displayed by employers towards trade unions in their attempts to subjugate workers certainly provided a 'jolt' which stimulated anti-capitalist sentiment. But without the development of a well defined socialist ideology, the labour movement had little chance of success. Socialist ideas were slow to take hold, and labourism continued to play a major role, but gradually the domination of Lib-Lab ideas was weakened. In the hosiery trade the leadership of the unions were strongly influenced by notions of solidarity and brotherhood, ideas which led them to seek the unionisation of all workers. In mining, the human needs of labour were recognised in the fight for the eight hour day. Moreover, masses of workers now looked seriously at the need for independent labour representation, recognising that they could trust only their own class to represent their class interests.

REFERENCES

[1] Council Minutes, Amalgamated Society of Lace Makers, November 1880.

[2] Trades Union Congress, *Annual Report*, 1883.

[3] See J. Saville, 'Trade Unions and Free Labour: The Background to the Taff Vale Decision, in A. Briggs and J. Saville (eds), *Essays in Labour History*, 1960, pp. 317-50.

[4] *Workman's Times*, 24 July 1891.

[5] Evidence of Samuel Bowers, *Royal Commission on Labour*, 1892.

[6] Report of an *Enquiry by the Board of Trade into Working Class Rents, Housing and Retail Prices*, 1906.

[7] Minutes, Nottingham Trades Council, 1 September 1890.

[8] *Workman's Times*, 29 October 1892.

[9] *The Knitters Circular and Monthly Record*, January 1896.

[10] Samuel Bowers claimed that the Board of Arbitration had been broken down: 'the employers who will not have it'. See his evidence to the *Royal Commission on Labour*, 1892.

[11] See the biography of William Collison, *The Apostle of Free Labour*, 1913.

[12] Minutes, Nottingham Trades Council, 20 January 1897.

[13] Quoted in A.R. Griffin, *Mining in the East Midlands 1550-1947*, 1971, p.114.

[14] *Nottingham Guardian*, 2 February 1892.

[15] Evidence of F.C. Corfield, *Royal Commission on Labour*, 1892.

[16] Percy Redfern, *Journey to Understanding*, 1946, pp. 19-20.

[17] Minutes, Nottingham Trades Council, 9 September 1893.

[18] Ibid., 4 October 1893.

[19] Theodore Rothstein, *From Chartism to Labourism*, 1929 (reprinted 1983), p. 266.

[20] For details of Bailey's campaign of opposition to Broadhurst, see the following; *Trade Union Congress*, Reports 1888 and 1889; *Nottingham Guardian*, 29 November 1890; *Workman's Times*, 8 December 1890.

[21] Henry Broadhurst, *The Story of his Life from a Stonemason's Bench to the Treasury Bench*, 1901, p. 243.

CHAPTER FIVE

Socialist Influences

Towns and cities in late Victorian England echoed with the shouts and cries of socialist or quasi-socialist movements. Certainly in large industrial centres like Nottingham these early propagandists found an interested audience. Open air socialist evangelising was at its height at the end of the nineteenth century, and the huge Market Square at the centre of Nottingham which had been the stage for great political meetings for over a hundred years, was often filled with speakers whose message varied from the traditional orthodoxy of Jimmy Dupe, a well-known preaching butcher, to the disturbing criticism of established society by the secularists and early socialists.

Throughout the 1880s the members of the Nottingham branch of the Social Democratic Federation (SDF), spurred on by an almost religious sense of right and wrong, were often to be heard speaking in the Market place, and on Sneinton Market in the west of the city. Their branch met weekly in Creswell's coffee house, but converts were made at the outdoor meetings which were often attended by huge crowds. By April 1884 *Justice*, the SDF newspaper, was listing more agents in Nottingham than in any other provincial town, and in August the annual conference of the SDF was told that the Nottingham branch was 'most active and has done good service'.[1]

Early in 1884 this group of early socialists derived added encouragement from the announcement that John Burns would become the SDF parliamentary candidate for West Nottingham. John Burns had been one of the delegates to the 1884 Amalgamated Society of Engineers rules revision conference in Nottingham. On the Sundays before and after the conference Burns spoke for the SDF at the Market Square meetings, and made frequent appearances in the town right through to the general election in 1885. At a Market Square meeting in June 1884 he addressed 1,000 people. The following Sunday more than 2,000 attended his meeting at Sneinton Market and 200 copies of *Justice* were sold. In the following week Burns spoke in different parts of the town on Monday, Tuesday and Friday, and in July, at a meeting of 3,000, a resolution was passed in favour of a labour candidate who 'must go in for a revolutionary programme'.[2] In September the socialists Proctor, Whalley and Keeling spoke at an open air meeting on the subject of 'Socialism and Representation', and money was handed up by workers who wanted to start an election fund for Burns. A week later a meeting in the Square unanimously passed a resolution in favour of Burns as the SDF candidate and on 26 September a great meeting in the Square of between 4,000 and 5,000 people clapped and cheered Burns until he agreed to stand.[3]

By October the SDF campaign was well under way with meetings in New and Old Radford, Basford, Bulwell and Hyson Green, as well as in the city centre. *Justice* fully supported Burns and late in October it vented some of the spleen for which the early socialist propagandists are justly famous by reporting the claim of Arnold Morley, the Liberal candidate in South Nottingham, that the 'moral condition of the working class was much improved'. This was due, said *Justice* to the presence in the midst of the Nottingham workers of the Nottingham Tabernacle, a religious edifice which enjoyed Morley's support. At least, added *Justice*, Morley had the grace not to say anything about the influence of the Morley hosiery factory and its starvation wages on the bodies and souls of the Morley workers, and went on to advise the town's workers to use the Burns candidature to show the world 'what they think about canting capitalists who steal the workers' labour to put in tabernacle plates'.[4]

A large meeting at the beginning of November resolved that 'as the Liberal Union refused to consider a memorial of working men asking for a Labour candidate, that Colonel Seely [the Liberal candidate] should retire in favour of the candidate John Burns.'[5] This impertinent suggestion was an early sign of the impatience felt by the most progressive elements of the working class movement with a Liberal Party which, in its attempt to become the party of 'the people', was increasingly caught between two stools. Later in the month Burns revealed just how worried the local Liberal Party was by his nomination. He announced that he had been approached by the Liberal agent anxious to see 'if any arrangement could be made for his withdrawal from the contest'.[6]

By the end of November the Burns campaign had enabled the SDF to establish three branches in the town. All three (East, West and South) were holding weekly business meetings as well as throwing their full weight into the propaganda campaign. Meeting after meeting of the town's workers reiterated their support for Burns. H.H. Champion of London and G. Smart of Salford were among speakers travelling to Nottingham to speak for Burns. On 5 December a large meeting stood in pouring rain to hear Burns and the local leadership. They passed a vote of confidence in the SDF candidate who by now was being harassed by organised Whig gangs, and also accused by the Liberals of being a paid agent of the Carlton Club, sent to Nottingham simply to split the working-class vote.

The Burns campaign was financed largely by the Fabian proprietor of the celebrated Bay Soap firm.[7] Joseph Burgess, an ex-lace-worker who became editor of the short-lived *Nottingham Operative*, was able to prove that the Liberals were active in offering Burns money to drop his candidature. Writing to Burgess, Burns, after dealing with these attempts, goes on to say that any Liberal visitor to his lodgings would have to go 'through a lively five minutes, should he call for the express purpose of inducing me to withdraw from the contest'.[8] Burns was attacked whilst on his way to a meeting in the Mechanics' Institute and when he arrived it was noticed that his lips were bleeding. The chairman had to explain that the candidate would not be able to speak for long because when he left home some villain had struck him in the mouth.

In the event it took a lot to silence Burns, who proceeded to make a speech in which he complained that the Liberals were asking his friends in labour organisations to rebut his candidature. It had been said, he went on, that he had come to split the vote, but there was no party for the labourers in the field ' … he was called a Tory tool, but would a Tory tool speak as he had done on behalf of the people?' There can be no doubt that the speeches of Burns and his principal supporters gave the Liberals a fright. Every attempt to smear and discredit him was made, and it is possible to detect an awareness in the attitude of the more perceptive representatives of the established political parties that Burns's growing popularity amongst the recently enfranchised proletariat represented the first erosion of their own position.

This fear deepened as the mood of the increasing numbers of unemployed in the town began to turn ugly. In October 1884 *Justice* reported that at large meetings of the unemployed in the town some said that they had not eaten for two days. Arising from these meetings a Committee of the Unemployed led by Mr Jones, a local miner, waited on the municipal candidates in order to demand work for the unemployed. During December the unemployed paraded the principal streets with a band and attendances at the SDF propaganda meetings continued to grow. Burns's election address contained the following ten points:

1. Free education, compulsory for all classes, together with the provision of at least one meal a day in Board Schools.
2. Eight hours or less to be the working day in all trades.
3. Adult suffrage.

4. Payment of members and all official expenses at elections.
5. Abolition of the House of Lords and all hereditary authority.
6. Triennial Parliaments.
7. Legislative independence for Ireland.
8. Free justice.
9. Nationalisation and municipalisation of land, mines, railways, machinery and banks.
10. The power of declaring war, making peace and making treaties to be vested in the people.[9]

These principles, Burns added, he put before the electors as a labour candidate and a social democrat, in the firm belief that only by a thorough change in the social and political system could the producing classes be benefited.

The echoes of Chartism which some of these demands evoke were also present in the riot which occurred on polling day. The ferocity of the running fights between the supporters of the various candidates have within them some elements of the pre-industrial popular disturbance. Writing in the *Sunday Express* in 1927, C.F.G. Masterman recalled the extraordinary version of events which Burns had told him:

> I shoved my wife into a fried-fish shop and said 'Stay there my girl.' The Market Place was paved with cobble stones. We levered up these stones with some instruments and, as he told me with delight, at the end of the evening there was not a pane of glass unbroken within the area of combat.[10]

This colourful account continued with Burns estimating the amount of damage done by the riot as £20,000, but Henry Snell told Burns's biographer that he considered this account highly imaginative. Imaginative or not, a major riot certainly did take place with the town's unemployed making up most of the crowd in the Market Place. The police effort to clear the square resulted in many broken heads, and at 9 p.m. the Mayor was forced to telegraph for the Hussars stationed at Leeds. The Leeds soldiers were, however, rendered immobile through lack of horse boxes, so an urgent appeal was sent to Sheffield. Eventually more than 100 men of the Lancashire and Yorkshire Regiment arrived in the town where a serious riot was in progress. Before the night was out a magistrate had been forced to read the Riot Act from a window of the Exchange Building and running fights had spilled from the Market Place into Dilkes Yard and Chapel Bar. When the poll was declared Burns stated that he was the man 'who refused to be greased' but, nevertheless, the Liberals had won easily.

Colonel Seely	(Liberal)	6,609
E. Cope	(Conservative)	3,797
J. Burns	(SDF)	598

So ended the Social Democratic Federation's first provincial campaign.

In August, the sixth annual conference of the SDF received a report that 'the candidature of Burns in Nottingham thoroughly permeated the town with Socialism and our candidate would undoubtedly have obtained a much larger number of votes had it not been for the lying reports concerning him which the Liberals set about on polling day.'[11] Although this claim may have pitched things a little high, it is clear that a great deal of propaganda work had been done. The big outdoor meetings and the steady sale of *Justice* showed that the Socialist evangelists were asking some very awkward questions, as the following report in the *Nottingham Figaro* reveals:

> At a neighbouring platform *Justice* is to be had for a penny. 'Cheaper than you can get it at the Town Hall' one of the vendors remarked. This must be Socialism, listen! 'What I can't understand is this … why should one man get £20 a week and another £1?' If you forward this poser, Mr Speaker, to the Editorial sanctum you will no doubt be requested to ask another.[12]

Two years later, in the year of Queen Victoria's Jubilee, conditions in the town continued to reflect the huge gap between rich and poor. In August 1887 the *Nottingham Daily Express* wrote:

> In this year of the Jubilee, there is a good deal of suffering in Nottingham from want of employment and there are many more than is generally supposed living on miserable pittances, in the hope of a better living. Living … no, existing on earnings which are barely enough to keep body and soul together.[13]

In this period, as Henry Pelling has pointed out, unemployment was helping to generate a situation in which desperate men were willing to threaten public order.[14] Not surprisingly, the SDF took the lead in organising demonstrations of those out of work whilst at the same time continuing their efforts to convert and recruit the Nottingham working class. In February 1887, two excellent open air meetings on 'Socialism and the Unemployed' and 'The Right to Live' were held, and the outdoor propaganda work amongst those out of work was bringing new recruits into the town's growing labour movement. In March the local socialists celebrated the anniversary of the Paris Commune with a tea and ball, held in the Secular Hall. Speeches on the Commune were delivered by Whalley, Cooper and Proctor in English and by Detre in French. The

'Marseillaise' was sung in French by Coutoux and songs and recitations were given. Among the decorations was a red banner inscribed 'Vive la Commune' and the names of Hyndman, Morris, Delescluze and Dombrowski were displayed. After singing the 'Marseillaise' in chorus, the meeting was brought to an end with three cheers for the Commune.[15]

Underneath comradely feeling of this sort, the traditional tensions of the left were as obvious in Nottingham as in any other area. These strains were reflected in a series of open air meetings during July which dealt with the rival paths of reform and revolution. This debate probably reflected the fact that the SDF had been losing members to the Socialist League. In August 1887 the SDF *Annual Report* included an item observing that although the Nottingham branch was held together by a group of energetic workers, local differences and intrigues meant that propaganda was not spreading as well as would be wished. But by October the SDF had opened a new clubroom in the town, and *Justice* was able to report that 'our old comrades Peacock, Knight and others have rejoined the SDF and we intend to start on active propaganda at once.'[16]

True to their word the SDF group immediately called a special meeting to condemn the murder of the Chicago anarchists. A fortnight later two campaign meetings were organised around the candidature of Whalley, who contested Wollaton Ward in the municipal elections. Whalley had a difficult fight, and not surprisingly, he lost by 287 votes to 1,242 for Smith, the Liberal candidate.

The result may have been poor, but the local group was not downhearted. The tea party held to celebrate Whalley's election fight was 'crowded to excess'. Some idea of the difficulties faced by the socialists in trying to return a candidate of their own can be gathered from the *Justice* report of the election:

> Though we did not poll many, the result is encouraging considering the conditions under which we fought. Our opponent was a publican and had the support of a number of Aldermen and Town Councillors. Having plenty of money he well advertised his meetings and held them in nice comfortable school rooms. We, having scarcely any money, and not more than 7 or 8 workers, had to hold our meetings in the open air on the bitterly cold nights, besides crying the meetings ourselves with a bell. Wollaton Ward is the worst possible ward we could have contested, being dominated entirely by the Liberal caucus. The people agreed with our comrade and even admitted that he was the best man, but they objected to him because he had not come through the legitimate channel.[17]

The reference in this report to the 'Liberal caucus' is an indication of the firm grip still held by the Liberals on a large section of the working-class vote.

Early signs of Socialist League influence in Nottingham date from January 1886 when Tom Proctor wrote to William Morris to ask for one quire of the Socialist League paper *Commonweal*. At the time Proctor was secretary of the Nottingham Council of the SDF, a fact that may be an indication of the fragmentation of SDF support in this period. The Socialist League was the product of the major SDF split, whilst another group which seems to have enjoyed some Nottingham support was the short-lived Socialist Union. Certainly, a series of letters written by three Nottingham socialists to the headquarters of the Socialist League would indicate that the town's socialists were fully involved in the internal arguments of the early movement. The writers' use of such terms as 'Social Union: Nottingham Section', 'Socialist Union' and 'Nottingham and District Social Democratic League' all suggest that the town's activists were fully aware of wider developments. At one point the possibility of Nottingham becoming involved in a 'Socialist Labour Party' is mentioned, and this may be a reference to the movement launched in the north by J.L. Mahon in 1887.[18]

In 1886 the Socialist League appointed a *Commonweal* sales agent in the town to overcome the difficulty experienced in obtaining copies of the newspaper. Newspapers played a crucial part in political propaganda and a journal such as *Commonweal* was not only a vital means of disseminating Marxist views and recruiting new members, but also an essential weekly morale-booster for existing members. The Nottingham socialists still had problems of supply; papers were late, over-supplied, and sometimes did not arrive at all. In May, Proctor wrote to complain 'this will make the third week they have not come'.[19] In March he had explained: 'We sell them not to make money but as a means of propaganda and we are not in a position to bear any loss, being all working men and many out of work.'[20] All of this helps to underline the correctness of Henry Pelling's view that the Socialist League was often inefficient[21] and gives added point to the claim of E.P. Thompson that to some extent the Socialist League members were part of a 'destructive' tradition which with its extreme individualism and desire to dispense with party discipline and serious organisation, was inherited from the ultra-Jacobin heritage.[22]

In November 1887 the municipal elections presented the League with an opportunity to try its strength at the polls. At very short notice Proctor, described by the *Nottingham Daily Express* as a 'labour or working man's candidate'[23] ran officially as an Independent in Byron Ward. Meanwhile, Samuel Tyler, an old member of the First

International, was nominated as an Independent candidate in St Mary's
Ward. Neither of these two Socialist League supporters did well:

Byron Ward

Berryman	(Conservative)	875
Mutch	(Liberal)	814
Proctor	(Independent)	61

St Mary's Ward

Young	(Conservative)	811
Sylvester	(Liberal)	466
Tyler	(Independent)	68

At a meeting in October, Bailey, the Miners' Agent, together with
Farmer, the Liberal agent in the Eastern Division, had asked Proctor to
withdraw in return for an undertaking that twelve months hence a labour
candidate would be selected by the Liberals. Proctor, however, refused
this offer and in the event, his campaign won enough votes to keep the
Liberal out. Although both Proctor and Tyler stood as Independent
candidates the local press made it quite clear that both men were
socialists, as it also did in the case of the SDF candidate who, it will be
remembered, polled 287 against the victorious Liberal in Wollaton Ward.
Whalley, at a mass meeting just before the poll, produced a letter from
Bailey of the NMA 'wishing him every success and urging workmen to
place him at the top of the poll'.[24] According to the *Nottingham Daily
Express*, however, Whalley also claimed to be a Liberal and a nominee of
the Labour Representation Committee, of which the newspaper
sarcastically remarked, 'nothing, to all intents and purposes, is known'.[25]
In reality, of course, this comment could be held true of all the early
socialist organisations.

Of the groups active in the 1880s the Socialist League was, in
numerical terms, amongst the smallest. Its contribution to the early
movement was, nevertheless, central. Under the direction of William
Morris the League took the lead in exposing the drabness of ordinary
workers' lives, in demanding a real improvement in the quality of life. The
disgust felt by William Morris for the philistinism and joylessness of the
middle class was, as E.P. Thompson has pointed out, a main feature of
the Socialist League's appeal and there is plenty of evidence that in
Nottingham his philosophy had a great deal of influence amongst the
town's socialists.[26] Something of the atmosphere of the Nottingham
Socialist League meetings can be gathered from Henry Snell's
autobiography in which, after telling of the tremendous influence which

Edward Carpenter had on him, he recounts

> memories of a Sunday fellowship meeting at Ambergate, midway between
> Nottingham, Sheffield and Leicester ... crowded into a local inn where
> Carpenter played the piano and we sang the best known Socialist songs.[27]

Later, he recalls

> small bands of young crusaders, including myself, carried the glad tidings to
> the 'heathen' living outside the Borough ... our practice was to ride out on a
> penny farthing from the saddle of which, the machine being kept in the
> perpendicular by comrades either side, I and others preached the gospel.[28]

The fervour of Snell and his comrades is difficult to understand until one
realises that underpinning the beliefs of the early socialists was the
certainty in their minds that radical change was not far off. The leading
propagandists underlined this view in their choice of subjects for the open
air meetings, for example, 'The Coming Revolution', and the Sunday
evening discussions in the group's clubroom were full of certainty that
the Socialist revolution was very close.

The Socialist League's great contribution to the socialist movement
was its vision of a great co-operative commonwealth. The emphasis it
placed on the cultural poverty to which large sections of the working
class were condemned by the capitalist system was tremendously
valuable, and something of its tone can be understood from the
Nottingham group's autumn lecture programme which included William
Morris speaking to an audience of 250 on 'Art and the Working Class', a
meeting on 'Monopoly', and a meeting in the Secular Hall at which
Morris lectured on the 'Origin of Ornamental Art'. The use of the Secular
Hall on this occasion underlines the fact that many of the early activists
had come to socialism via secularist agitation. Secularist lectures like that
given by Mr Shephard of Leicester in September 1887 on 'Christianity as
an elevating influence on Mankind' might not, on the surface, seem very
likely to produce socialist militants, but, as Snell recalled many years
later, they 'afforded opportunities for information and discussion'.[29] They
also allowed Snell and others to hear Bradlaugh, Holyoake, Edward
Aveling, Charles Watts and Annie Besant, and there is little doubt that
many who were to play a vital role in building the movement developed
their speaking and debating skills at its meetings.

The emphasis on the quality of working-class life, the major feature of
Socialist League propaganda, naturally brought many members of the
Nottingham branch into contact with the unemployed. As part of a
campaign on this theme Peacock, who had been elected to the School
Board as a socialist in 1886 and who was 'very popular' according to a

letter to the League from Clifton,[30] began to denounce the 'sweating' of teachers by the Nottingham School Board. This activity, together with an attempt by the lace manufacturers to reduce wages by 40 per cent, helped to bring recruits into the socialist organisations. In June 1889 *Commonweal* reported that several new members had joined the branch and that things were beginning to move; later in the month it reported that the Nottingham branch was progressing satisfactorily, both financially and numerically, and that it had been decided to run Peacock, Proctor and Whalley as socialist candidates in the November School Board elections.

Since Whalley was a member of the SDF this campaign represented an alliance between the Socialist League and the Social Democratic Federation. This had been cemented in July by a joint excursion to Charnwood Forest. The members of the various groups travelled in horse brakes and there was much waving of red flags and singing of the 'Marseillaise'. After dinner and tea at a farmhouse a single innings cricket match was played between socialists and secularists in which the former scored 67 to win the match against their opponents' 46. Sensibly, the socialist alliance was maintained in day-to-day propaganda and by August both groups were active in supporting a lace-makers' strike and in helping the gas stokers and other unskilled workers to organise themselves into a trade union.

In November, Annie Besant was in the town to speak at the Secular Hall on 'Education' and later she helped to inaugurate the socialist School Board election campaign at a Market Square meeting. Later in the month, three meetings were held each night in the week before polling day, propaganda which helped to push the socialist vote 2,000 above the vote recorded in 1886. Although no socialist candidate was returned, Peacock received 14,176 votes and Proctor 10,276. In December Proctor opened a series of indoor meetings with a talk on the 'Unskilled Labour Movement', and a tea party and socialist sing-song saw the old year out.

During July 1888 John Burns again visited the town to renew the contacts which he made during his election campaign, and to help the Nottingham socialists in their propaganda work. Writing in his diary Burns noted:

Went to Nottingham, arrived 4.30 p.m. Met by Whalley and Clarke. Town very depressed, many out of work. Measuring the poverty of the town by what I saw on the streets and in the Market Place, I should say that there was 40 per cent less money being spent than two years ago.[31]

On the Sunday morning following this entry Burns spoke to 2,000 at a meeting in Sneinton Market and in the evening he spoke to an estimated

6,000 in the Market Place before visiting the SDF members in their clubroom. At the discussion which took place at the club Burns noted that the Nottingham socialists expressed themselves as being in favour of amalgamation with other socialist organisations, so although the town was undoubtedly affected by the arguments and conflicts sponsored by national personalities, at a local level a good deal of co-operation was possible between the different groups and sectarianism was not a major problem at this stage.

Many of those in the audiences to which Burns spoke came from the ranks of the unemployed, and like other early socialists Burns depended on their support as well as that of unskilled workers. The concern of the Socialist League for these people was always conspicuous and in May 1890 it was well demonstrated when Tom McCarthy spoke to huge meetings in the town on 'My Experience in the Great Dock Strike'. From concern with the under-privileged flowed a natural concern for the plight of women workers; this was prominent in a *Commonweal* account of the daily life of Nottingham's working women:

> All sorts of minor tyrannies are imposed to break the spirit of the workers and render them docile serfs. The forewomen are selected especially for their ability to 'nag' and 'drive' the hands. One Nottingham factory manager occasionally strolls down the room, and if one of the women should turn her head to glance at the majestic passer-by she is instantly dismissed. This gentleman is a prominent Liberal and Churchwarden, and his master an MP who inherits the virtues of a pious father (Morley), is to be the Almighty's principal instrument in returning Mr Gladstone back to office at the General Election. In several large warehouses the girls are obliged to come half an hour earlier in the morning to have some hired parson preach and pray at them. One of these sky-pilots had the impudence to denounce his hearers because of the few ribbons they had obtained. The managers, sub-managers and chief clerks use their power to seduce girls and then cast them adrift. The gilded youth of two counties make Nottingham their pleasure house and the army of despair which lounges round the 'Clarendon', the 'Three Crowns' or that glorified gin-palace known as the 'Talbot' is recruited from the weaker sisters of the warehouse. The result is a social ulcer which permeates the bourgeois in spite of all efforts to conceal it. One hears of Aldermen slipping up back streets to brothels, or the disappearance of an unconvenient witness in a police prosecution because her evidence might compromise members of the Town Council, or the pillar of society who is said to have a kept woman in almost every street, and who turns up at mission meetings. Our MPs are a curious medley worthy of their supporters; Broadhurst, who has sold and betrayed the workers like the Judas he is; Morley, the superior person; and Smith Wright, a jingo banker. Not one has an idea above the level of the grocer's shop, and not one cares two pins for the welfare of the workers.[32]

Such comment makes clear that the Nottingham branch of the Socialist League was concerned at the overall corruption of late Victorian society.

To get away from poverty and the smoke and grime which went with the poverty of the period, the Socialist League members together with those of the SDF enjoyed getting out into the nearby countryside. In June 1890, after a ramble to Stoke Ferry, delegates from Sheffield, Leicester, Chesterfield, Derby, Newark and Long Eaton met with Nottingham representatives to form an East Midland Federation. After this meeting a joint demonstration in Nottingham Market Place with two platforms drew crowds of between 3,000 and 4,000. A month later the annual picnic visited Charnwood Forest and an enjoyable day was spent rambling among the bracken and foxgloves, mounting the ricks and trespassing in the woods in defiance of 'Law and Order'.[33]

Back in the town unemployment and poverty remained a tremendous problem, and Proctor in particular continued with his efforts to organise the unskilled. Conditions in the town seem to have been extremely grim, with the *Workman's Times* reporting in November 1890 that Nottingham 'has been passing through a period of depression never before experienced for length of time or acuteness. Distress is very alarming and serious indeed.'[34] As the situation continued to deteriorate the opportunities for socialist propaganda multiplied. Unfortunately, in 1891 Proctor, together with the other leading socialist Whalley, left the town and *Justice* reported that the local movement was flagging as a result. Two successful meetings in September, however, provided a fresh start, and the SDF reported that the Trades Council was beginning to play an important part in local agitation. These new links with the town's trade unionists are best illustrated in the development of the Independent Labour Party (ILP), the first seeds of which were being sown in this period.

The socialism of this early period had undoubted shortcomings, although it made very real contributions in the fields of organisation and theory. Although ideological disputes all too frequently led the membership of the early socialist groups into pointless and bitter argument, cutting them off without good reason from the mass of the working class, the Nottingham membership of both the SDF and the Socialist League seem for the most part to have done their best to break down sectarian divisions. The SDF played a decisive role in beginning the conversion of the unskilled to socialism, whilst the Socialist League contributed a concern with the quality of life which is still a major theme of the modern socialist movement. Evaluated in their own terms, both groups did indeed play an important pioneering role in laying the foundations of the Nottingham labour movement.

REFERENCES

[1] *Justice*, 9 August 1884.

[2] Ibid., 6 June 1884.

[3] Ibid., 26 September 1884.

[4] Ibid., 10 October 1884.

[5] Ibid., 7 November 1884.

[6] Ibid., 14 November 1884.

[7] William Kent, *John Burns: Labour's Lost Leader*, 1950, p. 22.

[8] J. Burgess, *John Burns: The Rise and Progress of a Right Honourable*, 1911, p. 22.

[9] Kent, op. cit., p. 20.

[10] *Sunday Express*, 2 January 1927, quoted in ibid.

[11] *Justice*, 7 August 1886.

[12] *Nottingham Figaro*, 22 August 1885.

[13] *Nottingham Daily Express*, 18 August 1887.

[14] Henry Pelling, *Origins of the Labour Party*, 1976 edn., pp. 42-4.

[15] *Justice*, 2 April 1887.

[16] Ibid., 18 October 1887.

[17] Ibid., 19 November 1887.

[18] Mahon was involved together with SDF militants in helping to establish a North of England Socialist Federation during the course of the great miners' strike of 1887. See Pelling, op. cit., pp. 54ff.

[19] Letter from T. Proctor to the Socialist League, 11 May 1886.

[20] Ibid., 5 March 1886.

[21] Pelling, op. cit., pp. 27-32.

[22] E.P. Thompson, *William Morris*, 1977 edn., p. 376.

[23] *Nottingham Daily Express*, 2 November 1887.

[24] Ibid., 1 November 1887.

[25] Ibid., 2 November 1887.

[26] During these years William Morris made visits to Nottingham.

[27] Henry Snell, *Men, Movements and Myself*, 1936, p. 56.

[28] Ibid., p. 60.

[29] Ibid.

[30] Letter, Clifton to the Socialist League, 7 June 1887.

[31] John Burns, Diary entry, 30 June 1888.

[32] *Commonweal*, 24 May 1890.

[33] Ibid., 16 August 1890.

[34] *Workman's Times*, 21 November 1890.

PART TWO

Young Turks and The Making of The New World 1895 to 1918

CHAPTER SIX

Pressures for Change:
The Labour Movement 1895 to 1914

The period 1895 to 1914 represents a watershed in the history of the British labour movement, for it saw a restructuring of working-class institutions and the politicisation of sections of the proletariat previously unorganised and unrepresented. Crucial to the process of politicisation in Nottingham was the decline of both the lace and hosiery industries and the general threat of unemployment. In the period between the turn of the century and the outbreak of the First World War, the accelerating developments in industry forced a change of focus in the labour movement. New machinery, new work and new ways of making traditional articles all constituted a major threat, not only to the economic status of the working class, but also to the pattern of the local community. Against this background it is not surprising that defensiveness born of fear became an important factor in shaping political development.

Those industries which had provided employment and high wage rates for the skilled craftsmen of the mid-Victorian period were most seriously affected by economic change and new technology. Entrenched in a philosophy of respectability and self-advancement, workers in these industries responded to the new conditions by attempting to defend a position which was no longer tenable. An identification with labourist political ideology prevented more imaginative strategies, such as unionisation of all auxiliary workers in order to strengthen the workers' bargaining position. In particular the negative attitude towards the unionisation of women workers had long-term effects on the local labour movement. This defensive stance of workers and their unions was typical of those employed in hosiery and lace, but can also be found in most trades which had skilled craftsmen. Thus, although engineers did not face the same levels of unemployment as those found in hosiery, they practised the same union exclusiveness.

Throughout the 1890s the former collaboration between employers and unions in the Nottingham lace and hosiery trades became increasingly difficult to sustain, as old arrangements and understandings were undermined by technical change and the effects of competition. This breakdown was particularly marked in the hosiery industry where the unions' efforts to maintain the old price list and some semblance of collective bargaining were continually eroded. In the hosiery industry, technical change and skilful manipulation of surplus labour allowed employers successfully to combat union activity. To a limited extent lace workers were able to resist employer encroachments, but their nadir was reached in 1899. In this year the employers took the offensive by demanding a reduction of 40 per cent in the wages of the Curtain branch, 25 per cent in the Levers branch and 15 per cent of all other rates. A mass meeting of the men in the Mechanics' Hall refused to concede to these demands or to go to arbitration. As a consequence the workers were locked out and for several weeks 2,500 operatives were out of work. Eventually, following the intercession of the Mayor, agreement on a return to work was reached, pending an award by the Board of Conciliation which eventually fixed a $12\frac{1}{2}$ per cent reduction. Giving evidence to the Parliamentary Commission on Home Work in 1907, Appleton the Lace Makers' general secretary claimed that since 1895 there had been a constant attack by the employers on the wages of the work-force. Agreeing that wage and profit levels had originally been very high, Appleton made the point that the introduction of modern machinery had gradually been bringing them down. He went on to complain about the activity of 'middlewomen' before admitting that the men's union had no control whatsoever over the rates paid to outworkers. This admission raises the question of whether the Lace Makers' Society really wanted to help other workers in the industry, or whether their craft exclusiveness persuaded them that their own interests were best served by ignoring other groups. In February 1900, for instance, the Lace Makers' executive were visited by a deputation from the Trades Council who argued that the loss of members recently suffered by the unskilled Auxiliary Union was a consequence of 'lack of interest on the part of the lace makers'. Earlier, in November 1897 there had been a lot of discussion about the desirability of admitting supervisory grades to the organisation. Eventually it was agreed that 'it was illogical to drive them from the Society when by retaining them we could control to a certain extent their activities.'[1]

Women and girls employed as outworkers suffered appalling conditions. Mrs Bartlett, a Nottingham lace worker explained to Sidney

Lace workers near Goose Gate, 1914

and Beatrice Webb that most lace manufacturers gave all or most of their work out through middle men or women.

> These 'sharks' usually hire a small ill-ventilated and insanitary workshop into which they squeeze far too large a number of girls and women ... their hours are dreadfully long and the Factory Acts are being systematically ignored.[2]

Against this background the efforts of male-dominated trade unions and political groups to involve women in the local labour movement were pathetically inadequate. During the 1890s the Lace Makers' Society did spend both time and money on efforts to establish a Female Lace Workers' Organisation, but their attempts were never more than half-hearted. According to the Webbs the women's union was totally controlled by the male lace workers, the secretary of the women's organisation being a member of the executive of the men's organisation. Its committee consisted of nine elected women and three members of the executive of the men's union, but in fact the organisation was run by men: 'the women members hardly ever speak and never vote against proposals made by the men.'[3]

As both the lace and hosiery trades continued to decline, the problems of organising women workers became more acute and it is reasonable to assume that as unemployment increased latent chauvinistic hostility to the idea of female trade unionism became more of a problem. In November 1905, for example, Mrs Brooks and Mrs Clifford attended the Trades Council on behalf of the Female Lace Workers, requesting organisational help which was not forthcoming. During the course of a Trades Council discussion on unemployment in 1905, a delegate from the Amalgamated Society of Engineers opposed the introduction of female labour into the engineering industry.[4] Although an examination of the Trades Council minute books for these years reveals occasional reference to the 'problem' of women workers, there is no real evidence of any widespread recognition of the need for women to organise themselves into trade unions. By the end of 1908 the Trades Council itself estimated that there were 'not more than 1,000 female workers organised in the city'.[5] This estimate followed a meeting at which Julia Varley, a member of the Bradford Trades Council and a *Clarion* writer, had urged the need for female organisation.

Since the established labour movement failed to organise women workers effectively it is not surprising that neither in the political field does there seem to have been much understanding of the legitimate demands and aspirations of the female population. The total exclusion of women from the electoral registers was actually supported by many men and this, together with the low economic status of women's work, made the female population highly vulnerable to 'deferential pressure'. In 1909, for instance, Higginbottom, the ILP secretary, reported his distress after wandering through the slums on a hot day and seeing women workers 'sitting at the doors of their hutches, manipulating lace heaped on the filthy pavement'.[6] This state of affairs undoubtedly helped to reinforce the conservatism and traditionalism of much of the working class. This was demonstrated at a Trades Council meeting in June 1906 when a letter from the Women's Social and Political Union (WSPU) asking for help was simply allowed 'to lie on the table'.[7] As late as 1913 a letter from the WSPU protesting at the introduction of the 'Cat and Mouse' Act was ignored by the Trades Council delegates and a later offer by the Suffragettes to provide the Trades Council with a speaker was rejected by 56 votes to 34.[8] The reports of the ILP activity in Nottingham reveal a patronising attitude whenever they mention women members and it seems likely that even progressive elements found it difficult to accept that women were entitled to equal political and economic status. The leaders of the Women's Suffrage movement often spoke in Nottingham but there is little evidence that their appeal made much impact on the working-class women of the town. In 1910 the Nottingham branch officers of the Women's Suffrage Society described themselves as being 'of liberal views', but by itself this did not guarantee that the organisation would make any real effort to recruit members of the working class. An examination of the branch records reveals just over 100 members living in working-class areas of the town, but it is impossible to estimate just how many of these were potential activists in the working-class movement.[9]

In the period of mounting industrial unrest around 1910 and 1911 there are several signs in the town of an increasing willingness to try and help women establish themselves as trade unionists. The Trades Council during 1910 collected £45 for striking members of the Female Cigar Workers and in November 1911 the Trades Council agreed to give assistance to the Nottingham branch of the Women Workers' Federation in organising an open meeting. This followed an appeal from Mrs Young and Mrs Gosling who asked the Trades Council to support locked-out lace workers. It seems that some 200 members of the newly formed Women Workers' Union were in dispute with the employers after refusing to sign a 'contracting out' form agreeing not to demand the new lace finishing rate fixed by the Board of Trade until the compulsory implementation date.[10] During the course of the Trades Council discussion it was claimed that 2,000 women had joined the union and.

even allowing for exaggeration, this report indicates that progress was beginning to be made at the industrial front.

In the case of other groups in the lace industry, specialist craft organisations seem to have developed without the Lace Makers' Society attempting to build solidarity within the industry. The Carriage Straighteners' Society, the Bobbin and Carriage Makers' Union, the Bobbin, Carriage, Comb and Dropper Makers' Society, the Amalgamated Society of Lace Pattern Readers, Correctors, Press and Piano Punchers, as well as the Lace Designers and Auxiliary Workers, all had separate organisations and there were no serious attempts to establish a unified approach to the problems of the industry's work-force. This was a serious failure given that the developments in the lace trade reflected deeper underlying trends in the British economy. As the marginal productivity of labour began to fall rapidly, the twist-hands' standard of living deteriorated sharply and the years 1898 to 1914 saw a reversal of the trend in real wages. In addition, some of the troughs in the trade were very deep; in 1904, for instance, unemployment in Nottingham was more than 21 per cent and short-time working was very common.[11]

As the position in the trade continued to deteriorate, a good deal of tension developed between the different sections of the Lace Makers' Society. In November 1904, a deputation came before the union's executive to report on a mass meeting held on the Forest. This meeting had passed a resolution of protest at 'the outrageous reduction agreed to by the General Purposes Committee'. It seems that during a period when real wages were falling the union official had offered a 15 per cent reduction on the rates of all new machines erected in Nottingham. The unofficial meeting had gone on to demand that the general secretary be asked to resign at once 'and that he be paid all that is due to him'. These demands were coming from the Levers section and they were only successfully deflected after the executive council had placed on record its own protest at the 'slanderous and unscrupulous' attacks being made on Appleton.[12] The general secretary survived this particular attack but the tensions which caused it continued with the industry's decline.

Arbitration proceedings in 1905 demonstrated that lace was continuing to expand in rural centres outside the town where there were no fixed rates. In addition, lace factories in Nottingham itself were being turned over to other manufacturers including cycles, jam and tobacco. It also became clear that despite allegations of restrictive practices, wages in the Levers branch were little more than £1 a week with some twist-hands being unemployed for three to nine months of the year. Real wages for those in full-time work were undoubtedly in decline at least from the turn of the century. Charles Wardle, in presenting the union's case, declared that working conditions were very bad, with many twist-hands able to earn only a poor wage on the machine provided. The modern Nottingham machine, declared Wardle, was 20 years old and besides this 'the Long Eaton machine was a machine and a half'.[13] During this period it was claimed that there were 1,595 lace machines outside Nottingham, employing 2,409 men, of whom only 549 belonged to the union. Of 2,805 Nottingham members in 1905, only 2,214 were working and there is little doubt that, had it not been for the growth of tobacco, pharmaceuticals and cycle-making in the town, Nottingham would have suffered serious decline.

The defensiveness of unions representing the traditional industries of hosiery and lace played an important role in the political mentality of the Nottingham labour movement in the period from 1895 to 1914. The inappropriateness of the labourist political outlook of so many of the early union leaders to the changed economic conditions was becoming apparent. Skilled men faced short-time working and unemployment, and employers no longer feigned interest and paternalistic concern for their labour force. In these circumstances it was difficult to maintain an ideology based on concepts of self-help, equality of opportunity and identity of interests between employer and worker. This fracture in the cohesivenesss of labourist attitudes certainly encouraged the development of socialist thinking and its adoption by a section of the labour movement. Nevertheless, it was the defensiveness of the traditional unions and their inability to break fully from labourism which prevented socialist ideas from reaching greater numbers of working people. Not only did such thinking hold sway in the older industries, but it was also present in the emerging industries on which Nottingham's twentieth-century wealth was based.

Of the industries which had established themselves in Nottingham towards the end of the nineteenth century, cycle-making was perhaps the most important. In 1897 it was estimated that 5,000 people were employed in the trade in and around Nottingham.[14] At this time some of the work-force were members of the Amalgamated Society of Engineers (ASE), whilst others belonged to the Filers' Union or one of the labourers' associations. In 1897 the filers struck successfully for an advance and shortly afterwards a branch of the National Union of Cycle Workers was formed. So great was the response that two more branches were quickly formed. These developments were viewed by the manufacturers with some apprehension and they eagerly supported the action of the National Engineering Employers' Association who, in opposition to the demands of the ASE for the introduction of an eight hour day, declared a national lock-out.

There was marked sympathy for the cycle workers in the town, and during the lock-out immense crowds hooted and jeered at blacklegs on their way to and from work. As a consequence of these incidents the employers' federation prosecuted several trade unionists for assault but, despite the publicity which these cases attracted, support for the engineers continued to grow. At one stage the *Nottingham Daily Express* inaugurated a 'Nothing to Eat Fund' and the Trades Council raised subscriptions and organised benefit concerts, but the dispute ended in victory for the employers and the cycle workers returned to work, with some manufacturers offering lower rates than they had paid hitherto. Encouraged by this victory, the engineering employers in the town tightened their grip. In April 1898 the *Labour Leader* pointed out that the employers in Nottingham were following up the fight with better organisation. 'They are bent on keeping the mastery', reported the ILP newspaper, before going on to quote from a circular issued by Sir Ernest Jardine, the president of the Nottingham and District Employers' Association:

> Your Committee have decided to keep a register of non-society men wanting employment. In order that this may be carried out all members are requested to at once report full particulars of all good men they may (from any cause) be discharging, also the same particulars of any likely men applying to them for employment ... the Committee feel that this register will assist greatly in keeping good free labour men in our district.[15]

Part of the motivation which lay behind this circular was the employers' need to control the growth of militant attitudes amongst the engineering labour force. The public arguments during the lock-out had centred on the eight hour day, but the crucial issue for the employers was the union's increasingly aggressive attitude towards technical change.

Rapid and fundamental change in the engineering machine shops of Nottingham began about 1890. The capstan and turret lathe, improved varieties of milling machine, external and surface grinders, the vertical borer and the radial drill, all threatened the fitter and the turner with the problem of dilution. Works engineers, planners, inspectors, rate-fixers and progress-men all appeared in these years, as did the introduction of detailed specification, close inspection and tighter supervision. All of these changes encouraged the growth of 'speed-ups', as well as the use of the payments-by-results system. In resisting these developments, members of the ASE and other unions tried to strengthen their traditional defences, as well as attempting the complete banning of piece-work. George Allcroft of the ASE, had told the Webbs in 1893 that the piece-work system was always strongly objected to in the town. 'No task-work or piece-work in any form whatever is now allowed in Nottingham,' insisted Allcroft, before explaining that the local union's district committee had passed a special rule which they strictly enforced, not allowing any man to operate more than one machine. This evidence underlines the fact that the strength of the engineers in the town was firmly based on the work process having been divided by the workers on the basis of demarcated skills. Men like Allcroft sought strength through exclusiveness. For a time the location of the engineers in expanding industries enabled them to achieve a level of collaboration with the employers on the basis of perceived mutual interest, but towards the end of the nineteenth century this began to break up, as competition and the introduction of new machinery forced their interests apart.

The men's concern to avoid encroachment and protect their union was demonstrated in the Nottingham ASE's attitude to the Cycle Workers' Union. In April 1897 the ASE No.4 branch wrote to the Trades Council protesting against the giving of assistance to the newly formed Cycle Workers' Union. The Trades Council pledged to give the new union 'heartiest support', and a month later ASE's No.2 branch withdrew from the Trades Council in protest at this decision, but this did not prevent the Trades Council from accepting the affiliation fees of the Cycle Workers' No.3 branch in September. Six months later, however, it emerged that the Cycle Workers' No.2 and 3 branches were now defunct. The Beeston No.1 branch was also in difficulty and it was claimed that there were only 64 members remaining. These revelations sparked a major row and the Trades Council ASE delegates moved a resolution calling for an inquiry into the financial position of the Cycle Workers' Relief Fund and its connection with the *Nottingham Daily Express* 'Nothing to Eat Fund'. Later the ASE questioned the veracity of statements made by officials of the Trades Council that the fund-raising work had been carried out without any regard to mercenary conditions, but when their demand for an investigation was put to the meeting it registered only seven votes.[16]

Meanwhile Sir Ernest Jardine and other members of the Employers' Federation were trying to push home their advantage. Jardine was a virulent anti-unionist and over many years he did his best to break trade union organisation. In 1896, for example, a Trades Council deputation visited Jardine but later had to report that 'Mr Jardine was emphatic in his refusal to allow the men to join the Trade Union.'[17] Jardine was involved in the manufacture of lace machinery and at the end of April 1898 the Trades Council decided to call a special conference of trade unions with members employed by the firm. 27 societies sent representatives to the conference which decided to ask the trade unions who were involved if they would be prepared to support a possible strike. The subsequent dispute sought to win union recognition but Jardine used blackleg labour and after several weeks about 30 of the men decided to return to work. Then the bobbin and carriage hands were forced back, and although the carriage straighteners stayed out for a little longer they too were eventually forced to call off the industrial action.

The struggle between the employers and the engineers continued in the form of sporadic engagements rather than a set-piece battle until the outbreak of the First World War. In October 1908 Jardine made it clear that he was as anti-union as ever when, at a dinner of Nottingham accountants, he advised all employers to 'fight the trade unions to the death'.[18] Jardine's concern centred on the continuing growth of the engineers' organisation. In 1903 the ASE had affiliated its fifth Nottingham branch to the Trades Council and for the employers there were worrying signs that the younger men in particular were coming under socialist influence. Even more worrying for the employers was the shift in opinion being expressed by the labour aristocrats who had been the backbone of the industry for so many years. Many of these exclusive older workers were abandoning, in this period, any serious attempt at workshop control or collaboration with the management. In September 1905 one ASE delegate to the Trades Council attacked the importation of American bonus schemes and the specialisation of labour:

> The system whereby a worker was kept at work upon part of a product was a Yankee importation, but it had taken an immense hold and in many a trade where formerly skilled men had to be employed the work was now divided into small portions which needed little learning.[19]

The shift in attitudes which these changes were generating was beginning to be important. In time they would work their way through into the political field to play a crucial role in the electoral victories of the town's socialists from 1908 onwards.

Despite these political victories, the attitudes of many members of the élite craft unions continued to pose problems for the socialists. Writing in 1910 Harry Quelch complained:

> The English working class is not less able, less intelligent or more stupid than the working class in other European countries; but it is certainly more completely imbued with bourgeois ideas, less conscious of its own subject

position as a class ... more reverential towards the master class than any other working class I know ... [20]

The Nottingham evidence suggests that this judgement contains a good deal of truth. Certainly, the relatively slow development of the political wing of the labour movement in the town had something to do with these factors, but deference to employers was under serious question from 1905 onwards. George Hodkinson, for instance, remembered the collapse of the Humber Cycle Company, the main engineering employer in Beeston in 1908. Financial gambling and share-rigging resulted in bankruptcy, throwing hundreds onto the labour market, but had the side effect of politicising many workers. The men put out of work by this closure were not comforted by the knowledge that the financiers involved were also pillars of the local church. The management of the Beeston Foundry Company also had a reputation as poor employers. The Pearson family dominated the Board of Directors and the type of management which they practised was that of the 'benevolent despot, and not too benevolent at that'.[21] Many of the key personnel of this firm, the foremen and charge-hands, were said to be 'pillars of the Tory Party' and there is little doubt that this was repeated at many other Nottingham factories, with the consequence that the management structure also played its part in helping to radicalise many workers.

The political significance of these changes in attitude was well demonstrated in 1908, the year in which Ernest Gutteridge became the town's first ILP councillor. In May a deputation consisting of three ASE members, two bobbin carriage makers, and two others, attended a meeting of the Trades Council, in order to ask if it were true that a Trades Council nominee was about to contest Robin Hood Ward. The concern of this deputation was that their employer, Mr Pycroft, was also about to contest the ward as a Liberal nominee. The deputation proceeded to explain how good an employer Mr Pycroft was, before trying hard to persuade the Trades Council delegates to abandon their own plans. This episode demonstrated that some engineers at least were still firmly in the political, as well as the industrial, grip of the employers; that the deputation was unrepresentative was indicated by the following intervention of the ASE district committee. The deputation, insisted the district committee, were 'private individuals and *not* official'. Furthermore, a workman who had questioned the right of the deputation to approach the Trades Council had subsequently been victimised. After ASE protests the discharged worker had been re-engaged but he had been told to find other work.[22] Only five months later the Nottingham socialists won their first council seat, probably because they had increased their influence amongst the engineers by putting themselves in the forefront of aggressive opposition to technical and organisational change.

The politicisation of the Nottinghamshire miners in the period 1895 to 1914, moved at a far slower pace than that experienced by the engineers. Solidarity in Nottinghamshire, unlike other coalfields, was fragmented and it is possible that two features of the Nottinghamshire men's lifestyle may have been responsible. Firstly, the mining villages of Nottinghamshire were strongly influenced by agricultural social relations; many miners were recruited from surrounding agrarian districts and radicalisation was slowed by their rural cast of mind. Secondly, those miners working pits in the south of the county lived in areas where other industries and their workers were present. It is possible that this proximity prevented the emergence of a mining identity on which solidarity depended. These two features appear to be responsible in part for the strength of the concept of 'community' as opposed to 'class' amongst the Nottinghamshire miners. Certainly this was true of the Lib-Lab leadership of the NMA. Miners' leaders such as Bailey, Hancock and later Spencer, stressed the virtues of industrial 'co-operation' as being in the interests of the 'community', rather than looking to the 'class' interests of miners. It was, of course, crucial to such thinking that each miner should somehow *feel* an identity of interest between himself and the coal owner.

The process of radicalisation amongst the Nottinghamshire colliers was also slowed by the pragmatic and opportunist attitudes which prevailed during the years of relative prosperity. These attitudes were expressed in the official leadership of the NMA, firstly by William Bailey who died in July 1896, and then by John George Hancock. At one level, Bailey was an effective leader – he worked hard to build the membership of the NMA and to put it on a sound footing. Beatrice Webb writes of him at the miners' conference in 1896 'in a perfectly clear speech' arguing the case against involving workmen in responsibility for the safety of the mine. Mrs Webb considered Bailey an 'excellent speaker' but did not exclude him from her criticism of the miners' leadership:

> Though they abound in common sense they have very little intellectual initiative, their very self-complacency is of a passive character. Revolution to these men would be impossible ... step by step reform is difficult ... they are barring a traditional radicalism intensely conservative and slow to move or convince.[23]

Hancock if anything was even more pragmatic. Like many others imbued with Lib-Lab attitudes, he seems to have formed the habit of forever genuflecting toward those he considered his social betters. A Gladstonian Liberal in politics, Hancock was a Methodist lay-preacher and active temperance worker. He and other leaders like Aaron Stewart played a crucial role in the local Liberal Party establishment's efforts to win working-class support for Liberalism.[24]

The cultural dominance of Liberal Nonconformist ideology was underpinned to some extent by the way mining in the Nottinghamshire coalfield was organised. The main characteristic of the job of digging for coal in the Nottingham pits was the way in which sub-contractors or butties acted as the leading man in a work group, virtually becoming a small master employing a subordinate group of hewers. Although the butties sometimes operated a whole face, or even a complete pit, their status during this period was declining to the point where they ranked as superior workmen rather than employers. They were the driving force behind the union, electing checkweighmen and dominating policy, but an influx of day-wage men in the years around the 1893 lock-out began to change the union's outlook. From this time the NMA began to seek increases for the 'banksmen and an agreed price-list for the "boys" '.[25] Nevertheless, the butties retained a great deal of power and influence within the union.

Despite the changing status of the butty, the politics of the NMA remained firmly wedded to the Liberal Party. Indeed, amongst Nottingham miners a kind of 'shared incoherence' is the most striking feature of NMA politics during the 1890s and the early part of the twentieth century. Compared with the miners of Derbyshire, for instance, the Nottingham colliers with at least one strong constituency and another where careful planning could have won the seat, were only able to return Hancock to Parliament and his victory was in a Derbyshire constituency.[26] Very few miners seem to have played any significant role in either the ILP or *Clarion* organisations; it seems clear that the conservatism of men like Hancock, Stewart and Bunfield had a stranglehold on the politics of the NMA which would not be broken for many years. Certainly the itinerant propagandists of the ILP found it difficult to make any significant political progress amongst the Nottinghamshire miners. Bruce Glasier wrote of Hucknall in his diary in 1896 'it is about the poorest miners' town in all the land ... wages do not average 10 shillings a week.' Two years later the *Labour Leader* reported that at the Nottingham collieries 'some men are only getting two days' work a week and an application to the union for relief from union funds was refused.'[27] A month later the ILP newspaper was reporting that 'the miners of Nottinghamshire and Derbyshire want 10 per cent or nothing,' but, despite the potential unrest which these reports indicate, there is little evidence of any shift in the political attitudes of the mining community.

Of the remaining groups of Nottingham workers in this period the railwaymen were the most significant. In 1906 it was estimated that over 3,000 lived in the town, which was served by four different railways. The Midland Railway had a large depot in the town and the Great Northern, the North Western and the Great Central had passenger stations and goods sidings in various parts of Nottingham. The railwaymen had been very slow to organise industrially. Many of the early recruiting meetings were undertaken by the Trades Council and it was not until 1892 that a branch of the Railway Servants affiliated to the Trades Council. Politically the railway workers were even more backward than the miners: conservatism and traditionalism seem to have been at the centre of their thinking, reinforced by the deference which was an important qualification for many of the uniformed working class.

The railway companies were particularly hostile to the growth of trade unionism. In November 1887, for instance, Tom Ball of the Nottingham branch of ASLEF was sacked by the Midland Railway Company for having been one of a delegation of engine drivers to the company. He was later to become the first full-time officer of the union. To break the men's organisation the employers subsidised compulsory friendly societies and operated a severe disciplinary code. The companies also insisted on dividing their 'servants' into elaborate grades and made a point of paying gratuities to the most 'loyal' of their employees. In the face of the combined resistance of the companies the Railway Servants could do little. Drivers, firemen, guards and signalmen were the most active but even the strength of these key workers was too patchy to sustain a general movement. As a consequence the men's representatives were reduced to forming respectful deputations in often unsuccessful attempts to improve the pay and conditions of the men. The authoritarian nature of the Victorian and Edwardian railway companies, when combined with the economic insecurity of these years, produced a more or less quiescent generation of union leaders.

This was clearly demonstrated in the Nottingham branch of the Railway Clerks' Association which was founded in 1897 with 68 members. Nottingham was the pioneer branch of the Railway Clerks' Association, but its black-coated members seem to have been of very doubtful spirit; in January 1898 the branch was worrying itself because Sir John Turney, a local employer and Liberal town councillor, had not replied to their invitation, asking him to become the president of the branch. A year later, Thomas Edney, the branch secretary, reported with much regret that he had to report that the previous day he had had a very stormy interview with Mr Viner, the Assistant Superintendent. Mr Viner had informed Edney that he was of the opinion that he was not a fit person to be employed by the company as 'he was a very dissatisfied fellow himself and tried to make others dissatisfied.' Edney was told that he would be reported to Euston with a recommendation for instant dismissal and two weeks later he was forced to resign 'because of recent events'.[28]

Other groups of railwaymen in the town found it very difficult to make either industrial or political progress. In January 1899 the Amalgamated Society of Railway Servants (ASRS) wrote to the Trades Council complaining about victimisation and expressing 'alarm and regret at the action of several railway companies in dismissing their employees without adequate cause'.[29] The union went on to claim that these men were discharged chiefly on account of their activity as members of the ASRS. Nine years later, in 1908, the Trades Council condemned the Midland Railway for sacking 100 guards, which it saw as yet another 'vindictive attempt to crush the spirit of the railway workers'.[30] Against the background of this kind of harassment and systematic victimisation the railway workers seem to have retreated into a political ghetto and in the years before the First World War it is rare to find individual railway workers involved in the life and work of the wider labour movement.

The one exception to this rule came in 1911 when the pent-up anger and frustration of a generation of railwaymen flared up into the first national rail strike. The origins of the strike are to be found in the pressure of falling real wages, but opposition to long-winded conciliation procedures was also important. Strike action was initially unofficial, and the railwaymen depended on the solidarity shown by other workers. In the Nottingham area miners held up trains still operating on the Mansfield branch of the Midland Railway, whilst the Trades Council organised solidarity action and protested at the government's action in sending troops to Nottingham during the dispute.[31]

The direct result of the strike was the setting up of a Royal Commission to examine the railwaymen's grievances and the working of the scheme of conciliation that had been agreed upon in 1907. The Commission held nearly 30 meetings and finally approved a scheme whereby the men's most outstanding grievances were modified. The recommendations of the Commission, published in November 1911, did little to deflect militancy among the railwaymen and it seems certain that many of them had learned deep political lessons. Certainly the 1911 strike produced little in the way of material advance. Politically, however, it helped to break thousands of railwaymen from the ties of deference and its political expression, Lib-Labism. It is from this time that areas like the Meadows in which a high percentage of railwaymen lived finally slipped from the grip of the established political parties to become Labour Party strongholds in the years between the two World Wars.

Throughout the 1890s and well into the new century the trade union movement faced a great deal of hostility from the employers, the press and many middle-class elements. In Nottingham this hostility made the job of organising unskilled and female labour particularly difficult. It was well expressed in 1894 during a strike of hosiery workers at Blackburn and Halgates, the Trades Council found it necessary to protest at the use of the police force to break up picket lines. A month later Samuel Bowers, the men's full-time official, was complaining that the union was faced by 35 summonses for intimidation and that the men were having to 'fight the police and the magistrates'.[32] Bowers also believed that in the hosiery industry a determined effort to break the union was under way.

Other unions were experiencing similar difficulties. The Farriers' Society reported in 1896 that they were having great difficulty with the Clifton Colliery Company, whose foremen appeared to have been instructed to 'have nothing to do with the Society men'. In April 1897 the Bestwood Iron and Coke Company sacked 11 men for alleged 'neglect of duty'. The Gasworkers' Union, however, claimed that the men had been sacked 'owing to a desire of the men for better conditions of labour, having become known to the management'. Later, 183 workers came out in support of the sacked men, and were paid 10 shillings a week after Will Thorne had appealed to the Trades Council for help. Faced with difficulties like this, many unions reacted with a policy of centralisation and the creation of a strong officialdom. The rank and file, however, felt that they had no alternative but to resort to coercion and intimidation to hold their organisation together. In 1897, for instance, the engineers' lock-out generated a good deal of hostility on both sides. The Trades Council had set up a special committee to co-operate with the engineers and in September 1897 this committee found it necessary to protest at 'the general offensive and overbearing attitude against legitimate picketing'. The Trades Council went on to demand 'an immediate and searching enquiry by the Chief Constable and the Watch Committee'.[33]

Despite, or possibly because of employer opposition to trade union organisations, the movement continued to grow between 1895 and 1914. The growth in size and strength was often demonstrated in the support of the Nottingham Trades Council for unions in dispute. In January 1894 the Trades Council handed over £69 3s 7¼d to the NMA who had been involved in the 1893 lock-out; the Trades Council also raised £27 19s 0½d in the same period for a special appeal for Mrs Briant of the Female Cigar Makers who had been taken ill. In 1896 the Trades Council sent £137 7s 9d to help support engineers on strike on the Clyde and in Belfast, and in 1897 it involved itself in a big row about the placing of the police clothing contract with unfair firms. This dispute involved the Trades Council executive in meeting in the Council House lobby at 9.30 a.m. in order that they could 'interview' Council members as they arrived. This campaign eventually succeeded in getting the City Council to withdraw the contract from the non-union firm by 23 votes to 21. This was achieved by using Lib-Lab councillors like Skerritt and Adams, although the Trades Council later had to hand over its documents on the case when the non-union firm tried to sue the *Nottingham Daily Express* for alleged libel.[34] In the same period the Trades Council joined with members of the Building Trades Council to lobby the members of the Board of Guardians on the question of contracts for a projected new workhouse. Subsequently, the Guardians agreed that only trade union rates would be paid. 1897 was also the year in which the Trades Council fully involved itself in solidarity action in support of the locked-out engineers. In October the Council organised a demonstration on the Forest which succeeded in raising £80 for the ASE. John Burns was the speaker and observed that the demonstration was a good example of the 'poor helping the poor'. Despite the demands of the lock-out which involved the Trades Council in a great deal of work, £22 2s 0d was raised in the same period for the widow of William Bailey, the first full-time agent of the Nottingham Miners' Association.[35]

Once the century had turned, the Taff Vale decision and political developments in the wider labour movement seem to have played their part in accelerating the growth in size and importance of the Nottingham Trades Council. In April 1903 a delegation of representatives from the Building Trades Council attended a Trades Council meeting and agreed to set up a system of joint executive council meetings. This breakdown of industrial sectarianism was an indication that the labour movement was at last drawing together; this was underlined in February 1903 when the Trades Council, the Building Trades Federation, the ILP, the Labour Electoral Federation and the Lenton and Nottingham Co-operative Societies all came together to invite the Penrhyn Choir to the town. The concert which followed was in aid of the Penrhyn quarrymen; it took place in the Clarion Club and was a great success, raising £57.[36]

During the years under review the concept of what were legitimate issues for the trade unions was the subject of constant debate. The left tried to redefine these around more aggressive policies and the taking up of a wider range of issues. In November 1904, after a militant speech from Mr Young of Ruskin College, Oxford, the Trades Council agreed to support the College financially, and in January 1905 the Gasworkers were urged by Pete Curran to work to 'make trade unionism in Nottingham much stronger'.[37] Perhaps taking this view to heart, Gutteridge of the ILP helped to form a Jewish Tailors trade union, as well as arguing at a Trades Council meeting that whenever anything of importance to labour was to be discussed by the City Council, consultation between the Trades Council and the 'progressive section' should be held.[38]

By 1905 the Trades Council had five members on the Board of Guardians, and Trades Council support for union candidates in School Board and Board of Guardians elections continued to be a feature of the Council's policy. During 1906 the Trades Council organised a large meeting in furtherance of the demand for old age pensions which showed an increasing concern for the well-being of the wider working class as well as for the role of labour in the civic life of the period. In January 1906 a resolution was passed, calling on the library committee to:

> obliterate all horse racing news from the press as we consider it to be in direct opposition to the good morals of our city.[39]

In March 1907 the delegates to the Trades Council protested at the making of a City Council grant to the Nottingham High School, before deciding to invite the town's MPs to a meeting to discuss the educational opportunities 'for poorer people' in Nottingham. At the same meeting voices were raised again at the use by the Corporation of 'sweated labour' and a month later it was agreed to give £10 to each trade unionist standing for the Board of Guardians as well as issuing a joint manifesto. By now Arthur Richardson had been elected as Lib-Lab MP for South Nottingham and it is significant that Richardson tried very hard to maintain his links with the Trades Council. In April 1908 Richardson attended a Trades Council meeting in order to ask 'for instruction' on how to vote on the government's Budget Bill which contained provision for the introduction of old age pensions and the retention of the sugar tax. After a long discussion, Richardson was told to put old age pensions first and to leave the problem of sugar tax until later.[40] Richardson undoubtedly recognised the growing importance of the Trades Council. During the course of 1908 five additional trade union branches affiliated, so that the annual report could claim that the Trades Council now represented 40,000 workers.[41]

In 1910 the Trades Council raised £48 14s 1d for the striking miners at Clifton Colliery and in October they were involved in organising a propaganda meeting for the Nottingham bakers who were demanding a fifty-four hour working week. Thundercliffe told this meeting that:

> So far as the Nottingham bakers and confectioners were concerned there were some very bad places ... machinery was displacing men and steps needed to be taken so that there were fewer working hours a day.[42]

Both of these disputes were part of a national wave of industrial discontent which was then sweeping the country. Richardson, the Lib-Lab MP, told the Bakers' meeting that 'wherever there were civilised men there was unrest among those who were called the working classes.' A week later the *Nottingham Express* reported that in Nottingham a number of disputes were under way:

> Several thousand workmen attached to a number of different trade unions were involved ... the plumbers were on the verge of a lock-out, the joiners have given and received six months' notice to terminate their engagements ... the printing and allied trades are taking a ballot on the question of handing in their notices and the bricklayers' union are said to be greatly dissatisfied with the recent arbitration award and threatened to strike if its provisions are enforced.[43]

During the course of 1911 the rising tide of industrial unrest continued. In that year the Nottingham bricklayers came out on strike and the Trades Council sent various sums of money to other workers in dispute. Throughout the year stoppage after stoppage made it clear that a widening social gulf was opening up between the workers and the rest of society.

At one level this gulf manifested itself in a letter which the Trades Council received from the mayor of Nottingham. This letter explained that even though the Trades Council had been meeting in the Exchange Building for the previous nineteen years, permission would now be withdrawn 'unless the Trades Council abandons the discussion of political questions'.[44] In June of the same year the Trades Council was forced to decide that in view of an injunction granted against the NMA forbidding it to use its funds for political purposes, the Trades Council would not itself be able to seek contributions from affiliated societies for political campaigning. The reaction to these attempts to restrict political activity indicated that beneath the outward prosperity of Edwardian England a deep-felt unrest was growing in the hearts and minds of the local labour movement. For a time it seemed that no section of the working class was immune from the agitation which characterised these years. In September 1911, for example, it was reported that Nottingham schoolboys were on strike, demanding that the school leaving age should be lowered to 13. In October, Will Thorne and Arthur Hayday set up two new branches of the Gasworkers' Union, one for engineering labourers, the other for general and chemical workers, and in December 1911 the Trades Council appointed a deputation to ask the corporation for a 2s a week increase in the pay of school caretakers.[45]

The Nottingham labour movement had advanced a long way in the period between 1895 and 1910. This was not merely illustrated by increased union membership and financial assistance given to fellow workers, but was also apparent in the nature of their political debates. Little more than 15 years prior to this, the Trades Council had aspired to a 'non-political' identity, and liberalism was their watchword. By 1912 they could openly engage in a thorough discussion on the relative merits of syndicalism. The national coal dispute of 1912 precipitated this assessment in as much as it revealed the extent to which employers would go in using the law to undermine the trade union movement. The imprisonment of Tom Mann generated a resolution which condemned the persecution of

> men of advanced views on industrial and political matters, merely because they appealed to the sons of fellow workers in the Army not to maim and murder their fathers, mothers, brothers and sisters during any dispute between labour and the forces of capitalism.[46]

In the discussion which followed, Staton, of the tailors, said that it would be a disgrace to the working people if they did not pass the resolution. He did not believe in syndicalism, but fully associated himself with the advice given to the soldiers. Later Mr Garness wanted to know 'who sent for troops for Nottingham during the railway strike', before going on to say that 'Tom Mann was known throughout the length and breadth of the land; he wished we could get a few more like him.' Hayday, who spoke with the knowledge that 2,300 of the 3,300 Nottingham gasworker members of his union were out of work because of the coal strike, wound up the debate by declaring 'Syndicalism was justified. It was using the power of their organisations to force the conditions their members were entitled to.'[47] This discussion seems to indicate that even though only a tiny minority were actively involved in propagating them, the theories of syndicalism were beginning to influence a growing number of trade unionists. Only a few individuals like Tom Mann or James Larkin could be positively identified but many others, without having seriously studied syndicalism, were directly influenced by its vision. One such was probably the ex-Ruskin College student who in December 1909, after addressing the Trades Council on 'The Shortcomings of Ruskin College from a Labour Standpoint', persuaded the delegates to support the new Central Labour College.

In May 1912 the Trades Council joined with the British Socialist Party in a protest meeting which wrote to the Home Secretary demanding the release of Tom Mann, and later in the year it joined with the ILP and Fabian Society in a 'War Against Poverty' campaign. Throughout the year the organising work of the Trades Council was very successful and the *Annual Report* for the year noted 'increased activities and increased membership for many unions'.[48] The Gasworkers in particular seem to have made considerable progress by 'energetically organising the labourers in the engineering trades'.[49]

Throughout the period from 1895 until the outbreak of war in 1914 unemployment was the single biggest issue concerning both the industrial and political wings of the labour movement in Nottingham. Before the 1890s this was not a matter in which any but the SDF was particularly interested. From the 1890s, however, a gradual change began to take place. In April 1892 the Nottingham Trades Council's concern at rising unemployment led them to co-operate with the Blackburn Trades Council in any moves to check the 'wholesale introduction of destitute foreigners into the country'.[50] This was an attitude regrettably widespread among trade union circles at this time and was directed against the considerable Jewish immigration from Eastern Europe. In 1893 the Council campaigned to pressurise the City Council to provide relief work for the unemployed. Unemployment was rarely forgotten and was even a factor in the fight for old age pensions: it was considered abhorrent that old people were required to work when younger men and women could not find employment.

During the winter of 1903/04 unemployment rose sharply, and the Nottingham Trades Council agitated for public work schemes, as well as supporting the local Right to Work Committee. This organisation had been set up on the initiative of the SDF. In February 1906 an unemployed march organised by the ILP, entered Nottingham on its way to London and the Trades Council provided hospitality in the Socialist Hall. Attitudes towards unemployment were contradictory, however, and often reflected the fear expressed by skilled craftsmen. On the one hand there was a desire for humanitarian treatment, but on the other a determination not to allow the unemployed to affect the skilled craftsman's position in the labour market. Only gradually did labour leaders perceive the wider issues raised by unemployment. In 1908, one delegate on the Trades Council, appalled at the lack of clarity concerning unemployment, roundly attacked his fellow members and demanded that the Council 'take a more militant attitude and not play with the question of unemployment as the Liberal Party was doing'.[51]

During the course of 1909 William Beveridge wrote that unemployment was fundamental to the whole question of poverty:

> Workmen today are men living on quicksand, which at any moment may engulf individuals, which at uncertain intervals sinks for months or years below the sea surface altogether.[52]

Many of Nottingham's trade unionists would have agreed with this description, and the 1909 *Annual Report* of the Trades Council made the point that unemployment needed much attention. Unemployment according to the Council was 'without doubt *the* question of the day'. The solutions posed by union activists were no advance on those proffered by the Liberal establishment, and it is easy to be critical of the local labour movement. What is important however is the shift represented by the consideration of unemployment. In 1880 the Trades Council would not have been willing to consider the subject, whereas by 1909 they at least recognised that it was integral to their own struggle. This perception was indeed partial, but it was emerging gradually.

The period covered by the years 1895 to the outbreak of the First World War was one fraught with contradictions. It was a period which spawned the ideas of socialism, and provided industrial struggles which found their strength and inspiration in those ideas and at the same time it was a period when workers suffered great oppression in the workplace, severe poverty and intolerable restrictions on their human rights. At one moment the labour movement appeared to forge ahead stimulated by leaders with imagination and verve; at the next moment it seemed tied to a heritage of Liberalism and bureaucratic officialdom. The years 1895 to 1914 saw a massive expansion in union membership *and* the inability of key sections of workers either to organise effectively or to obtain basic bargaining rights.

Economic transformation and technological change undermined the bargaining strength of traditional unions, a process which radicalised large sections of the working class but also produced a defensive response not conducive to political change; the labour movement, was therefore, at one and the same time progressive and deeply conservative. There can be little doubt that socialist thinking played a crucial role in the radicalisation of the movement and in providing the inspiration which

encouraged those progressive elements to struggle forward. The socialist
individuals and organisations prominent in the Nottingham labour
movement in the period 1895 to 1914, were a small minority, but their
influence was widespread.

REFERENCES

[1] Minutes, Lace Makers Society, 13 November 1897.
[2] *Webb Trade Union Collection*, Section A, vol. XXXIX.
[3] Ibid.
[4] Minutes, Nottingham Trades Council, 20 September 1905.
[5] Ibid., 9 December 1908.
[6] *Labour Leader*, 12 August 1909.
[7] Minutes, Nottingham Trades Council, 27 June 1906.
[8] Ibid., 13 July 1913.
[9] Minutes, Nottingham and Nottinghamshire Branch, National Union of the Women's Suffrage Society.
[10] Minutes, Nottingham Trades Council, 8 November 1911.
[11] *The Lace Trade in Nottingham and District*, pamphlet 1905.
[12] Minutes, Lace Makers' Society, 5 October and 12 November 1904.
[13] Nottingham Lace Trade, *Arbitration Proceedings and Award*, 1905, pp. 20, 33, 37.
[14] *Nottingham Daily Express*, 18 February 1897.
[15] *Labour Leader*, 23 April 1898.
[16] Minutes, Nottingham Trades Council, 16 March 1898.
[17] Ibid., 2 December 1896.
[18] Ibid., 14 October 1908.
[19] Ibid., 20 September 1905.
[20] *Social Democrat*, March 1910.
[21] George Hodkinson, *Sent to Coventry*, 1970, p. 24.
[22] Minutes, Nottingham Trades Council, 27 May and 24 June 1908.
[23] Beatrice Webb, Diary, 15 January 1896.
[24] Aaron Stewart, son of a victimised miner, helped establish the NMA and appeared on the platform of the first NMA demonstration in 1884. Between 1884 and 1886 Stewart was the part-time secretary of the NMA. In 1886 he published a series of letters in *Labour Tribune* which were critical of the weaknesses of trade unionism amongst the Nottinghamshire miners. In 1886 he became president of the NMA and was active in support of the eight hour day. Stewart supported the withdrawal of NMA support for Broadhurst although he remained a Liberal all his life. See, Joyce Bellamy and John Saville (eds.), *Dictionary of Labour Biography*, Volume I, 1972, pp. 312-3.
[25] The Council of the NMA at its meeting in April 1892 agreed to claim the following rates for boys as the minimum day rate:
For boys starting work at the age of 12 ...... 1s 4d
For boys starting work at the age of 13 ...... 1s 6d
For boys starting work at the age of 14 ...... 2s 0d
[26] Hancock was elected as Lib-Lab MP for Mid-Derbyshire in 1909.
[27] *Labour Leader*, 16 July 1898.
[28] Minutes, Railway Clerks' Association, Nottingham Branch, 28 February 1897.

[29] Minutes, Nottingham Trades Council, 18 January 1899.

[30] Ibid., 7 September 1908.

[31] Ibid., 10 September 1911. Alse see, R. Holton, *British Syndicalism 1906-1914*, 1976, p. 106.

[32] Minutes, Nottingham Trades Council, 5 September 1894.

[33] Ibid., 1 September 1897.

[34] Ibid., 12 May 1897.

[35] Ibid., 22 December 1897.

[36] Ibid., 25 February 1903.

[37] *Clarion*, 13 January 1905.

[38] Minutes, Nottingham Trades Council, 18 March 1905.

[39] Ibid., 10 January 1906.

[40] Ibid., 29 April 1908.

[41] Nottingham Trades Council, *Annual Report*, 1908.

[42] *Nottingham Daily Express*, 17 October 1910.

[43] Ibid., 24 October 1910.

[44] Minutes, Nottingham Trades Council, 5 January 1910.

[45] Ibid., 6 December 1910.

[46] Ibid., 27 March 1912.

[47] Ibid.

[48] Nottingham Trades Council, *Annual Report*, 1913.

[49] Ibid.

[50] Minutes, Nottingham Trades Council, 13 April 1892.

[51] *Nottingham Daily Express*, 12 November 1908.

[52] William Beveridge, *Unemployment: A Problem of Industry*, 1909, p. 148.

CHAPTER SEVEN

Socialist Organisations

If the Social Democratic Federation and the Socialist League were the first truly socialist organisations to try to recruit the Nottingham working class, it was the Independent Labour Party which drew the many threads together. The first signs of the emergence of this new political party are to be found in the gradual change of outlook amongst Nottingham's younger trade unionists at the end of the 1880s. This generation had been exposed to socialist literature and propaganda during its formative years, and at the beginning of the 1890s their demands for independent labour representation began to dominate the agenda of Trades Council meetings. Against this background three Nottingham delegates travelled to Bradford for the founding conference of the ILP. Staton, of the Tailors' Society, was a delegate from the Fabian Society; the other two, George Smith and G.S. Christie, had both been active socialists for a number of years. Christie had been a member of the First International and at the founding conference was elected to the National Administrative Council of the ILP as the representative for the Midland counties.

By March 1893 the Nottingham branch of the ILP was well established. Its first secretary, Frank Kennedy, was the manager of a local hosiery factory, and he, together with Christie and a small group of activists, quickly began to organise propaganda meetings. At this stage in the history of the ILP many of its members seem also to have been members of the Fabian Society and in July this organisation was reported to be holding good meetings. Bowers, the secretary of the Rotary Power Hosiery Workers, was active in both organisations and at the beginning of July was reported as saying 'we intend making these meetings a great feature of labour and socialist propaganda.'

At the beginning of July 1893 the newly established Nottingham branch of the ILP suffered a blow when Jones, its first president, died unexpectedly. Jones had been a miners' delegate to the Trades Council and only a day or two before his death he had taken part in a debate on the question of the recent grants to royalty, during the course of which he had 'made pathetic appeals on behalf of the poor'.[1] Despite this setback both the ILP and the Fabian Society were holding 'splendid and enthusiastic' meetings. Some of these are vividly remembered by Percy Redfern, a young Nottingham shopworker:

> In the dark of the evening, after eight o'clock, I packed myself with the crowd, whilst Socialist lecturers simplified everything. Eloquent hands pictured the round cake of the national income. The workers made it: the capitalists and landlords took it. One slice only, a mere third, they gave back to the worker, just to keep their slaves alive! Thus did Marxian doctrine and Fabian diagrams reach the people.[2]

At the end of July and into August A.G. Wolfe held propaganda meetings at Trent Bridge every night for a week, with a further three meetings on Sunday to wind up. This first flush of enthusiasm carried the ILP through the summer and at the end of August the newly-established party announced that Sam Bowers would stand as its candidate for Wollaton Ward in the municipal elections.

October 1893 saw the ILP in the thick of the fight to get Bowers returned for Wollaton Ward. According to the correspondent of the *Workman's Times*, 'a fine time of it' was had by Bowers' supporters, since although he was the vice-president of the Trades Council, his candidature was actively opposed by Hardstaffe, the Council's president, and Skerritt, another leading member. As the election drew near the Liberal campaign against Bowers began to gather pace. Three or four days before the poll a *Nottingham Express* editorial said of Bowers:

> Mr Bowers is a man of ideas, of progress, a socialist ... but is he built of straight timber? ... we have a deal of sympathy with Mr Bowers ideas, we think the section he represents has not always found the elbow room inside Liberalism that it ought to have had ... but he will not gain it at all unless by very candid talk and consistent action he leads a wider circle of citizens to believe in him.[3]

The same newspaper later added that Bowers's faults were, 'all writ large on the surface of him. He loves a fight and is inclined to hit pretty nearly everybody with the handiest weapon.'[4] Certainly there seems to have been a good deal of truth in this judgement, but it needs to be remembered that politics in the 1890s was a rough-and-tumble business. In the campaign under consideration, for instance, Charles Smith, the Liberal candidate, waited until his eve of poll meeting to publish dire warnings against Bowers's religious views.[5] This charge against Bowers had been put about by Liberals during the campaign and it is evident that the Liberals were worried that they might lose the seat. During the course of one outdoor meeting Bowers earnestly contradicted the reports that he was an 'infidel' arguing that there was a great deal of difference between 'Churchism and Christianity'. Later at the same meeting Bowers set out his election programme, which included:

1. Eight hour day for all Corporation employees.
2. Evening sittings for the Town Council.
3. Public committee meetings.
4. Abolition of contract system.
5. Municipal colonisation on the democratic and non-competitive basis for the unemployed.
6. Municipal hospitals.
7. Abolition of slums.[6]

This meeting ended with an attack on brewing interests. If publicans prospered, according to Bowers, 'the working man could not thrive'.[7] This claim was probably motivated not just by a belief in temperance, but also by the realisation that the publican of the 1890s often played a crucial political role on the side of the establishment. This had certainly been the case in Wollaton Ward. The result was close enough to worry the Liberals:

C. Smith	(Liberal)	1,241
S. Bowers	(ILP)	919[8]

The election caused a good deal of press comment. According to the *Nottingham Express*:

One of the features of the 1893 election is undoubtedly the number of votes polled by Mr Bowers ... we doubt whether any very considerable number of Mr Bowers' supporters were Conservatives. They included temperance advocates and very advanced Radicals who believed in the forward policy of Mr Bowers ... it seems to us that the existence of so large a body of voters in a Liberal Ward ... is a fact that deserves earnest attention.[9]

The ILP supporters were, of course, elated at the success of their candidate and the celebratory mood continued through to the new year.

The votes won by Bowers seem to have stimulated a good deal of further activity, and by early 1894 the ILP had built a formidable political machine. This was well demonstrated at the first Labour Day celebrated in Nottingham on 7 May 1894. According to the *Nottingham Express* thousands marched in procession to the Forest where three platforms had been erected. Bowers took his place on a platform and amongst the surging crowd and brass bands the banner of the Tailors' Society, 'tattered, yet gaily bedizened, was in evidence and was cheered'. Bowers soon got into his stride, working himself up to a climax in which he told the crowd that 'their object was to protest against the action of an irresponsible body of nincompoops like the House of Lords in mutilating the Employers' Liability Bill'. He went on to claim that

> the terror of the workers today was the unemployed army. It was an injustice to allow one man to monopolize 8 or 10 hours whilst others worked 3, 2 or 1 and none ... employment of children was one of the biggest curses of the day. The taking of children into factories at such early ages was a crime. The whole matter would end in socialism and the sooner the better.

Another platform was surrounded by the miners who were headed by the Wollaton Colliery brass band and the Bulwell Ebenezer brass band. The platform was taken by Bailey, the NMA agent, Jepson, secretary of the Trades Council, and interestingly, four women speakers from either the lace or the hosiery workers. The third platform attracted many railway workers since it featured Hartford, the general secretary of the Railway Servants Union, as well as Christie of the ILP.[10]

The ILP organised out-door entertainment events to attract large numbers of working people to listen to their political message. High on the list of targets were the Liberal leaders of the Town Council. In particular the Nottingham Board of Guardians was accused of 'white slavery', a reference to the fact that of 1,915 boys apprenticed by the Board to the fishing smack owners of Grimsby, 628 had deserted and 118 died.[11] Such accusations, and the general threat posed by the new political party, led the Liberal group to attempt some form of alliance. These overtures were firmly rejected at this stage in its development the ILP's prime need was to distance itself from the Liberal establishment. The struggle with the Lib-Lab elements in the town was of major importance since there were large, articulate groupings of the trade union old guard in several of the town's major industries. It was essential therefore that the ILP should seize every propaganda opportunity.

In May 1894 the local ILP branch invited Tom Mann to the town. Mann was able to establish an ILP branch at nearby Stapleford, where he was joined by two brakeloads of ILP members from Nottingham. Later Tom Mann spoke to meetings of railwaymen at Hucknall and Netherfield and also helped to start a Nottingham ladies ILP branch, 'which promises to outshine the men's organisation'. Harry Quelch of the SDF was also in the town for a couple of Sunday propaganda meetings.

These, however, were only moderately successful, being 'consistently interfered with' by the presence of the yellow van of the Land Nationalisation League which was conducting a vigorous campaign of its own.[12]

All this activity generated enthusiasm and, of more importance, new members. At the second ILP conference in February Nottingham was represented by six delegates who were there on behalf of branches in West, East, Central and Manvers Wards. At the end of May the growth of the Nottingham ILP was acknowledged when the quarterly meeting of the administrative council of the ILP met at the Trent Ward club run by the Nottingham membership. Keir Hardie was in the chair and the meeting lasted for seven hours. In the months which followed the ILP organised a cyclist lecturing campaign to capture the adjoining villages, and after Tom Mann's rousing meetings branches were formed at Arnold, Hucknall, Netherfield, Beeston and Carlton. Later, Pete Curran came to Nottingham for a week of meetings, and in August a big crowd in the Market Place at which 'silk hats and other badges of respectability were much in evidence' heard Keir Hardie speak for the ILP.[13] A day or two before this meeting Edward Aveling had 'electrified the audience' whilst giving 'two of the most powerful and thrilling speeches ever heard in the Market Place.' Writing in 1934 Robert Meats, who acted as Aveling's chairman, remembered:

> He was little in stature and elderly, but his power, his voice, his fluency and the richness of his addresses generally so impressed me that I must place him bang in the front rank of Socialist propagandists. At one of his meetings, when there must have been 2,000 or more people present, I know that the collection was a record for outdoor meetings ... Dr Aveling's evening subject was entitled 'Masters and Men' and I do not exaggerate when I say one could fancy seeing the forces of capitalism and labour marching in opposition to one another, in the vivid exposition of society's rottenness, as given by the Doctor.[14]

The vividness with which the meetings are remembered forty years later is an indication of the strength and vitality of the early ILP. The comradeship and good fellowship of these early meetings were deepened by indoor and outdoor social occasions.

Although there is plenty of evidence that the ILP propaganda meetings attracted many new members, there are also signs that some of the early socialists were depressed and pessimistic at their inability to make more rapid progress.[15] In July 1894 the *Labour Leader* reported that the Nottingham Trades Council did not pursue a very vigorous policy with respect to the ILP's principles. So far as we are able to judge it is dominated by a majority of members who still believe in the Liberal Party. Our members should see that they send the most advanced men to represent them and then by steady and persistent work get the Council to join hands with the ILP.

The problem with this approach, of course, lay in the fact that the socialism of the ILP did not exist in a static world. The ILP could not isolate itself from other political activity; it did not breathe and grow in a sterile cultural vacuum. This fact of life was soon to dawn on the ILP activists who reported in July that the Liberal member for the Southern Division was making a fair bid for the labour vote. To judge from his speeches, he was prepared to promise anything. The tactics of the 'advanced Liberal candidates (we have two here) is strengthening the impression that these gentlemen have received the tip from HQ to go upon the sort of Harcourtinian lines of being all socialists now.'[16]

Later, commenting on the recently announced programme for the NMA demonstration, the Nottingham ILP expressed its concern at what it saw as 'an attempt on the part of the wire-pullers to work the organisation on Liberal lines'. On this occasion the ILP was upset because the announced speakers for the demonstration were Ellis, a local coalowner and Liberal MP for Rushcliffe, and Yoxall, the Liberal candidate for the Western Division. Further, Yoxall was introduced to the audience of coalminers as 'the Liberal and Labour candidate for West Nottingham unmindful of the fact that the ILP have adopted Councillor Beever of Halifax to do battle for Labour'. Outraged by these developments the ILP activists optimistically comforted themselves with the hope that since 'a good number of the Notts miners are members of the ILP when our candidate comes forward for the Western Division they will plainly show their disapproval of this caucus work.'[17]

By this time, only a year and a half after its formation, the ILP in Nottingham had 700 members, two club rooms and an 'eminent band of women workers whose energy and enthusiasm carry everything before it'.[18] Some idea of the strength of the ILP in the town can be gauged by the fact that it spent £3 on penny copies of Blatchford's *Merrie England*. By October 1894 the group felt strong enough to run its own candidates for the Town Council and fielded five candidates in the local elections. Commenting on the Nottingham campaign the *Labour Leader* reported 'good attendances, good collections, increased membership and great uneasiness in the old parties'. Concurrent with the municipal elections the general election campaign began, and in October Councillor Beever of Halifax opened the Nottingham ILP parliamentary fight at an evening meeting where the 1,000 strong audience was brought to its feet with ringing cheers for Tom Mann. In the local elections all five ILP candidates were well-known trade union members, and in addition two other Trades Council members stood as non-political trade union candidates. The actual contest seems to have been most closely fought between the socialists and the Lib-Lab elements. True, the Town Council was attacked for voting ratepayers' money to buy presents for the royal family, but most of the political in-fighting seems to have centred on Bailey, the Miners' Agent. According to the Nottingham correspondent of the *Labour Leader*, the local ILP 'besides the usual class opposition, have an active enemy in Mr Bailey, the Miners' Agent. Looking at some of his amazing talk, I should say that nothing could ultimately do the Notts ILP more good than his opposition.'[19]

Although none of the ILP candidates were successful on this occasion, the group won 24 per cent of the votes polled in the three-cornered fight, and this contrasted well with the 15 per cent poll for socialists in Liverpool. It was, however, a long way behind the 40 per cent vote in Keighley, or the 37 per cent achieved in nearby Leicester.[20] Reporting the Nottingham result the *Clarion* made the point that Bowers might well have won Wollaton Ward but for the 'foolish and unfair attack on the ILP by miners' agent Bailey', whilst the *Labour Leader* unleashed its full scorn on the ILPs strongest opponents:

those furious demons of political partisanship the amphibious Lib-Lab town councillors ... the most determined and unscrupulous of these, Councillor Bailey, in addressing the miners of Wollaton Ward, made a frenzied attack on the ILP ... no weapon was too base or too mean for the pseudo-trade unionist to use ... his cunning verged on Jesuitry ... his babbling tongue was allowed to run riot.[21]

William Bailey continued to oppose the politics of the ILP throughout the 1895 general election campaign. Whilst addressing the Labour Electoral Association in May, Bailey made an appeal to the ILP to consider 'whether they could not get what they wanted through constitutional methods'.[22] Since the ILP was busy contesting elections in a perfectly straightforward and constitutional way it is not surprising that the local militants replied with a certain amount of sarcasm:

Of course, we are all hairy chested, red-shirted monsters with bloodshot eyes who go about demanding eight-hour Bills and pensions for aged workers as well as retired speakers and who are even in favour of giving the poor, dirty miner the full value of his labour ... revolutionary destructive proposals all of them! For, says Mr Bailey, to try to run the country without landlords and mineowners would be 'Socialism run wild.'[23]

Bailey was not alone in his determination to crush the socialist groups. In September 1895 the *Labour Leader* reported that the Liberal trade unionists in the town were

> in high glee at having brought about another *coup d'etat*. This time it is the Liberal-Labour leaders and their fellow members of the Rotary Framework Knitters' Society whose prejudices against everybody and everything that savours of ILP-ism has led them to essay the hopeless task of blotting out socialism.'[24]

Unfortunately for the ILP the anti-socialist element were able to bring enough pressure to bear on Bowers, the secretary of the Rotary Power Society, to ensure his withdrawal as ILP candidate for Wollaton Ward in the forthcoming local elections. This setback, together with the temporary collapse of the SDF, must have created a crisis amongst the socialists and against this background the municipal campaign must have been very difficult.

Compared with the 1894 campaign the 1895 local election passed off very tamely. Bowers had been replaced as the ILP candidate for Wollaton by Harry Staton of the Tailors' Union. He polled 386 votes as against the 996 gained by Bowers the year before. To some extent the collapse of ILP support can be explained by the more forward-looking policies being advocated by some Liberals. In Bridge Ward, for instance, William Hamilton, the Liberal and Radical Association candidate, described himself in his election address as a 'progressive' and called for the municipalisation of the tramways as well as the building by the Corporation of workmen's houses. It was significant also that just before the election J.E. Ellis MP, a local coalowner, having voted for the Eight Hour Bill in the House of Commons, introduced the eight hour day into his collieries without loss of pay. Fortunately for the morale of the ILP, only a week or two after the local election defeat, Tom Moore, their candidate for the School Board, was able to win a seat, registering 19,458 votes despite a complete press boycott. This consolation prize was welcomed by the *Clarion* as the long-awaited 'thin end of the wedge'.

In many ways 1896 ought to have witnessed major progress in the history of the Nottingham ILP. The party was now three years old, it had about 1,000 members, many of whom were active in the town's trade unions, and at the end of 1895 it had won its first electoral victory. Everything should have been set fair for continued growth and influence. In fact, the ILP lost ground. It seems probable that there were personality conflicts in the Nottingham ILP branch centred around G.S. Christie, and this certainly weakened its capacity to mount vigorous election campaigns. The main reason for lack of advance was, however, the strength of the Lib-Lab trade unionists like Bailey and Hardstaffe. ILP militants argued that the 'pandering of the Liberals to Trade Union officials in Nottingham has for a long time proved the most successful weapon in their armoury with which to attack the ILP.'[25] The loosening of this grip was the major task facing the ILP and by the end of 1896 it was still more than a decade away.

According to the SDF publication *Justice*, the ILP in 1896 and 1897 was involved in little open-air propaganda and the SDF had the field to itself. The SDF, it will be remembered, had collapsed at the end of 1895. Propaganda meetings, continued to be held by the remnants of the group and in September 1897 the political secretary of the SDF was able to report that the branch had been reorganised. Towards the end of September 1897 the SDF held a Sunday evening meeting on 'Liberalism, Toryism and Socialism'; according to *Justice*, Nottingham at this time represented 'a good field for propaganda with ample opportunities for a good working branch to become strong and powerful'.[26] Later in September the SDF organised a meeting at Beeston where 'nearly the whole of the workers are directly or indirectly affected by labour troubles through a local dispute in the lace trade and the lock-out of the engineers at the Humber Cycle Co.'[27]

Despite the propaganda work of the SDF it was the ILP which in late October felt confident enough to announce that George Patchett, a foreman labourer at the local gasworks, would contest Wollaton Ward on behalf of the socialist cause. The engineers, who were locked out at this time, were fully supported by the ILP. The socialists had arranged a number of meetings for members of the ASE and a good deal of money was being passed across to the lock-out fund. Against this background the ILP had hoped a good result, but the poll revealed that Patchett had done very badly, receiving only 229 votes against the successful Liberal's 896. To rub salt into the wound, the Lib-Lab element had been successful in two wards, Skerritt winning in St Anne's and Hardstaffe winning at Manvers Ward in the face of opposition from a Conservative and an Independent Liberal.[28] Later, at the Liberal Club, these two members of the Trades Council heard Roberts, the Liberal Councillor who had beaten Patchett, declare that the best Liberal policy was to ignore the ILP, and the chairman made Hardstaffe blush by declaring that he was 'a thoroughly practical man who, like the other Lib-Lab members, would work to cement the alliance between Liberalism and Labour'.[29] In June the Trades Council had received a letter from the ASE which commended Roberts for his 'fearless and courageous stand amid the running fire of interruptions and jeers, whilst stating the case of the engineers before a hostile Town Council'.[30]

The Lib-Lab alliance of which Roberts was a part was by now coming under increasing strain. In January the *Labour Leader* published a report of the politics of the Nottingham employers involved in the lock-out, showing clearly that the majority were supporters of the Liberal Party. During the lock-out the Trades Council did their best to raise money for the engineers and one might have expected this to help in their politicisation. Certainly the ILP did its best to ensure that the right political lessons were drawn. The *Labour Leader*, for instance, when urging the Nottingham ILP to fight the South Nottingham constituency, claimed that Lord Henry Bentinck, the Conservative member for the constituency, had 'nothing to recommend him except his extraordinary resemblance to a young crust once of the Pall Mall Gazette'.[31] Subsequently, the *Labour Leader* told its readers that 'Billson, Walton and Furness and Co. have made the name of Liberalism stink ... the trade union 'leaders' who insist on sneaking up the coat tails of the trio are being measured for their political coffins.' This comment, however, was excessively optimistic. In April 1898, for instance, the executive of the NMA balloted on a list of possible speakers for their annual demonstration, placing Sir Walter Foster, a Liberal MP, at the top of the list with 204 votes, whilst Will Thorne, the Gas Workers' leader and a member of the SDF, was second from bottom with only 14 votes.[32]

As the 1898 local elections drew near the Trades Council sent the name of Appleton, general secretary of the Lace Workers, to the Trent Ward Liberal Association and he was subsequently nominated as the Lib-Lab candidate. Obviously, the intelligent section of the local Liberal establishment was as intent as ever on winning over the trade union leadership and at an election meeting in the Ward in October this was made clear when Councillor Radford on the platform with Appleton said that he was glad to 'welcome a fair proportion of labour representatives to the Council'.[33] The argument here centres on the definition of a 'labour representative'. The ILP in Nottingham was determined that the 'Johnny Facing Both Ways' of the Appleton type must not, in their terms, be allowed to 'dupe' the ordinary rank and file. In 1898, however, Appleton, Hardstaffe and Hancock were well in the saddle and the ILPs chances of unseating them were very remote indeed.

Signs that Lib-Lab control was beginning to crumble are difficult to find in Nottingham at the turn of the century. It must be remembered that this was the period in which imperialist hysteria had been whipped up around the issues of the Boer War, strengthening conservative and anti-political attitudes. Nevertheless, despite the jingoism there are signs of a gradual shift in attitude, not only of leading trade unionists, but in the hearts and minds of the rank and file. Some of this came to the surface at a Trades Council meeting in January 1899. On this occasion Ernest Gutteridge, a leading ILP member, was invited to attend to give his views on the subject of labour representation. During the course of a lengthy statement Gutteridge made the following points:

1. That the Town Council had adopted a standard rate of wages resolution, but had failed to carry it out.
2. That the City Corporation was increasing in power and numbers as an employer of labour.
3. That the Municipalisation of industry was growing.[34]

These factors, Gutteridge argued, pointed to the necessity of increasing labour representation. Against all the odds, Gutteridge's exposition seems to have carried the day and the Trades Council agreed to carry out a survey of the trade union branches to try to establish rank and file opinion.

In June Christie and Meats, in another ILP deputation, asked the Trades Council to join them in a programme of joint action. Despite an attempt to get this suggestion deferred a sub-committee of five was set up to confer with the ILP. A month later it was reported that the sub-committee and the ILP had agreed to recommend that a joint committee be set up to select wards and candidates, as well as to draw up a programme to be submitted to 'the various organisations for approval'.[35] The progress which this represented does not mean that the Lib-Labs and the socialists had suddenly decided to bury the hatchet, and in August Appleton was complaining of the insinuations continuously being advanced by a socialist delegate to the Trades Council with regard to the Trent Ward election. The October meeting of the Trades Council agreed to support a Lib-Lab candidate for Bridge Ward 'on purely personal lines' and Robinson, the Trades Council secretary, seems to have had no difficulty in persuading the Council to back him with the Lib-Lab ticket for St Albans Ward.

The mixed feelings represented by the argument and tension between the militant socialists and the Lib-Lab element present a confused picture which is difficult to interpret. The Trades Council 1899 'Labour Representation Fund' which was used to help finance Appleton and other

Lib-Lab candidates raised £44 17s 0d from different trade union branches. This might be taken to support the view that trade union politics were fully committed to Lib-Lab candidates, with no hope of socialist activists ever winning trade union support. At the end of the year, however, the Trades Council announced the result of its questionnaire on independent labour representation. Nine trade union branches had expressed themselves in favour, four against, with two returning a neutral answer.[36]

The dissemination of the ILPs socialist ideas was aided by the establishment of the Labour Church. The text adopted by the Labour Church was William Morris's 'Fellowship is Life', and the central objective was the achievement of salvation by solidarity and brotherhood. The main appeal of Labour Church teaching lay in the fact that it could be easily assimilated by those for whom much early socialist propaganda was too abstract and complex. For many of the workers in the northern and midland towns where the Labour Church was strongest, life was 'miserable, poor, nasty, brutish, short and insecure'.[37] The attraction of the Labour Church was the broad ethical appeal of moral regeneration which had a direct appeal to many young trade unionists aspiring to a better life and society.

By April 1896 a congregation was meeting in the Albert Academy adjacent to the Grand Theatre in Hyson Green. By May the Labour Church was so successful that it was able to publish its own monthly paper, the *Labour Echo*. The Labour Church had a clear political position that was evident in an article written in the August issue of *Labour Echo*. 'Socialism', it wrote,

> appeals to the worker logically and as none are so blind as those who will not see, it follows, then, that to support either Liberal or Tory when a Socialist is in the field is to purposely shut one's eyes and remain oblivious to the fact that we are not helping to unforge the fetters by which we are bound ... [38]

The appeal of the Church is illustrated by the large numbers who attended their meetings. In November Enid Stacy speaking on 'Religion and Socialism' drew a huge crowd of about 1,800.[39] In December similar audiences turned out to hear Miss Isobel Tiplady of Blackburn discuss 'Agitation and What is to be Done'.

Many of the Labour Church adherents were active socialists in one or other of the town's socialist organisations. Their work in the election campaigns of the time was enthusiastic and there is no doubt that they were a key element among the small group of militants actively fighting for the return of independent labour candidates. Initially, at least, the furrow which they had to plough was hard and stony and this was recognised in a realistic paragraph in the *Labour Echo* late in 1896:

The municipal elections have taken place but the result has proved that Socialism is not brought to the minds of the people in a day; nor is rapid growth so much desired as through permeation though it is to be hoped that our comparison with the oak will be respecting his strength and not in the comparative slowness of growth.[40]

'When all is said and done,' added the *Labour Echo*, 'the Nottingham Corporation is principally a Liberal clique, the gods help the poor aggressive socialist who enters the Nottingham municipal chamber.'

The appeal of the Labour Church gained strength from the social aspect of many of its activities which included summer camps, outdoor propaganda meetings and social evenings. The Sunday lecture was at the heart of such activity. G.D.H. Cole has noted the importance of fellowship for those involved in the espousal of new ideas, and certainly the young men who became involved in the Labour Church in Nottingham found support and encouragement in meeting with like minds.[41] William Robinson, the first president of the Nottingham Labour Church, was one of the young men attracted. Summing up the appeal of the Labour Church in 1896 he wrote:

The beauty of our movement is, we get such different speakers and such a variety of topics, this all tending to educate and refine the hearers. We have plenty of enthusiasm and are in touch and close sympathy with all socialist propaganda throughout the country. Every practical worker in our movement feels imbued with a religious sentiment which strengthens the will and determination in the fight for social emancipation. We realise the beauty and grandeur of the object we have in view. We possess the transparent honesty of being what we really are, and we take no steps to disguise our principles to the world, for we are unanimously one in our conviction and desire to further those natural and humanitarian principles which, when consummated, make the whole world kin. We feel that our religion must first of all be a social religion; that the true foundations of any abstract creed must necessarily consist in healthy bodies, healthy surroundings, and healthy minds ... [42]

According to Robinson, the Nottingham Labour Church was attractive because it did 'what no religious movement in the town has ever done', it allowed criticism and discussion based on the remarks of the 'preacher'. This gave an opportunity to expose mere rhetoric and the lecturers most appreciated were those who could 'educate and refine their hearers and not simply exhort them'.

At the turn of the century the Labour Church continued to extol the virtues of socialist thinking. Increasing emphasis was given to practical matters and special study groups and committees were established to discuss such matters as municipal housing, temperance reform and the like. The Sunday services were attended by an average of 250, whilst outdoor meetings attracted many more. The Nottingham Labour Church also provided the national president of the movement in 1904 in the person of T.A. Pierce. In this year the Church combined with the ILP to provide a three month open-air campaign which brought very successful results 'both in audiences and educative work ... The audiences have kept up and many members have joined.'[43] This campaign marked the increased co-operation between the Labour Church and the ILP which culminated in the election of Ernest Gutteridge as the first ILP councillor in Nottingham. This electoral victory was against the national trend of declining support for the ILP, and it seems certain that the role of the Nottingham Labour Church in uniting the divergent socialist groups was largely responsible.

Henry Pelling has described the Labour Church as 'a short-lived protest against the link which Nonconformity had established with the middle class and in particular, against the alliance with the Liberals'.[44] This was certainly true, but in Nottingham the Church enjoyed a vibrant life for a longer period than in many other towns. The main reason for this was the extent to which in Nottingham the Church identified with the secular religion of socialism. Its congregation provided most of the town's activists and there is little doubt that Eric Hobsbawm's claim that the chief function of the Church was 'to lubricate the passage of northern workers from Liberal Radicalism to an Independent Labour Party' holds good for Nottingham.[45] Throughout these years it is difficult to disentangle the complex mixture of politics and religion, so firmly wedded were the ILP and the Labour Church, and their political fortunes certainly appear to have followed the same course. The congregation in Nottingham was still in being in 1910 with about 150 to 200 supporters and then it gradually disappeared.

A second major influence on the development of socialist thinking during this period was the Clarion Commonwealth. The central concept of Clarion socialism, a co-operative commonwealth where the community would own, produce and distribute for the good of all, was immensely attractive. The idealism which lay behind the philosophy advocated by Robert Blatchford in the *Clarion* newspaper, and in his books *Merrie England* and *Britain for the British*, permeated socialist thinking of the early twentieth century. A plethora of organisations stemmed from the parent group, including the Clarion Cyclists and the Clarion Scouts. Too often this movement is dismissed as eccentric and irrelevant and yet, as Henry Pelling has pointed out, the Clarion movement helped to systematize the existing jumble of local labour and socialist organisations.[46] The ideas presented also had a profound effect on traditional labour leaders. After the lock-out of Nottingham tailors in July 1892 the Trades Council, influenced by Blatchford's ideas, agreed to help establish a tailors' co-operative, and in February 1893 they supported the Bakers' Union in the establishment of a co-operative bakery.[47]

The first signs of a separate Clarion organisation appeared in Nottingham in April 1895 when the newspaper drew the support of George Gee, a Nottingham socialist.[48] Within a few months the group organised a Cinderella club for Nottingham's slum children, and a summer camp at Woodborough.[49] By early 1897 the possibility of a Clarion propaganda-van tour of Nottinghamshire was on the agenda. Julia Dawson, a Clarion columnist, wrote that the mining districts of South Yorkshire and Nottinghamshire were 'crying aloud for some light to be shed into their darkness'.[50] During the summer of 1897 the van toured Hucknall, Bulwell, Daybrook and Basford, and also called at Nottingham's Market Place.

The Market Place meeting attracted a crowd of 1,500. Keeling of the Labour Church was in the chair and the first speaker was Ernest Gutteridge, a leading member of the Nottingham ILP. He was followed by Bacon and then Comrade Belt of Hull put in the 'rousements' in his usual vigorous style. Just after the meeting had commenced feeling was heightened by the arrival in the Square of a large contingent of Clarion Cyclists. In the afternoon another meeting was held on the Forest Fields and the thirsty propagandists adjourned to the premises of the Labour Church for tea where 'the light-hearted conversation and merry jests proved that socialists are not the perishing pezzers but people who enjoy life as well as most folk.'[51] The evening meeting attracted a huge crowd. The Watch Committee had refused the Clarion van permission to stand, so the Clarionites were forced to try to hold a meeting from two drays which they had hired as a platform. During the meeting a police inspector demanded the removal of the drays. Asked for his authority, he maintained that he had instructions from the Watch Committee and their 'factotums'. Later a resolution condemning the police action was carried unanimously.

The socialism of the itinerant propagandists involved in this meeting was utterly direct, unambiguous and comprehensive in the way in which it stripped the hypocrisy from a society wherein both secular class divisions and the dominant elements of established religion excluded human fellowship. The electrifying language of the vanners, the 'rousements' of men like Gutteridge and Christie, helped to stimulate a radical spirit which refused to be contained within the orthodoxies of the established political parties. The socialism which they propagated was a joyful and creative libertarian philosophy expressed in willing service to humankind. The enthusiasm and corporate spirit of the early Clarionites owed much to the fact that they were consciously reacting against a suffocating Victorian morality. Their rebellion against this aspect of the world in which they lived is seen at its best in the convivial atmosphere of the Clarion Fellowship. In Nottingham the Fellowship was founded at a meeting in November 1900. The ILP and other socialist groups came together with the object of organising a Fellowship dinner which became an annual event. Many of the young men prominent in founding the Fellowship and other Clarion organisations were young clerks. Clerical workers emerged as a distinctive social group at this time and many were active in the Nottingham socialist movement. The Clarion Cycling Club, for instance, had as its secretary more than one black-coated 'cuff and collar boy' from West Bridgford or other similar 'better class' parts of the town.

The Clarionites were in the main working class, and the strength of their movement was in the industrial towns of the north and midlands. Here, the isolation of many urban workers and their families, with few outlets for social activity apart from the church, provided a base on which to build. In Nottingham the increasing insecurity of workers in industries like lace and hosiery, both of which were undergoing decline or structural change, provided many eager converts. George and Harry Wheatcroft, father and son are not untypical. George Wheatcroft had left school at 14, nevertheless he became a prolific reader, and Harry, his son, remembered his father devouring Ingersoll, the American free thinker, Ruskin, Bradlaugh, Darwin and Huxley. When Harry was born in 1898 the family lived in Sneinton Bottoms with 'no indoor sanitation or bathroom. Rows of back-to-back houses, many of which were in a very poor state of repair being bug infested, it was a very very poor area.'[52] Wheatcroft senior in this period was a jobbing builder, and Harry remembers that because of his membership of the ILP and general outspokenness, he lost the custom of many property owners. Despite these pressures Harry sold the *Clarion* and the *Labour Leader* and in 1908 the entire family took part in the campaign which returned Ernest Gutteridge as the first Nottingham ILP councillor.

Making socialists continued to be the main preoccupation of the Clarion supporters. In February 1906 the Clarion Cyclists in Nottingham decided at their annual general meeting 'to lay themselves out for propaganda work on a larger scale than formerly.' The club had £25 9s 8d in hand and the membership of 150 decided to spend much of this on propaganda material. The period from 1906 to 1909 were the years of greatest Clarion propaganda activity since the mid-1890s. Six Clarion vans were on the road during this period, reinforcing the political work being done by the local groups. The effort and enthusiasm which went into this activity in Nottingham in the years between the 1906 and 1910 general elections surpassed anything which had gone before. 'We are continually making new members, and the attendances are better than ever' reported *Clarion* of the Nottingham group in May 1906.[53]

The increasing tempo of Clarionite political activity in these years was no doubt a response to an intuitive feeling that after years of electoral defeat the socialist cause in Nottingham was at last bearing fruit. Certainly the growing membership of the socialist organisations, together with signs of political change amongst key sections of workers, like lace workers and coal miners, gave hope to those who had worked so hard to advance the socialist cause. Undoubtedly, there were tensions in the movement concerning questions of political strategy and the most appropriate way to advance the socialist cause. These tensions and differences combined with the effects of the First World War, were to lead to the disappearance of all the political organisations so active in the period 1895 to 1914. Nevertheless, without their stamina and zeal there could have been little hope of breaking with labourism, or of providing the political education and experience crucial to the formation of the British Socialist Party and other socialist parties.

REFERENCES

[1] *Workman's Times*, 8 July 1893.
[2] Percy Redfern, *Journey to Understanding*, 1946, p. 19.
[3] *Nottingham Daily Express*, 26 October 1893.
[4] Ibid., 30 October 1893.
[5] Ibid., 1 November 1893.
[6] Ibid., 19 October 1893.
[7] Ibid.
[8] Ibid., 2 November 1893.
[9] Ibid.
[10] Ibid., 7 May 1894.
[11] *Labour Leader*, 7 April 1894.

[12] Ibid., 25 August 1894.

[13] *Labour Leader*, 11 August 1894.

[14] *Nottingham Forward*, November 1934.

[15] Lib-Labism was particularly strong amongst miners and lace workers.

[16] *Labour Leader*, 21 July 1894.

[17] Ibid., 11 August 1894.

[18] Ibid.

[19] *Labour Leader*, 10 November 1894.

[20] The ILP percentage of the vote in major centres was: Bristol 36, Salford 31, Rochdale 38, Burnley 32, Stockport 16, Bradford 29, Halifax 30, Nottingham 24, Keighley 40, Glasgow 34, Leicester 37, Southampton 34, Liverpool 15. Figures given in *Labour Leader*, 10 November 1894.

[21] Ibid.

[22] Ibid., 4 May 1895.

[23] Ibid.

[24] *Labour Leader*, 10 November 1894.

[25] Ibid., 5 December 1896.

[26] *Justice*, 18 September 1897.

[27] Ibid., 2 October 1897.

[28] Election results: St Ann's Ward

Skerritt	(Lib-Lab)	651 votes
Danbney	(Conservative)	446 votes
Manvers Ward		
Hardstaffe	(Lib-Lab)	1,423 votes
Barnett	(Conservative)	1,124 votes
Wells	(Independent Liberal)	423 votes

[29] *Nottingham Daily Express*, 2 November 1897.

[30] Minutes, Nottingham Trades Council, 9 June 1897.

[31] *Labour Leader*, 15 January 1898.

[32] Minutes, Nottinghamshire Miners Association, 30 April 1898.

[33] *Nottingham Daily Express*, 8 October 1898.

[34] Minutes, Nottingham Trades Council, 25 January 1898.

[35] Ibid., 2 August 1898.

[36] Ibid., 25 October 1898.

[37] E.J. Hobsbawm, *Primitive Rebels*, 1978 edn, p.131.

[38] *Labour Echo*, August 1896.

[39] Ibid., December 1896.

[40] Ibid.

[41] Some sense of this is conveyed in William Robinson, *The History of the Nottingham Cosmopolitan Debating Society*, p.4.

[42] *Labour Prophet*, May 1896.

[43] *Clarion*, 27 January 1905.

[44] Henry Pelling, *Origins of the Labour Party*, 1976 edn, p.143.

[45] Hobsbawm, op. cit., p. 142.

[46] Pelling, op. cit., p. 97.

[47] Minutes, Nottingham Trades Council, 22 February 1893.

[48] See Gee's letter on this: *Clarion*, 27 April 1895.

[49] See, *Labour Leader*, 14 December 1895, and *Clarion*, 27 June 1896.

[50] *Clarion*, 9 January 1897.
[51] *Clarion*, 23 July 1898.
[52] Harry Wheatcroft, *The Root of the Matter*, 1974, p. 8.
[53] *Clarion*, 18 May 1906.

CHAPTER EIGHT

The Need for a New Political Party

The single most important achievement of the early socialists was that of providing the drive behind the establishment of independent labour representation. In retrospect it is difficult to grasp how enormous this task was unless one remembers the pervasiveness of Liberal influences on the labour movement. In February 1900 the TUC issued a circular convening a national conference to consider the question of 'Labour Representation'. The response in Nottingham was half-hearted and reflected the fact that the political agenda in the town was still set by the Lib-Labs. The response from Nottingham's Trades Council stated that 'we express our fullest sympathy with the movement but cannot see our way clear to being represented.'[1] Despite their disappointment with this response, those delegates on the Trades Council who identified with socialist thinking managed to win a resolution to organise a special meeting to 'obtain the views of the rank and file'.

This special meeting took place in April 1900, and was chaired by the unbending Lib-Lab miners' leader J.G. Hancock. Hancock, like many leaders of the Nottinghamshire miners, was a member of the Liberal Party and not surprisingly he and the group around him had little enthusiasm for the resolutions adopted. The meeting affirmed the advisability of securing direct representation of the working class upon various local administrative bodies, forming a Workers' Electoral Federation (WEF) and instructing the Trades Council to take immediate steps to establish such a Federation. Christie and Gutteridge, who represented the lace industry and were both members of the ILP, were the driving force behind all these resolutions.

The constitution of the Nottingham WEF was formulated at a meeting in September 1900, attended by 300 representatives from the Trades Council, trade union branches, co-operative societies and independent labour organisations. G.S. Christie and J.A. Murray, both active in the ILP, were elected president and secretary respectively. Despite this success, the Lib-Lab influence continued as strong as ever. The 1900 general election saw a continued support for Liberal candidates, and the attempt by the Liberal leadership of the Trades Council to suppress the influence of socialists. In October Christie, whilst trying to speak in a debate on the National Housing Council at a Trades Council meeting, was stopped by a resolution 'that we have no politics in the Council.'[2]

In August 1901 Ramsay MacDonald issued a circular to all trade unionists in which he maintained that 'The recent decision of the House of Lords ... should convince the unions that a Labour Party in Parliament is an immediate necessity.'[3] Certainly the deliberate use of the legal machine to undermine trade unions, in cases like the Taff Vale decision played a role in bringing the working class closer to support of independent labour representation. During the first six months of 1902 the affiliated membership of the Labour Representation Committee (LRC) rose by 238,000 to well over 700,000. In Nottingham the Lib-Labs seem to have successfully blocked the affiliation of the Workers' Electoral Federation to the LRC. Appleton, the general secretary of the Lace Makers, and president of Nottingham Trades Council, was determined to isolate the militants active in the WEF, and he advised the LRC to reject their affiliation on the grounds that the WEF was neither a trade union nor a Trades Council. This was despite the fact that the Nottingham Trades Council had affiliated to the WEF in February 1902. This rebuff infuriated the WEF whose secretary, Murray, commented:

> It is no use hair splitting when such important work is to be done, nor bantering over trifles when the enemy is thundering at the gate. Organise, mobilise, affiliate, federate, *aim straight*, then victory is assured.[4]

Appleton was determined that the socialists should not gain any credence and was prepared to adopt any tactic, including character assassination, to undermine their credibility. For a man so deeply tied to the interests of the Liberal Party it may appear strange that Appleton should have been in such close contact with MacDonald and the LRC. Patently Appleton was prepared to keep all options open in the changing political scene. His one insistence was that his own power should not be threatened, as is apparent in a letter written to MacDonald in December 1902 in which he expressed his opinion of the difficulties facing Nottingham's labour movement:

> The first of these difficulties is termed the WEF. Unfortunately the Trades Council sanctioned the formation of this body, never dreaming at the time that it would be bossed by people who were outside the Trade Union movement ... unfortunately the Trades Council has undercurrents and the

desirable will not be accomplished without a very severe struggle, during which it would be unwise for the WEF to become affiliated with the LRC. If this organisation with its outside control became the recognised political factor it would not become the dominant one for the miners and lace makers who form the back bone of the Trades Council will never permit domination of men outside the trade union movement.[5]

During this period the lace makers were still the dominant force on the Trades Council. Appleton was president for the years 1901-2, 1902-3, 1906 and 1907, and whilst Appleton himself was thoroughly Lib-Lab his membership was moving towards the left. This was the main reason for Appleton keeping open his options on the question of independent labour representation. The changing attitudes amongst lace workers were the subject which Appleton chose to write of in the *Annual Report* of the association at the end of 1902:

> To talk about labour representation at a lace makers' meeting in the 'nineties' would have been to invite trouble, for not 10 per cent of the members were in favour of it. Today the position is changed and there are not 10 per cent who dare speak against it. The Taff Vale and other decisions have taught the trade unionist bitter lessons, and if he does not adopt the only obvious method of self defence, he desires to be kicked, and kicked hard ... the seriousness of the position and the need for action become more apparent every day, for following upon the Taff Vale comes the Denaby Main decision, which actually prohibits the Yorkshire Miners' Association from paying strike pay.[6]

Appleton's response to the changing mood of the rank and file was to adopt a totally opportunist political strategy. He was prepared to support the LRC at the same time as courting the favour and support of Nottingham Liberals. In February 1903 the Southern Division of the Nottingham Liberal Party wrote to MacDonald to suggest that 'if possible ... the candidate for the next Parliamentary election be a direct labour representative.'[7] MacDonald was highly suspicious of this approach[8] but his reservations were side-stepped by Appleton's political manoeuvring.

Arthur Richardson, a local wholesale grocer and tea dealer, was proposed by Appleton as the possible candidate for Nottingham South. He was to stand as the 'labour' candidate, and his campaign was to be financed with Liberal money. It was generally recognised that Richardson, 'though not a Labour man is prepared to accept the Labour ticket,'[9] and this questionable commitment created a deal of dispute amongst Trades Council delegates. Appleton worked hard to unite the Lib-Labs behind Richardson and succeeded in gaining the support of the

NMA, the Railway Servants and the Certified Teachers. Despite opposition from socialist delegates the Lib-Labs succeeded in their bid to adopt Richardson.

Beneath the surface of all the manoeuvring around the question of the Richardson nomination, long-lasting and fundamental political changes were at work. In March 1904, for instance, Appleton had spoken to the Nottingham Cosmopolitan Debating Society on 'the Egotism of Socialists'. By October, however, he was writing to tell MacDonald after a ballot of the Lace Makers that a decision to affiliate to the LRC had been taken by 1,029 votes to 106. A fortnight later he wrote again to add that he had now 'resigned all connection with the Liberal Party in order that I may bring myself into line and have a free hand'.[10] Other important trade union leaders were beginning to change sides in the same period and it is possible to sense a new atmosphere developing in which an increasing number of important activists were prepared to drop the 'no politics' pretence.

In January 1904 the Trades Council had run six candidates for the Board of Guardians at a cost of £67 1s 7d,[11] and in May delegates had heartily cheered Mr E. Knight, the delegate of the Colwick branch of the Railway Servants, on his election to the chair of his local Urban District Council. In October the Trades Council had decided that it could not afford to run any direct candidates in the local elections, but only a month later it agreed to sponsor Hancock of the NMA for a vacancy in Broxtowe Ward. The November local elections were contested by the ILP in Sherwood Ward where, in the absence of a Conservative candidate, Gutteridge successfully pushed his vote up by over 200 to come within striking distance of the Liberals:

Wright	(Liberal)	844
Gutteridge	(ILP)	640

This improvement in the ILP vote was long overdue, and it seems likely that it was achieved in the face of Lib-Lab opposition since at the December meeting of the Trades Council several letters were read which condemned the part played by Allcroft, the well known Lib-Lab, in the Sherwood Ward election. Despite Lib-Lab hostility the ILP decided to contest the seat again when a by-election became necessary a month or two later.

Added encouragement was given to the ILP when at a meeting on 2 May 1905 the Trades Council decided to support Gutteridge. Gutteridge was asked if he was prepared to be under Trades Council 'instructions on all labour matters'; he replied in the affirmative and the secretary was instructed to write to the Conservative and Liberal Associations informing them of the Trades Council decision.[12] A week later, the Sherwood Ward Liberals wrote asking the Trades Council to withdraw, but after a long discussion a resolution was passed which made it clear that the Trades Council was not prepared to give 'any pledges'. Some idea of the strength of Gutteridge's support can be gauged by the fact that 63 Trades Council delegates handed in their names as being willing to help him.

Gutteridge did not win the by-election, and it seems likely that there might have been some residual Lib-Lab hostility to his nomination. Councillor Hancock at the Trades Council meeting which followed the campaign was asked why he had failed to support Gutteridge, and his reply that his 'absence from the election was due entirely to the business of his society', seems a little weak, since at the same meeting he opposed a resolution moved by Appleton that the time had now come for the Trades Council to affiliate to the LRC. Significantly, Hancock could only get support of 14 other delegates, and the Trades Council which had just paid out £44 5s 6d to finance Gutteridge's campaign, agreed to affiliate to the LRC at a cost of £40 a year.[13]

Later in 1905 the Trades Council supported Appleton's candidature in Trent Ward, and his victory (by 1,009 votes to the Conservative candidate's 924) was hailed by the *Labour Leader* as a victory for the ILP. In reality the *Labour Leader* was over-enthusiastic. Appleton was far from being a socialist and the absence of a Liberal candidate in the Trent Ward contest suggests that some kind of deal might have been struck. A later account of these years implies that once the Trades Council had joined the LRC it had thought 'that having purged itself of politics by handing over that part of the business to the new organisation it would be able to devote itself to purely trade union matters'.[14] If this was a sincerely held belief, then it was naïve, for the years that followed were to demand more political commitment from the Trades Council than ever before.

Over the course of 1905 and 1906 the LRC was in the process of becoming the Labour Party, a development which generated some tension in the Trades Council. In July 1906 an attempt to move a resolution endorsing the change was postponed. A month later, during a long argument about the creation of a Labour Party, one delegate accused the president of 'sitting on him and telling an untruth'. Subsequently, a resolution calling for affiliation to the Labour Party was lost by 44 votes to 27. This defeat led one delegate sarcastically to suggest that the Trades Council should get in touch with the local Conservative Association in order to arrange for the running of joint candidates.[15] Later the Trades Council resolved to fight the November elections and to contest the three seats already held by Lib-Labs. It also seems that a good deal of Lib-Lab manoeuvring was going on with Appleton at its centre.

In September 1906 the *Nottingham Star* drew attention to some of the double dealing:

> We remember the frantic efforts Mr Arthur Richardson has always made to disclaim any connection with the Liberal Party, especially during the municipal election contests, and how on the close of the poll he was always to be found in the Liberal Club along with the remainder of his colleagues.[16]

This damaging accusation went on to suggest that both Richardson and Appleton could best be described as tightrope walkers, before saying of the Lace Makers' secretary:

> Our good friend Mr Appleton is evidently going to attempt the difficult task of running with the hare and hunting with the hounds. He has contested Trent Ward as a Lib-Lab candidate on two occasions and last November was elected with a majority of 84. When the question of affiliation with the LRC came before the Trades Council a short time ago he resisted the proposal along with Messrs Hancock, Pendleton and others. The contention was that it was impractical under the present circumstances, in as much as the three of them held their seats on sufferance, and a dissolution of their alliance with the Liberal Party would forfeit those seats, and be a cutting off the nose to spite the face. Since then the lace makers' secretary has become the prospective labour candidate for the Ilkeston Division, against Sir Walter Foster ... will the Nottingham Liberals (and the Trent Ward ones especially) overlook this treason, and continue to cherish the traitor? ... we have great admiration for Mr Appleton's talents, and should not be surprised to find that he succeeded in wearing the different coats to the satisfaction of both the factions concerned.[17]

In fact, Appleton's victory was the result of a deal with the Liberals which had allowed him to be elected for one year in a by-election, whilst a straightforward Liberal was elected to fill a seat in the same ward for three years. The disagreements surrounding these events were directly responsible for the reconstitution of the LRC to run independent labour candidates.

The controversies surrounding the 1906 local elections were sharpened by yet another defeat for the faithful Gutteridge. On this occasion his

vote, although smaller than previously, had the effect of keeping the
Liberal out:

A. Baker	(Conservative)	963
J. Perry	(Liberal)	962
E. Gutteridge	(ILP)	361

His campaign as always had been honest and straightforward and it led
the *Nottingham Star* to comment:

> One almost loses count of the number of times Mr Gutteridge has contested
> this ward. He has certainly stood as a single candidate against a Liberal and
> a Conservative, and against the two combined, with varying support but
> never with success ... his attitude is consistent and places him and his party
> in a different category to those labour candidates who make all their attempts
> on Conservative seats and leave religiously alone those occupied by
> Liberals.[18]

Only six weeks after this defeat for Gutteridge, the socialists in the town,
after a special meeting at the Clarion Club, decided to unite their forces,
formally abandon the Lib-Lab element and set up a Labour Party. Mr
G.O. Richards was the first secretary of the new organisation and in
December 1906 he wrote to tell MacDonald:

> A local Labour Party having been formed here ... wants to affiliate to the
> National Labour Party. For information I might state that a local LRC
> existed before but through the action of the Trades Council in not agreeing to
> any independent labour policy it was dissolved. But the Nottingham and
> District Building Trades Federation along with other branches of the Trades
> Unions decided to start an organisation on the lines of the national party and
> up to now the scheme has progressed as well as can be expected in a place
> where the leaders of the societies connected with the staple industries are
> simply hangers-on to the Liberal Party.[19]

The ILP seems to have played a crucial role in this significant
development. During the course of 1906 the local branch enjoyed a new
lease of life, and its out-door propaganda work was attracting huge
audiences. During the first week of May Pete Curran was the speaker at
a number of meetings which were attended by crowds of about 2,000.
Three times the usual number of *Labour Leader* copies were sold, and
large meetings throughout June gave the local group every
encouragement.[20] During July, Councillor Arthur Hayday of West Ham
spoke at ILP meetings in the town; this seems to have been his first

contact with the Nottingham movement which he was to represent as a
Labour MP from 1918.

Throughout July the Nottingham ILP was registering increasing
success. Sales of the *Labour Leader* were rising constantly and new
members were joining the party. In August Gutteridge organised a
meeting on 'Labour Representation' at nearby Hucknall with the result
that an ILP branch was quickly formed in the town. In September
another ILP branch was opened at Bulwell, and at huge meetings in
Nottingham addressed by Fred Richards MP 'monster crowds and
collections broke the record'.[21] Clearly, a new mood was abroad and it is
not surprising to find the *Labour Leader* reporting that the workers of
Nottingham were 'jubilant at the prospect of the coming fight'.

This jubilation was as so often, premature. The socialists were again
defeated in the 1906 local elections, and the 1906 ballot on Labour Party
affiliation which was conducted by the NMA must have deeply
disappointed the local militants. Of the miners balloted, 9,492 voted
against affiliation, whilst only 1,806 registered votes in favour. Since
the membership of the NMA in 1906 was 23,774, most of the men were
simply too apathetic to participate.[22] The ILP was keen to win the
miners' support and in July, Pierce, the secretary of the Nottingham ILP,
wrote to MacDonald:

> The miners are about to ballot on joining the Labour Party ... the officials
> seem to be against affiliation with the Labour Party but on the other hand
> there is a very strong movement amongst the rank and file in favour of
> independent action through the Labour Party.[23]

Subsequently, Pierce asked MacDonald to help provide a speaker for the
miners' annual demonstration but MacDonald replied:

> My EC is taking no part in working up opinion regarding these ballots; if it
> did it would be open to unpleasant attack.[24]

Despite this refusal the Nottingham ILP joined with the Mansfield
Federation of the Party in what was a most successful demonstration.
Katharine Glasier was in the town at the time and she was reponsible for
three excellent meetings on the Forest at which she 'ridiculed the popular
notion of today that those who worked the hardest received the most'. As
a result of these meetings 11 new members joined the women's section of
the ILP whilst 12 men also applied to join.[25]

Arthur Richardson, standing as a 'Labour' candidate won the 1906
general election taking the seat for the South Nottinghamshire division.

In 1907 he commenced giving reports on parliamentary affairs to the Nottingham Trades Council, telling the assembled delegates that

> It was with considerable pleasure that he stood before them the only body of men to whom he was responsible, to give an account of his stewardship ... he acknowledged no other authority than the trade union organisation as represented by the Nottingham Trades Council.[26]

Despite these assurances Richardson's position was becoming increasingly vulnerable as the socialists in the labour movement began to assert themselves. Many members of the ILP saw themselves as the conscience and spearhead of the labour movement, and in 1907 this group led a national revolt against the Liberal alliance. In April, 11 branches came together to form a Nottingham and District Federation and later those who saw the alliance in the terms of a straight-jacket were able to tighten the rules governing the selection of candidates at the ILP 1907 annual conference. In the same year the victory of Victor Grayson in the Colne Valley by-election on an uncompromising socialist ticket encouraged all those who saw working-class interests being stifled by irrelevant parliamentary conventions.

These developments were mirrored in Nottingham at a meeting in the Albert Hall addressed by Ramsay MacDonald, then the chairman of the ILP. According to a letter written to the *Labour Leader* it seems that on this occasion, after the chairman had closed the meeting and whilst the aisles were still thronged with people:

> A man arose and in strident tones read out a resolution setting forth the claims of the class war as a solvent of all problems ... this spread confusion in the public mind, and what is even more important, did no good to the 'cult' ... it was nothing more than a childish tilt at the chairman of the ILP. This done, they made for the door, wildly gesticulating, and shouting 'It is carried'. Doubtless the 'class' journals of the world will by now have been appraised of the great victory.[27]

On the face of it this was an attack on SDF supporters, but there is no doubt that many amongst the ILPs membership there were also supporters of the 'class war' approach. As the year turned the ILP in Nottingham seemed to be on the crest of a wave. At the end of January 1908 the *Labour Leader* reported that the ILP had 'grown in numbers and the cause of socialism is spreading so rapidly in the town that the secretary cannot give the attention he would desire to the affairs of the branch'.[28] Because of these problems the branch decided to appoint a paid organiser, and in March a most successful social event was held to welcome Sam Higginbottom of Blackburn, the newly appointed full-time secretary.

Higginbottom quickly picked up the reins and on the Sunday after his appointment he addressed a large audience on 'The Work Before Us' with such effect that 12 new members were enrolled at the end of the meeting. In March the branch literature secretary reported that the members were 'elated by the way our ILP literature sells', and when the summer propaganda got under way members began to flood to the local branch. At the end of June things were going so well that the *Clarion* reported:

> The Nottingham ILP is making history in the City. Six successful socialist meetings were held last weekend, large central premises have been taken as an HQ, a municipal candidate has already been selected and systematic distribution of literature started in the ward to be contested.[29]

Three weeks later the ILP staged an impressive demonstration at the NMA annual demonstration at Eastwood. In contrast with earlier demonstrations, the platform was occupied not by Liberal coalowners but by Robert Smillie and Katharine Glasier as well as Bunfield, the Nottinghamshire Miners' president. The job of weaning the miners away from the Liberal Party was still an uphill task, and in the 1908 ballot on the question of Labour Party affiliation the NMA still voted heavily against the suggestion.[30]

The *Labour Leader* was far from downhearted and it reported that, despite the large majority against affiliation, 'so great was the impression made by the speakers ... that many were converted to the policy of political action.'[31] Many of these converts must have been at the ILP demonstration and procession which followed the miners gala; this featured Charles Duncan MP, Alderman Banton of Leicester and Councillor Arthur Hayday, all wearing large red rosettes. Like all the other ILP meetings during the summer of 1908, this meeting attracted 'record crowds, record literature sales, record collections'.[32] The excitement and enthusiasm which the ILP was building up reached a peak in September when the TUC visited Nottingham for its annual congress.

The Congress was held in the Mechanics' Hall and there were aspects of it which were as significant for the future of the local labour movement as the huge socialist meetings. Writing in the *Labour Leader*, Bruce Glasier drew attention to the almost complete lack of 'distinguished strangers'. For the first time for many years not a single titled personage ornamented the platform, nor was there to be seen 'the usual galaxy of

intellectuals, the Sidney Webbs, Sir John Gorsts and the professors'.[33]
Equally significant were the comments of the chairman of the
Nottingham Trades Council, Thundercliffe, described by Glasier as 'a
very stout man, with a very thin voice who declared that in Nottingham
labour had hitherto failed to conquer the City Council, because it was
divided against itself'. Despite Glasier's perceptive comment that
Thundercliffe's remarks 'were a cryptic utterance seeing that Mr
Thundercliffe had been an opponent of labour representation', the shift in
Thundercliffe's position was symptomatic of the change of philosophy
being undergone even by an 'old obstructionist' like Thorneloe, the
Trades Council secretary.

Later the three Nottingham MPs addressed the Congress. Predictably,
Sir Henry Cotton delivered a homily on the desirability of peace between
employers and workers. James Yoxall 'urged that education was a
greater force than Parliament or the trade unions', without making it
clear what kind of education he referred to. Finally, Richardson who was
introduced by the Congress chairman, Shackleton, 'with doubtful felicity
as a "labour member",' was called to the rostrum. His opening allusion
to the labour movement as the 'children of Israel in the wilderness' was
not very propitious. He went on, however, to attack Blatchford's
militarist utterances before making a stirring and even passionate appeal
against the misery of the unemployed. During the course of the civic
welcome there had been much solemn speech 'and nearly all waxed
eloquent over the beauties and glories and superlative excellence of
Nottingham'. Richardson, however, pictures the '2,000 unemployed who
now tramp aimlessly through Nottingham's streets' before pointing out
that as the delegates had passed in procession on their way to the official
congress church service 'through Leenside and Hockley, we saw not
dozens or scores but hundreds of little children without boots or
stockings, with scarcely any clothing'. Glasier commented, 'Somehow,
Mr Richardson seems to have a good side to us all – ILPers,
Clarionettes, and Liberals.'[34]

Another indication of the important political changes which were
under way came in the municipal election campaign which represented
the second major peak in ILP activity during 1908. In the late summer
the branch had selected George Watts, a small businessman, to represent
them in Manvers Ward, although Ernest Gutteridge had to fight the seat
because of Watts's withdrawal. The election address issued by
Gutteridge explained:

Finding that our friend Mr Watts could not be beaten by fair play the foulest tactics have been used to drive him from the field. He is not a wealthy man, and the boycott of his trade has been such a big financial strain that the Labour Party have accepted his withdrawal to save him from financial disaster.[35]

Stepping in at the last moment, Gutteridge concentrated his campaign on the unemployed, arguing that with 4,000 out of work in the city, it was the duty of the City Council to find work for the unemployed. Later, the ILP attacked the appalling housing conditions in the city and Gutteridge's election address pointed out that the death rate of children under one year old in Manvers Ward was 20 per cent. To remedy this situation he claimed the Council should build houses with baths and modern conveniences to let at rents within the reach of the workers.

Reporting Gutteridge's adoption meeting, the *Nottingham Express* records him as saying that he believed 'in the collective ownership of everything that is essential to humanity'. A week later, Victor Grayson, now suspended from the House of Commons, spoke at an election meeting in support of Gutteridge. With Gutteridge in the chair and the leaders of the Nottingham unemployed marchers on the platform, the ILP band played before Grayson spoke. He wasted no time on the social niceties but went straight onto the attack:

> Look at some of the types of humanity you see in the great hotels and restaurants, little, podgy, rounded, palpitating, complacent protoplasms I call them. If I had a chance of making everyone of you like that tomorrow I would not. It is not food only we want. It is the vistas of life which exist beyond food ... we are idealists here tonight; we have a vision and a dream and if we sometimes seem rude, it is not that we love etiquette less but that we love humanity more.[36]

Predictably, Grayson's climax brought the packed audience to its feet to sing the 'Red Flag' and to pledge themselves to ensure Gutteridge's victory. The opposition described all this as 'brag and bluff', but there is no doubt that Dr Brown Sim, the sitting Liberal Councillor, was worried that his occupation of the seat was at risk.

This anxiety was well placed for when the result was announced the Liberals were bottom of the poll:

Gutteridge	(Labour)	1,156
Armitage	(Conservative)	1,144
Sim	(Liberal)	795

This result must have come as a great shock to the established political parties; for the first time a genuine socialist had been returned for a

Nottingham Council seat. Armitage, the Tory candidate, tried to explain what had happened by claiming that 'the working man was very much like a child; he was very easily led by figures and statements which he did not understand.'[37] This patronising dismissal of the working-class vote infuriated the ILP who replied:

> The workmen of Manvers Ward will make a note of what this rich Tory businessman thinks and says about them after the election. While he was seeking their votes they were all 'gentlemen', 'free and intelligent electors' etc. Now, when Armitage is sacked he loses his temper and speaks what he really thinks. Keep cool Stephen, there were 1,156 men in Manvers who had enough sense to vote against *you* anyhow.[38]

It had taken Ernest Gutteridge six electoral campaigns to win a seat on Nottingham Council. His victory mirrored the many years of often unrewarding propaganda work undertaken by the activists of the ILP. Their work had been aided by structural changes in the economy which rendered many thousands of working people unemployed, and by the offensive campaigns mounted by employers to destroy the trade union movement. Whilst the success of Gutteridge cannot be said to mark a victory over the Lib-Lab traditional leadership of the labour movement, it did represent a break in their ability to control that movement. Over the course of the years 1895 to 1914 the ILP had persistently argued that social and economic change could not be achieved without independent labour representation. The election of Ernest Gutteridge suggests that many working people had come to agree with that interpretation.

REFERENCES

[1] Minutes, Nottingham Trades Council, 14 February 1900.

[2] Ibid., 24 October 1900.

[3] Frank Bealey and Henry Pelling, *Labour and Politics 1900 to 1906*, 1958, p.77.

[4] Letter, Murray to MacDonald, 17 September 1902.

[5] Letter, Appleton to MacDonald, 23 December 1902.

[6] Lace Makers' Society, *Annual Report and Accounts*, 31 December 1902.

[7] Letter, Nottingham South Division Liberal Party to MacDonald, 20 February 1902.

[8] For details of MacDonald's reservations, see letter, MacDonald to Appleton, 31 December 1902.

[9] Letter, Thorneloe to MacDonald, 14 May 1903.

[10] Letter, Appleton to MacDonald, 4 November 1904.

[11] Minutes, Nottingham Trades Council, 20 January 1904.

[12] Ibid., 1 May 1905.

[13] Ibid., 31 May 1905.

[14] *Souvenir Programme*, Nottingham TUC, 1930.

[15] Minutes, Nottingham Trades Council, 22 August 1906.
[16] *Nottingham Star*, 11 September 1906.
[17] Ibid.
[18] Ibid.
[19] Letter, G.O. Richards to MacDonald, 29 December 1906.
[20] *Labour Leader*, 11 May 1906.
[21] Ibid., 21 September 1906.
[22] Roy Gregory, *The Miners and British Politics 1906–14*, 1968, p.29.
[23] Letter, Pierce to MacDonald, 31 July 1906.
[24] Letter, MacDonald to Pierce, 2 August 1906.
[25] *Labour Leader*, 17 August 1906.
[26] Minutes, Nottingham Trades Council, 12 November 1907.
[27] *Labour Leader*, 22 November 1907.
[28] Ibid., 31 January 1908.
[29] *Clarion*, 26 June 1908.
[30] Gregory, op. cit., p.32.
[31] *Labour Leader*, 24 July 1908.
[32] Ibid., 21 August 1908.
[33] *Labour Leader*, 11 September 1908.
[34] Ibid.
[35] Ernest Gutteridge, 'Election Address', 1908.
[36] *Nottingham Daily Express*, 24 October 1908.
[37] *Nottingham Labour Journal*, November 1908.
[38] Ibid.

CHAPTER NINE

Consolidation of the Labour Movement

In May 1909 the progress which had been made in uniting the different forces of labour was demonstrated by the holding of a joint May Day demonstration in which the Trades Council, the ILP and the Labour Party all took part. The procession of 3,000 included five bands, and most of the major unions took part, their gay banners filling the Market Place. The ILP, wearing red rosettes, turned out in force and a waggonette full of happy youngsters from the ILP Sunday School was a noticeable feature. J. Thorneloe JP, the secretary of the Trades Council, presided on No. 1 platform where Gutteridge moved the resolution, seconded by Sadler of the Typographical Society. The No. 2 platform was chaired by Ben Hewing, the president of the Labour Party and the resolution was moved by Hayday. At 12.15 p.m. the bugle sounded and a resolution recognising that the 'private monopoly of land and capital is the root cause of unemployment and poverty' was moved and carried.[1]

The Nottingham ILP followed Gutteridge's victory in November 1908 with a full programme of winter lectures and socials, and at the beginning of January 1909 the branch rallied in large numbers to welcome Katharine Bruce Glasier. Nottingham was proud of its new rooms and of the way in which new members were flocking to the branch. The city, predicted the *Labour Leader*, would 'make history during 1909'. During February the branch sponsored a highly successful series of four Fabian lectures on 'Modern Socialism' and later that same month they invited Captain Morrison, the Conservative candidate for East Nottingham, to speak on 'The Fallacies of Socialism'.[2]

The progress of the ILP continued throughout 1909 and in May they established a group of ILP scouts who announced that they were 'going strong. We have an interesting campaign planned for the summer. Netherfield and Beeston are to be the principal points of attack.'[3] In fact their first activity was in the electioneering surrounding a by-election campaign in Meadows Ward which took place at the end of May. Herbert Bowles, an ILP member, had been nominated as the Labour candidate and in the absence of a Liberal he was able to capitalize on Gutteridge's earlier victory. When the poll was declared Bowles had won the seat by a relatively narrow margin:

Herbert Bowles	(Labour)	912
W.E. Walker	(Conservative)	849

This success had much to do with the mood of unity which was pervading the Nottingham labour movement in these years. As the Trades Council noted, Bowles's return had 'demonstrated what can be done by united effort'.[4]

Throughout the summer the ILP maintained its now traditional out-door propaganda programme and in August Higginbottom was organising five meetings on each Sunday in different parts of the city. In addition, two meetings a week were being held in the wards which the ILP had decided to contest in the November local elections. The ILP, with the scouts as their spearhead, were already laying systematic siege to the wards selected, and as the summer continued the pressure was increased:

> Every week we hold at least two street corner meetings until every street has been visited ... besides this we own a little sheet, *The Nottingham Labour Journal*, which is systematically distributed each month to every house in the wards to be fought. The same man or woman visits the same houses every month. ILP 'Commonsense' leaflets are also given out at all street corner meetings ... as to our policy we work at elections as part of the Labour Party. There is a full and frank understanding between the ILP and the trade unions. There is no idle chatter about 'capturing'. Most of the leading trade unionists are socialists and members of our ILP branch. In the natural course of events the candidates of the Labour Party are ILP men. The Trades Council also is rapidly changing its complexion. Its old Lib-Labism is dead, having given way to our vigorous policy of complete independence.[5]

By late October the ILP branch was 'going very strong, with new members joining every week', but despite an overall sense of optimism amongst the socialists it became obvious as the municipal elections approached that Lib-Labism was far from dead.

The residual strength of Lib-Labism in this period is best demonstrated by the career of J.G. Hancock, the NMA full-time Agent. In July 1909 Hancock was selected to contest the parliamentary vacancy of Mid-Derbyshire with the support of the Derbyshire Miners' Association. During the campaign which followed the socialists in the constituency grew restless as it became clear that Hancock, like so many other

Lib-Lab candidates, was trying to face both ways. The Sheffield Telegraph asked: 'Is he a Liberal, is he a Socialist, or is he a mixture of Liberalism and Labour on the pattern of Mr Harvey, who has done so little since the North East miners sent him to Parliament?'[6]

The answer to this question soon became clear. Bruce Glasier wrote in his diary during July that although the Mid-Derbyshire election had gone well 'doubtless there will be grumbles and allegations of a Liberal deal.'[7] In August MacDonald wrote to Hancock enclosing a report from the *Nottingham Express* of a Liberal victory celebration:

> I need not say that this is making things very awkward. We have to defend the position against a very aggressive attack made by considerable numbers of our own members ... it was a Liberal meeting, called to celebrate a Liberal victory, and you attended although you signed our constitution ... surely there must be some mistake.[8]

During this period Hancock, who had been sent a telegram of support from the Nottingham Trades Council during the Mid-Derbyshire election, was also involved in a campaign to retain his Nottingham City Council seat and there is no doubt that his political balancing act was causing a good deal of embarrassment. In September, MacDonald wrote to Hancock again about reports that he had been speaking under the auspices of the Brixtowe and Walton Liberal Club:

> You have done this after my talk with you ... we are anxious to give you time to build a bridge from the past into the future but I think you are behaving in a most indiscreet way.[9]

A week later Higginbottom the secretary of the Nottingham ILP, wrote to MacDonald to complain bitterly:

> We in this city have striven hard to build up the idea of political independence for Labour and we are just beginning to reap good results. It will hamper and destroy our work if Mr Hancock is allowed to pursue his way unchecked.[10]

Hancock, it seems, was prepared to throw caution to the winds with the consequence that during the course of his campaign he alienated important groups amongst the town's socialists and trade unionists. In September MacDonald wrote to Hancock yet again to say that 'things seem to be getting worse rather than better ... resolutions are coming from Nottingham, objecting ...'[11]

As the local election campaign continued the Liberal candidate for Wollaton Ward wrote to ask the Trades Council for support. This request intensely annoyed the increasing number of socialists who made

Why all Progressives should

VOTE FOR HANCOCK.

1. —BECAUSE **LABOUR** should be fairly represented on the City Council. At present only **Four** out of the 64 members of the Council are Labour Members. The Tories are trying to push one of these out.

2. —BECAUSE Broxtowe Ward is essentially a Labour Ward and ought to return a Labour Member.

3. —BECAUSE he is striving to secure better pay for the worst-paid employees of the Council. The Tory "business man" blocks the way.

4. —BECAUSE his opponent is not recognised by Trades' Unionists as a Fair Employer and does not employ **ONE** *bona fide* Trades' Unionist in his Bakery Business.

5. —BECAUSE the **QUALITY** of the work he has done is a better recommendation than any record of attendances can be.

6. —BECAUSE he is a **VOTER** in the Ward.

7. —BECAUSE the *Nottingham Guardian* says:- "This year the Municipal Elections will have a strong bearing upon the fate of the Budget."

All Progressives therefore are STRONGLY urged to

VOTE FOR HANCOCK.

Printed and Published by J. Exton, Black Boy Yard, Long Row, Nottingham.

Election address issued for Hancock, a Lib-Lab standing as a 'Progressive' to avoid any suggestion of socialism the point that 'He has no right to put Labour on his bills; we cannot recognise him as a Labour candidate, in any circumstances.'[12] In June the Labour Party had offered the services of Gutteridge and Bowles to the Trades Council and it seems that the socialists' presence was becoming increasingly significant. This was underlined in September when G.F. Berry, the ILP candidate in Manvers Ward, was allowed to tell the Trades Council that 'he would get rid of private capitalists and private interests', after an attempt to stop him speaking had secured only two votes.[13]

At his final election meeting in Broxtowe Ward, Hancock was supported on the platform by Bunfield of the NMA and Sir Edward Fraser of the Liberal Association. Questioned about his position, Hancock explained that

> he was not a socialist in the ordinary acceptance of the term, and never was; he might be on the way to socialism and there might be a good deal in the socialistic scheme … he, however, was no more or less than a labour candidate.[14]

Hancock had also been supported by the president, secretary and treasurer of the Trades Council, as well as old Lib-Lab supporters like Pendleton and Hardstaffe. Significantly, none of this was enough to enable him to win the seat:

A.B. Gibson	(Conservative)	1,358
J.G. Hancock	(Liberal)	1,185

Perhaps predictably, in view of the confusion surrounding the concept of a 'Labour' candidate, the other 1909 electoral contests fought by genuine socialists were also lost. In Manvers Ward G.F. Berry failed to win the seat by 324 votes and in St Ann's Ward an SDF candidate polled only 118 votes after a campaign described by the *Nottingham Guardian* as a 'burlesque'.[15]

The political atmosphere in Nottingham began to change in 1910, as national events and pressures came into play. The rejection of the Liberal Budget by the House of Lords in November 1909, led to a general election which was to have a devastating effect. Against this background the existing political tensions on Nottingham's Trades Council re-emerged in full force. Predictably a difference of opinion emerged between those who argued against supporting any candidate not run under the constitution of the Labour Party, and those who were still in favour of backing Lib-Lab candidates. In the end it was resolved to send 'fraternal greetings' to John George Hancock, whilst hoping that the 'workers of

Mid-Derbyshire will again return him as their representative'. Additionally, the Trades Council issued a manifesto on behalf of Richardson, the Lib-Lab MP for South Nottingham, and sent a letter to the electors of West Ham recommending 'our old comrade, Will Thorne'.[16]

The main platform of the Conservative opposition during the 1910 election was tariff reform, and Joseph Chamberlain was quick to recognise its significance in capturing the vote of Nottingham workers and manufacturers alike. Writing to the local Conservative candidates he noted that:

> Nottingham will understand it is in our interest to move quickly in the direction of Tariff Reform. In fact, without something of the sort I do not believe Nottingham can hold its present position.[17]

The *Nottingham Guardian* popularised this opinion by running continuous articles on the theme, and by asking emotive questions of their readership. 'Men of Nottingham, are you going to allow this to go on much longer? You know what will happen in the end. Then do your duty today and plump for Tariff Reform.'[18] In the Eastern Division of Nottingham, Captain Morrison, the Conservative candidate, tried to generate the same fears in the minds of the town's hosiery workers by arguing that 'preference helped the hosiery trade'.

The Conservative Unionists were successful in winning two of the three Nottingham seats. Sir Henry Cotton, the Liberal candidate, and Richardson for 'Labour', were defeated. The second general election of 1910 did nothing to change this position. It is of interest to note that the position of the Trades Council had hardened in the period between the two elections. Although the Council agreed to support one Liberal candidate, it refused to back the Liberal Stewart-Smith because of his questionable attitude on the Osborne judgement upheld by the House of Lords in December 1909, by which trade unions were restrained from using their funds for political purposes. In fact, there are indications that the Liberal establishment and the leadership of the labour movement were becoming increasingly incompatible. W.E. Smith, an outspoken member of the Trades Council, declared that 'they were banded together to protect themselves against the Tories and Liberals alike.'[19]

The election of two Conservative MPs for Nottingham, revealed that despite the strength of the socialist movement it was representative of only a small minority of the town's working class. Further evidence of this was provided by the reaction to left-wing comments by a delegate on the Trades Council. Following the death of King Edward VII, the Trades Council had written a letter of condolence. This action spurred Hayday, a delegate, to comment 'I am pleased that there is one less parasite upon society.' Rebuked by the chairman, Hayday returned to the attack:

> There has been too much slobbering and fawning in consequence of the death of this particular individual ... I am of the opinion that the church and throne are stumbling blocks in the way of democracy entering into its own.

Not surprisingly, both Nottingham newspapers were outraged at Hayday's remarks and both attacked him under banner headlines, 'AMAZING DISLOYALTY' and 'SCANDALOUS OUTBURST!'. More significantly, however, Hayday was supported by only four Trades Council delegates, and was attacked by others.[20]

In October 1910 the Trades Council decided to print 25,000 copies of a manifesto advising local trade unionists not to support municipal candidates who refused to support Trades Council demands. In the discussion that followed Hayday took the view that this effort would be futile because there was evidence that the Tories and Liberals were combining to give candidates 'walk-overs' to keep the socialists out. Once the replies to a Trades Council questionnaire were analysed it became clear that Hayday's suspicions were well founded. Many Liberal candidates declared themselves in favour of the Trades Council manifesto, whilst all the Liberal nominations declared themselves in favour of a 6d an hour minimum for council employees.[21] In the confusion generated by these developments the Trades Council tried to issue a recommended list of candidates, but a *Nottingham Express* report under the heading 'A DIVIDED CAMP' made it clear that the meeting was a far from unanimous gathering:

> The socialist wing freely criticised the action of the Council in supporting the Liberals at the recent General Election ... Mr G.O. Richards, the secretary of the Labour Party wanted to know how it was that the Trades Council held aloof in Manvers Ward ... Cockerill, one of the socialist delegates, accused Thundercliffe, the secretary, of saying that the Liberal candidate was 'absolutely the best'. Mr Askew, one of the socialist miners delegates, said in Robin Hood Ward they had to fight against 'wealth, organised liars and even the resurrection of the King'. Referring to Dr Milner's designation of Mr Hayday as the 'thing', the speaker said that if ever he had to be carried into Nottingham Hospital and attended by Dr Milner he would 'spit in his eye'.[22]

Once again, confusion was allowed to reign with the predictable result that as the November elections approached the socialist organisation showed signs of serious strain.

Despite the disagreements amongst the Trades Council the ILP, acting on its own initiative, nominated Berry for the Manvers Ward seat. At the adoption meeting the chairman claimed that Berry had the support of the trade unions and the candidate told the meeting that:

> Talk about setting class against class was mere cant. These men to whom he had referred stood for their class, it was for working men to stand for theirs.[23]

Later, Hayday was nominated in something of a hurry for Robin Hood Ward, and at a big meeting with Sadler the president of the Trades Council in the chair, Will Thorne told the audience that they were 'moral cowards if they refused to vote for a man like Mr Hayday'.[24] Three days before polling Thundercliffe, the Trades Council secretary, confirmed earlier suspicions about his loyalty by coming out in favour of the Liberal candidate in Castle Ward. Against this background of muddle and uncoordinated chaos the defeat of both Labour candidates was predictable:

	Robin Hood Ward	
Clarke	(Conservative)	1,286
Hayday	(Labour)	591

	Manvers Ward	
Morris	(Conservative)	1,347
Berry	(Labour)	1,139
Wells	(Liberal)	501

Following the success of the two previous years 'keen disappointment was felt', at the meeting in the ILP rooms which followed the declaration of the poll but it ended as usual with the singing of socialist songs.

Only a few weeks later a municipal by-election in Bridge Ward provided Nottingham socialists with another chance. George Richards, a carpenter and joiner and secretary of the local Labour Party, was quickly nominated, and the Trades Council agreed to issue a manifesto on his behalf. Supported by a large group of trade unionists, Richards ran as an ILP and LRC candidate against Buckingham, the political agent of Lord Henry Cavendish-Bentinck, the Tory MP. Richards according to the *Nottingham Express* had the support of the ILP, the Trades Council, and some Liberals including Sir Jesse Boot, who sent a motor car to help with the campaign. Concentrating all of their forces in the ward the socialists worked hard for Richards and he was able to achieve a respectable majority:

G.O. Richards	(Labour)	1,209
V.C. Buckingham	(Conservative)	985

This victory allowed the Nottingham socialists to round off the year in the knowledge that real progress was at last under way.

In April 1911 the socialists were successful in persuading the Trades Council to pass a resolution calling for a 'full measure of electoral reform including adult suffrage for men and women'.[25] At the same meeting one delegate complained bitterly of the unsympathetic attitude of the Corporation towards the trade unions, and by implication to the Labour councillors. Sir John McCraith and Sir Edward Fraser it was claimed

> sat on anything they brought forward ... these two gentlemen put their heads together and opposed anything the trade unions suggested. The Trades Council ought to take steps to deal with this sort of thing and if the present lot of Councillors had got such weak backbones as to follow the lead of these people, they ought to do their best to shift them and show Sir Edward and Sir John that they were not going to 'boss' the working men of Nottingham.[26]

In this period the town's ILP branch was continuing to recruit new members. In July 1911 a vigorous summer campaign was being conducted. Five outdoor meetings were being held each Sunday and new districts being opened up. Early in September a highly successful demonstration was held in the Victoria Hall. Councillor Richards presided whilst councillors Gutteridge and Bowles moved and seconded a resolution expressing 'satisfaction at the growth of solidarity amongst the workers as shown by recent strikes'. George Lansbury was the main speaker at this rally and after being given a rousing reception he expressed the hope that 'next time there was a great strike he hoped the men would strike for big things, for the nationalisation of the mines and railways.'[27] Following this meeting it was reported that 'new members are joining the branch each week', and it seems likely that the branch was confident of further expansion. At the 1912 annual general meeting, Higginbottom the secretary, reviewing the three years since the Party had been reorganised, claimed that they had

> held six large demonstrations, 157 indoor meetings, 270 outdoor Sunday meetings, fought five municipal elections, two auditors elections and one Guardians and secured the return of three members to the City Council and one to the Board of Guardians. The branch also ran a monthly *Labour Journal* of which 12,000 are systematically distributed door-to-door.[28]

Another indication of increasing confidence came in May when the annual labour demonstration showed that it was still possible to build a united movement. The organising committee was made up of delegates from the Trades Council, the ILP, the Labour Party and the Social

Democratic Party and the speakers included two South Wales miners as well as J.R. Clynes.

Within the political wing of the labour movement of this period there were many differences in both tactics and philosophy. Writing in April 1909 the *Clarion* had claimed:

> We have for years been treated as enemies by the official wing of the ILP ... Hyndman, Grayson, Blatchford, the *Clarion* and the scouts have been looked upon by a section of the Labour Party with more hostility then if they had been Liberals or Tories.[29]

The disagreements referred to here eventually led to the formation of the British Socialist Party, a branch of which appeared in Nottingham early in 1911. Slightly earlier, in July 1910 there was other evidence of a degree of political dissatisfaction amongst some activists when the *Socialist*, the newspaper of the Socalist Labour Party, listed cash collected for the press fund of the party by ten Nottingham contributors. By December a small branch of the SLP had been formed. This development followed a meeting held under the auspices of the Cosmopolitan Debating Society at which Yates of London spoke to the motion 'Can the Working Class Achieve their own Emancipation?' Yates wound up with an exposition of the objects of the SLP and the Industrial Workers of the World. This meeting helped to lay the foundation of the town's SLP branch. The Socialist Labour Party was strongest in Scotland and although Paul of nearby Derby was one of its leading lights it seems that his many visits to Nottingham failed to give the town's branch of the SLP appeal for any more than a small minority of the local activists. Throughout 1912, however, the branch was meeting weekly in the Cobden Hall and in December the secretary, H.F. Smith, reported that 'the branch has put in some good work for the cause of the revolution ... membership of the branch has now reached 14 with more to follow.[30] Nottingham also had a branch of the Socialist Party of Great Britain (SPGB), but it appears to have been very small indeed.[31]

The established political parties were by 1912 becoming increasingly worried by the threat posed by the socialists and were busy trying to consolidate their position. In June, Pendleton, who had been a Lib-Lab councillor for some time, wrote to sever his connection with the Trades Council. In July the ILPs *Labour Journal* was complaining of a Liberal-Conservative ploy, and as the local elections approached it became clear that both of the major parties were in the process of working out an alliance aimed at defeating the labour candidates. Early in October it was announced that G.O. Richards would defend his Bridge

Ward Labour seat at the forthcoming municipal elections. His election address called for the introduction of evening Council meetings, a universal penny tram fare, 6d an hour and one rest-day a week for Corporation employees and the establishment of a Works Department for the use of direct labour. Richards argued that the City Council was as yet

> composed of men who represent solely the interests of the property owning and capitalist class. It is imperative, if progress is to be made, that a more powerful Labour group should have a say in the administration of City affairs; four men out of sixty-four can but act as pioneers.[32]

Later, Berry and Hayday were nominated for Manvers and Wollaton Wards respectively. A week later E.H. Lee was adopted as the Liberal candidate for Bridge Ward; he made the point at his opening meeting that 'the Liberals and the Conservatives face a common enemy.' That some kind of Liberal-Conservative deal had been struck was soon obvious as the Conservatives neglected to nominate for the Labour-held seat.

Lee was certain that many Tory voters would support him, but to make certain of winning he made great efforts to capture the Lib-Lab vote, making use of W. Trustwell, 'a trade unionist of long standing', who was produced at meetings by Lee to say 'working men should support Mr Lee because he had passed from the ranks of a trade unionist to become a master ... I am a labour man but I can't stand the socialists.'[33] Later at a meeting in support of Lee, Councillor Atkey and other well-known Conservatives were present to hear Sir Edward Fraser, the Liberal leader, say:

> In this town we have a small, unscrupulous body of men who are trying by any and every means to promote their propaganda, if you vote for the socialist candidate you vote for the promotion of principles which can only spell disaster in the city and in an imperial way, disaster for the country.[34]

The socialists, however, remained confident and only two weeks before polling they sprang a surprise by nominating a further three candidates. Eatough, well known in the town as the leader of the 1911 railwaymen's strike and a member of the Trades Council executive, was nominated for the Meadows Ward. T.B. Griffin, a local dentist and a member of the Fabian Society, was named for Trent Ward, and Harry Taylor, secretary of the Prudential Insurance Agents' Association and a well known ILP speaker agreed to fight Robin Hood Ward.

The Liberals and Conservatives seemed to have been in alliance in almost every ward which was being contested, and Lee at his eve of poll meeting made it quite clear that it was the socialist threat which really concerned them. 'I would never have consented to oppose a Labour candidate,' Lee claimed, 'but I do not consider Mr Richards a Labour candidate. He is a member of the ILP, a socialist body.'[35] The campaign itself was fiercely fought by the socialists who used as their main weapon a specially printed ILP pamphlet, *All About Stoke Farm*. This pamphlet pointed out that on the first opportunity after his election in 1908 Councillor Gutteridge had demanded a special inquiry into the working of the Corporation-owned farm. Subsequently it was proved that the farm's wage-sheets contained the names of 'persons who were not and never have been employed upon the farm as workmen', but the scandal surrounding Stoke Farm was insufficient to enable the socialists to win any of the six seats that they had contested. Immediately after the poll was declared the *Nottingham Express* was able to gleefully proclaim, 'SOCIALIST ROUT IN NOTTINGHAM'.

This setback is a useful illustration of the fact that the history of labour has never run smoothly. For the Nottingham socialists the loss of the seats held by Berry and Richards was a serious set-back, and the failure to make progress in other wards came as a real disappointment. For some amongst the local activists these defeats were only explicable in terms of a straightforward Liberal-Conservative plot. The *Labour Leader*, reporting the results explained that;

> in Nottingham a great tribute was paid to the growing power of our movement by the Liberals and Tories combining for the purpose of defeating our candidates. The Liberals and Tories have won one seat each from us in consequence, but our greatest victories are not always those in which we have majorities.[36]

These electoral defeats coincided with the departure of Sam Higginbottom who had been appointed as a full-time National Organiser for the Labour Party and the ILP's year ended on something of a low note at a special meeting to bid farewell to the secretary who over the previous four years had done so much to rejuvenate the local group.

During the course of 1913 the local labour movement seems to have been on the defensive. The City Council spurred on perhaps by the ILP's electoral defeats of 1912 prohibited out-door meetings of the NUR and laid down prohibitive restrictions as to meetings held in hired halls. This provoked a mass protest meeting against the action of the Watch Committee with speakers from the trade unions, the BSP, the ILP and the Labour Party. This protest was not sufficient to deflect the Watch Committee and they refused the Trades Council permission to sell shamrocks in the streets in aid of locked-out Dublin workers.[37] Early in the year the Trades Council had called a special conference at which it was alleged that Nottingham had the 'worst Corporation in England'. After a long discussion about the Council's use of sweated labour, Councillor Gutteridge told the meeting that he wanted the Trades Council to realise that 'every committee of the Corporation was prepared to fight to the last ditch any advancement of trade union principles.'[38]

Politically, the town's socialists insisted throughout 1913 that they were making significant progress. The BSP, which was meeting weekly at the William Morris Institute, claimed that

> the branch is making considerable progress thanks to the strenuous work of a few comrades and their determination to refuse to allow their activities for socialism to be hampered or deadened by petty personal disputes.[39]

The ILP in the same period declared in the columns of the *Labour Leader* that 'Nottingham is not asleep'. the branch, it was claimed, was making a canvass of the Eastern Division 'with a view to showing the way to win a parliamentary seat in the near future'.[40] In June a new branch was formed at Beeston and it was claimed that

> at last those interested in the Socialist movement in this ancient city show signs of arousing themselves from a spirit of 'dolce far niente'. During the coming week the HQ of the branch will be moved to healthier and more compact premises ... and we will celebrate this event by a reunion of all members, and will, it is hoped, secure the support of a large band of the rank and file to set to in real earnest to realise the object of the NAC and double the membership.[41]

Later, at the ILP's annual demonstration in the Victoria Hall it was announced that W.C. Anderson, an ex-chairman of the ILP, would be fighting for a Nottingham parliamentary seat.

The realities presented a far different picture of the health of Nottingham's labour movement, and give justification to the ILP Councillor Murby of Leicester who characterised the town as 'Poor Old Stick-in-the-Mud Nottingham'.[42] At the end of a long period of struggle the industrial organisation of the town's workers still left a great deal to be desired. Residual differences between the skilled and the unskilled still bedevilled trade union organisation, whilst the Lib-Lab ideology of important individuals amongst the local leadership continued to be a major drawback. Meanwhile the Nottingham socialists were now split into five separate organisations. Of these the SPGB branch was tiny and unwilling to enter the political fray, retaining its political purity at the cost of failing to produce anything at all; the BSP and the SLP were slightly stronger but still relatively ineffectual; the ILP, which was the largest and most influential socialist group, had lost some of its earlier strength and its efforts to make progress in the electoral field had been unsuccessful.

Despite this, it is fair to suggest that the period from 1909 to 1914 was one of consolidation. The period ended in weakness, as the working class, influenced by tariff reform arguments and jingoism, deserted the socialists whom they had elected in 1909 and 1910. Nevertheless the socialists had made an essential impact on the labour movement in establishing the credibility and political reality of independent labour representation. The ground had been laid and from 1909 onwards the leadership of the working class was committed to a recognition of the Labour Party as the 'natural' party of the labour movement. Thus, even in the negative mood which dominated the movement in the year immediately preceding the First World War, the Trades Council in Nottingham met with the Labour Party to provide a joint reaction to the Trade Union Act of 1913. This unity both saw as crucial in order to ensure that

> the forces that make up our movement can be more effectively united ... we sincerely hope that everyone will sink their personal feelings and give the scheme their support in order that the aspirations of our movement may be urged with increasing strength in the Council Chamber.[43]

Unfortunately it was not until five years later, after a catastrophic World War, that the seeds sown by Gutteridge and his band of pioneer socialists would flower, repaying the personal sacrifice which so many of them had made.

REFERENCES

[1] *Labour Leader*, 7 May 1909.
[2] Ibid., 23 February 1909.
[3] Ibid., 7 March 1909.
[4] Minutes, Nottingham Trades Council, 18 August 1909.
[5] *Labour Leader*, 12 August 1909.
[6] *Sheffield Telegraph*, 2 July 1909.
[7] Bruce Glasier, Manuscript Diary, 16 July 1909.
[8] Letter, MacDonald to Hancock, 25 August 1909.
[9] Letter, MacDonald to Hancock, 8 September 1909.

[10] Letter, Higginbottom to MacDonald, 14 September 1909.

[11] Letter, MacDonald to Hancock, 15 September 1909.

[12] Minutes, Nottingham Trades Council, 15 September 1909.

[13] Ibid.

[14] *Nottingham Guardian*, 1 November 1909.

[15] Pegg, the SDF candidate was a lace designer and draughtsman. His campaign included a demand for a 30s minimum wage and a 48 hour week. See *Nottingham Daily Express*, 2 November 1909.

[16] Nottingham Trades Council, *Annual Report*, 1910.

[17] *Birmingham Weekly Post*, 1 January 1910.

[18] *Nottingham Guardian*, 19 January 1910.

[19] Ibid., 1 December 1910. For the background to the Osborne judgement, and its consequences, for the trade union movement, see H.A. Clegg, A. Fox and A.F. Thomson, *A History of British Trade Unionism Since 1889, Vol. 1, 1889-1910*, 1974, pp.413-22.

[20] Minutes, Nottingham Trades Council, 15 May 1910.

[21] Ibid., 18 October 1910.

[22] *Nottingham Daily Express*, October 1910.

[23] *Nottingham Daily Express*, 15 October 1910.

[24] Ibid., 27 October 1910.

[25] Minutes, Nottingham Trades Council, 26 April 1911.

[26] Ibid.

[27] *Nottingham Daily Express*, 8 September 1911.

[28] *Labour Leader*, 20 January 1911.

[29] *Clarion*, 23 April 1909.

[30] *The Socialist*, 12 December 1912.

[31] Robert Barltrop, *The Monument*, 1975, p.30.

[32] George Richards, 'Election Address', 1912.

[33] *Nottingham Daily Express*, 16 October 1912.

[34] Ibid., 24 October 1912.

[35] Ibid., 30 October 1912.

[36] *Labour Leader*, 7 October 1912.

[37] Minutes, Nottingham Trades Council, 5 November 1913.

[38] Ibid., 12 May 1913.

[39] *Socialist Record*, October 1913.

[40] *Labour Leader*, 17 April 1913.

[41] Ibid., 19 June 1913.

[42] *Labour Leader*, 18 July 1914.

[43] A special joint conference with the ILP was held on 31 January 1914.

CHAPTER TEN

The Labour Movement in Wartime 1914 to 1918

In February 1914 a resolution placed before the delegates of the Nottingham Trades Council condemning the action of the Labour papers which carried army advertisements was narrowly lost. Six months later with the onset of hostilities the brave rhetoric of those behind the resolution quickly evaporated, like many other aspects of pre-war society. The threatened strikes and anti-war protest did not materialize. The secretary of the Trades Council summed up the feelings of many:

> We find ourselves plunged into a catastrophe without our knowledge or consent. This action is not of our seeking, nor is it the will of the industrial workers of those nations now urging war, neither can the people at this stage stop the war although they may at any rate do much in the direction of mediation at the appropriate time ... in the meantime people are suffering as they always suffer. Most of us will not only lose those who are near and dear to us, but also wives and children will undergo privation.[1]

The incipient anti-war sentiments being expressed here were shared by many of the activists of the Nottingham labour movement. The vast majority of the wider working class, however, seem to have been swept up by the chauvinism and anti-German hysteria which greeted the outbreak of the war.

The German invasion of Belgium had the effect of converting most of the labour movement to a vigorous though not uncritical prosecution of the war. Most activists other than those whom Royden Harrison has characterised as the 'super patriots' were usually confused in their attitudes, and it is too easy to claim that the unions supported the war whilst the socialists did not.[2] Some members of the BSP like Hayday, the president of the Nottingham Trades Council, demonstrated strong jingoistic tendencies, whilst the ASE was genuinely divided. For the most part those active in the Nottingham unions during the First World War were as patriotic as any in the country, and the Trades Council was

Trades Council Executive, 1913-14
left to right (*back row*) A.V. Guy, E. Bradley, W. Hargood (*inset*), T. Cripwell, G.M. Sadler (*middle row*) Miss K. Akins, G. Thundercliffe (Secretary), A. Hayday (President), G. Allcroft (Treasurer), W. Askew (Vice-President) (*front row*) C. Wardle, G. Butler

proud to be able to claim that the town's workers were as keen 'to answer the drum' as the men of any other district.[3]

In the early stages of the war most Nottingham workers were carried along on a patriotic wave which drew its strength from the vigorous assertion of the common traditions of the total population, and by February 1915, according to statistics compiled by the War Emergency Workers National Committee, 3,500 members of the Nottingham Miners' Association had already enlisted.[4] G.D.H. Cole has pointed out that 'a nation at war (we are told) must set aside for the time being all minor antagonisms: industrial and social dissentions must give way before the supreme need of the nation as a whole.'[5] Certainly this was true throughout the First World War and constant references in the newspapers to the 'National Tradition' or the 'National Heritage' helped to undermine a class perspective. The strength of patriotic feeling amongst Nottingham's organised workers was underlined when a pacifist resolution that the Trades Council not be represented on the parliamentary recruiting committee was lost by a large majority and Arthur Hayday was elected to serve on the committee.

The Trades Council echoed the nation-wide pro-war sentiment by forming the War Emergency Committee early in 1915; the committee included Richards and Bowles of the Labour Party, Taylor and Turney of the ILP, and Oakden and Keble of the BSP. The committee's main concern was recruiting work. Even convinced socialists rushed to volunteer. Cyril Goddard remembers his 49 year old father joining the army:

> He had been active in the SDF but he thought we had got to defeat German militarism, you see ...[6]

Later, Goddard senior deserted and his son recalls that at his Court Martial which took place in Leeds towards the end of 1917, he threatened to desert again once the opportunity offered. According to Cyril Goddard, an army captain who was present told his father that he did not blame him. This anecdote, apocryphal though it might well be, was used by Goddard to illustrate not only the extent of patriotic feeling at the beginning of the war, but also as a pointer to the onset of war weariness by the end of 1917. By this time war weariness was a feature of civilian as well as military life and, as the working class in particular came under pressure from shortages of food and housing and rising prices, institutions like the Trades Council came into sharp conflict with the local Council as well as the national government.

At the beginning of the conflict unemployment remained the major concern of the town's workers. In October 1914 the local Labour Party protested that

> over 100 men employed in the Nottingham Postal Service have responded to the country's call ... to replace them some 70 temporary auxiliary men were engaged ... all of these men have received notice and many were discharged on Saturday last and to meet this shortage of labour the postal service has been cut from six to four deliveries a day.[7]

At the same time the Trades Council War Emergency Committee demanded that the local Council begin public works in Nottingham to help the unemployed, whilst reporting that '76 out of 110 Trade Unions in Nottingham returned 1,064 of their members totally out of work and 4,409 partially.'[8] As the nation began to establish itself on a war-footing, unemployment receded as whole industries were restructured to meet the specific needs of a war economy.

The war accelerated the decline in Nottingham's lace industry, and it was never to recover. By December 1914 the Board of Trade reported that the skilled engineers who built lace machines were on short-time, and most either went into the army or were directed into the manufacture of munitions.[9] Many of the female lace workers were drafted into both the hosiery and armaments industries. Despite these trends, and the fact that by 1915 the majority of lace operatives were on half-time, the unions still tried to retain control over workshop practices. The male work-force remained deeply hostile to the introduction of women twist-hands and sent delegations to the Home Office to argue against the practice.[10] Their ability to oppose 'dilution' was limited and by November 1916 several Nottingham firms were employing women and girls on machines previously operated exclusively by men.[11]

The job of directing the substitution of women for men in Nottingham's industries was undertaken by a local sub-committee of the National Advisory Committee upon Women's War Employment. This organisation was active in helping major undertakings like the Raleigh Cycle Company and Boots to support the war effort by using large numbers of women workers. In the case of the Raleigh company the war initially brought a great sales boost. By September 1914 the government had ordered several thousand bicycles. In addition many motorists turned to cycles as the most economical form of transport. Shortly after the outbreak of hostilities a large part of the factory was turned over to the making of munitions. The automatic machinery used for the making of Sturmey-Archer gears was ideally suited for making fuses, and the giant presses used for making sheet-steel parts were converted to the manufacture of magazines for the Lewis machine gun. By the end of 1915 the company was employing a work-force of 2,000 which had risen to 5,000 by the end of 1918. Many of these additional workers were women, yet there is no evidence to suggest any unrest among male skilled workers in opposition to this dilution of their craft and traditional agreements.

The first reaction of Boots to the war was to produce a range of goods 'for the men at the front'. These included water sterilisers, anti-fly cream, vermin powder, foot comfort, 'tinned heat' (a pocket stove at $7\frac{1}{2}$d), pocket air pillows and a pocket case of compressed medicines. Later, aspirin, phenacetin and atrophine were produced in very large quantities for government contracts. The firm was also involved in trying to combat the effects of poison gas. Simple respirators, flannel helmets and a more elaborate box respirator were all manufactured in Nottingham. Since the need for these products was very urgent a night shift was introduced in September 1916; the work-force involved in making these items reached a peak of 900 in April 1918.[12] Most of the workers were girls, and their output reached a maximum of 85 tons of granules and 90,000 respirators a week. The assembly of the gas masks took place on a moving belt and the flow-system of production was so intense that it led to a good deal of unrest amongst the women workers. As a result the management reduced the working-week by stages from 53 to 48 hours early in 1917, and total output increased, much to management's surprise. As the war continued the number of women workers increased so that by 1918 the firm was employing 2,966 against 1,546 in 1914.[13]

A great many women were directly employed in the making of munitions. By the end of 1915 the ratio was three women for every man in the munitions industry but it was not until the spring of 1916 that any significant number of women entered the shell and gun factories in Nottingham. This delay came about because the factories in which the work was undertaken had to be built specially. In November 1915 the Nottingham press reported that men were working day and night to complete a new gun factory in the Meadows district of the town. A month later it was claimed that articles in the press concerning the wages which the Nottingham lace girls would be able to earn when the local munitions factories began production was causing consternation among the lace manufacturers. Lace girls earning between 10 and 15 shillings working short-time in the lace factories would, it was claimed, be taking home 35 shillings a week with overtime after a week's work in an arms factory.[14] On 30 December 1915 the *Nottingham Express* claimed the 5,000 hands would shortly be needed. Several thousand applications had already been received and between 500 and 600 women had been accepted. Most of these, it was reported, were women who had not previously worked in a factory and three-quarters were estimated to be the wives or mothers of serving soldiers. Nottingham's second major munitions factory was built in the same period at Chilwell, about four miles from the city centre; by the end of the war 10,000 were employed on this 260 acre site.

In December 1918 it was estimated that 35,000 women were employed on war contracts in the Nottingham area.[15] Many other women had entered commerce, the banks and office work of all types. Others were used by the Post Office on both deliveries and sorting, and the town's trams made use of female workers from February 1916 when 62 women conductors were taken on. By July 1915 the Chamber of Commerce was urging the government to relax the Factories Act in order to help utilise female labour and three months later a firm of window cleaners had replaced its entire male labour force with women. The vast majority of the women and girls involved in these changes had little or no trade union consciousness. The record of the town's trade union branches in organising women was poor, and it seems likely that even in those cases where women had previously been employed many had remained outside the unions' organisation. Some months after the outbreak of war the Trades Council began to realise the importance of bringing women within the unions' sphere of influence. During 1915, of 163 authorised Trades Council delegates, only six were women. By early 1916, however, the Council, after recognising that 'a number of societies, through the dilution of labour, have been placed in a difficult position, many of the unions not being open to female members,'[16] decided that the time had come to sponsor a 'definite system of organising'. This campaign seems to have had some success and in June it was reported that nearly 500 women workers had joined the General Workers Union in a six week period.[17]

The hosiery industry also found itself transformed as a consequence of the war. Within weeks of its outbreak enormous orders from the War Office for socks, underwear, pullovers, balaclavas and gloves had been placed. By May 1915 at least a quarter of the hosiery machinery in the town was employed on government contracts. At the end of that month it was reported that 'despite the increased productive capacity of this district for the supply of hosiery, the demand continues to be greater than the possible output and most firms are only booking fresh business for delivery at a long period ahead.'[18] Because of demands of this kind, and pressure from the government and the manufacturers, the hosiery unions

Nottingham and District Trades Council.

9, HEDDERLEY STREET,
NOTTINGHAM,
OCTOBER 24th, 1916.

ORGANISATION OF WOMEN WORKERS.

DEAR SIR OR MADAM,

At the last meeting of the Trades Council a report was given of meetings of the Engineering, Textile, Distributive, Printing, Vehicular, and Miscellaneous Trades Groups having been satisfactorily held for the furtherance of the above object, and the following scheme received unanimous approval :—

1. That a Manifesto inviting the organisation of women on general lines be issued, the same to be separately headed for each specialised section, with the names of the affiliated societies attached.

2. The societies recommended should then undertake the distribution of the Manifesto, with any suitable explanatory literature of their own, and defray the cost proportionately of the Council's printing bill.

3. The Executive to be authorised to arrange, in conjunction with the societies, for indoor, or where suitable meal time, meetings, the union or unions affected to supply the principal speakers, supplemented by Trades Council speakers. The expenses of any room or meeting place necessary to be borne by the unions concerned, who are also to defray any outlay in connection with the provision of their own speakers. The Trades Council to meet the same as regards the Council speakers.

4. In groups, where more than one society is recommended, joint organising meetings should be held.

The Manifesto has been drafted and is now in the hands of the printers. I shall be pleased if you will at once inform me of the number you will require.

The Executive earnestly requests that if your Branch is directly concerned they will arrange for organising meetings at the earliest possible date, and promise you their full support. It is also desirable that they should be kept informed of your intentions in order to prevent clashing. Co-operation between the societies is advisable, and given sufficient interest being shown by the rank and file, this movement should be of great benefit to all concerned.

Yours faithfully,

GEO. THUNDERCLIFFE, *Secretary*.

Wartime leaflet issued to recruit women workers into the trade unions attended a special conference convened by J.H. Rogers, Superintending Inspector of Factories in December 1915. The conference discussed the terms on which women could be admitted to the hosiery factory departments which had previously been restricted to men, and the agreement which followed had an immediate effect; before the month was out it was reported that the male labour shortage had been 'largely surmounted'.[19]

As the war continued economic pressures began to generate a serious clash of interest between different groups of workers. Skilled workers of all kinds resented the breakdown of old agreements and the introduction of unskilled labour. In July 1915 Arthur Hayday, the full-time official of the General Workers, assured a mass meeting arranged in order to appeal for munitions workers that 'at the termination of hostilities any relaxation of trade rights that had been permitted would not be allowed to react to the prejudice of the workmen.' Amongst the craftsmen of all trades resentment was expressed about the use of women and unskilled labour. Later, as the awe which had been felt by many before the mystery of 'craft' began to evaporate, and as the wages of machine-minders threatened to rise well above those of their mentors, the elaborate structure of rules and restrictions began to splinter and break down. As it did so, the grudging acceptance by organised labour of these fundamental and far reaching changes signalled that the government could not expect the workers' patriotism to last for ever.

Soon after the outbreak of war the Trades Council had begun to organise action in an attempt to enforce food-rationing, rent control and the scaling-down of conscription quotas. This agitation was to become vital in helping to create a locally-rooted mass labour movement. This process began in August 1914 when the Trades Council questioned the authorities on the problems which they expected the working class to face. At a special meeting after the declaration of war the Council called on the government to 'take over official control of the staple foodstuffs and arrange for its equitable distribution'.[20] The same meeting also demanded the introduction of rent control. As the war continued the conflict between the organised workers and the government sharpened in intensity. The Trades Council campaigned vigorously against high food prices and the profiteers 'who sought to take advantage of the people's needs'.[21] At the same time an attempt to increase rents of working-class dwellings led the Council to protest to the Nottingham Property Owners' Association and the *Nottingham Express* reported that 'there is a strong undercurrent of discontent sweeping among certain sections of the labour movement.'[22]

The experience of war accelerated the divide between union leaders and rank-and-file members. The right-wing leaders of the NMA, Hancock and Spencer, attempted to direct their membership away from the National Miners' Federation towards a more Liberal political identity. Opposition was mounted by Herbert Booth and W. Askew, the NMA delegate to the Trades Council. Aided by the ILP, these two men distributed 30,000 leaflets entitled 'Trade Unions and Political Action' amongst the Nottinghamshire miners. The success they had is indicated by the results of a poll of NMA members held in December 1916. Asked if they were in favour of contesting the Mansfield Division at the next general election, 7,511 voted for the idea, and only 2,427 against, a majority of 5,084. Asked if they favoured nominating a Labour Party candidate, the majority was 3,405. This result was an indication that right-wingers like Hancock and Spencer were losing control and it prompted the *Labour Leader* to remark:

> For the last eighteen months there has been an agitation in Nottinghamshire for secession from the MFGB for political purposes springing mainly from local official sources. On the other hand, there has been a counter campaign carried on by a non-official rank-and-file committee.[23]

Later the rank-and-file militants were able to force the issue at a special ballot which effectively squashed the attempted breakaway. In retrospect this struggle was only the first round in a fight which George Alfred Spencer was to win after the 1926 General Strike when he established the Spencer Union.

Spencer and Hancock were motivated by a desire to break away politically from the ILP anti-war group in the MFGB. To the left of the ILP other elements were active. In June 1917 the NMA Council passed a resolution which called attention to the 'mischievous agitation a few men are trying to create in the country'.[24] Hancock, Spencer and the rest of the official leadership are here concerned at the propaganda of syndicalists. Of these, Jack Lavin, an Irish exile who had been a member of the Socialist Labour Party of America, was the most prominent. Lavin had helped to found a branch of the SLP which was influential amongst miners in the north of the county. In addition a left-wing group which included Tom Mosley, the Gedling checkweighman and the secretary of the Nottingham Cosmopolitan Debating Society, was also active.

Industrial unrest was not a major feature in Nottingham during the war years, although there was a short period in May 1917 when the town's engineering workers responded to the national mood and came out on strike. Two government decisions were responsible for precipitating the strike: the decision to abolish the Trade Card scheme and the decision to extend dilution to private work. The strike, as James Hinton has pointed out, originated in Lancashire which, like Nottingham, was heavily involved in the manufacture of textile machinery.[25] Consequently, the threat of dilution on commercial work represented a potent issue and gave rise to the fear that the war was being used to undermine living standards. At the May Day rally held on the 6 May, Dick Mee of the Printers gave voice to this fear when he said that the workers must

> hold fast to their rights or he was convinced that every bit of liberty would be whittled away. The game had been played insidiously and even now some of their leaders had misled them. (Hear Hear). Winning the war on the cheap at the expense of the workers was a policy they were determined should not continue.[26]

On 17 May 1917 the *Nottingham Express* reported that at

> one of the principal works in the city between 400 and 500 skilled men came out on strike yesterday. There is no friction between the men and the local management, the stoppage is due to the men's antipathy to the action that is being taken by the Government in regard to the card system.[27]

The strike was unofficial and not supported by Nottingham's ASE leaders. It lasted a mere five days and did not display any of the militancy shown elsewhere in the country. It is difficult to assess why this was so, but certain explanations can be advanced. Underlying, and to some extent explaining, the unofficial movement in other centres were the militant ambitions of the Workers' Union. This organisation did not exist in Nottingham, and there is no doubt that the Gas Workers' Union in Nottingham was much less militant. James Hinton has suggested that the modernity of the engineering industry in Coventry diminished the power of the shop stewards' movement, and the same argument helps to explain its weakness in Nottingham. Both towns had light engineering industries developed from the bicycle boom of the 1880s and 90s. In Nottingham the early introduction of semi-skilled workers had weakened the control of the labour process which was at the heart of the strikes of 1917. The final reason for the weakness of the unofficial movement in Nottingham must be sought in an assessment of the labour leadership. Clearly the revolutionaries in Nottingham were isolated from the great mass of workers and the social base from which the strike movement drew its strength in the north did not exist in Nottingham, and although mounting casualty lists, rising prices and stories of profiteering undermined support for the war amongst militant elements, these alone were not enough to sustain a significant unofficial movement.

The socialist movement had been fundamentally split by different attitudes to the war. Pierce, from the Nottingham ILP was officially opposed to the war, resigned and enlisted to fight. In May 1915 a group of socialists associated with the *Clarion* newspaper launched a patriotic pressure group known as the Socialist National Defence Committee. A local branch was established in Nottingham, and amongst its early supporters were H.J. Kebbell of the BSP, and J. Cockerill of the ILP.[28] Those who retained their commitment to internationalism included Dick Mee and Arthur Statham. Although political opposition to the war was limited to a small minority, there was, in spite of widespread patriotism and much jingoism, a considerable movement against conscription, and this was especially notable among trade unionists and Labour supporters. At the outset of war the Trades Council had insisted that;

> The workers of Nottingham will never be compelled or driven. They have said they will not have conscription and they mean it.[29]

This determination to resist compulsion, together with the indignation generated by profiteering helped to provide a fertile soil for the socialists, and they were quick to take advantage of it. In August 1915 R.C. Wallhead spoke for the ILP at two open-air meetings on the Forest. Faced with the predictable patriotic heckling, Wallhead, according to the *Labour Leader*, was able to 'trounce in true Wallheadian style the exploiters of the people'.

Other aspects of socialist activity seem to have been continuing almost normally at this stage of the war. The Clarion Fellowship held its annual whist drive and dance in February 1915. The Clarion Cycling Club continued to meet on Saturdays and Sundays and from June to September throughout the war the Clarion supporters were in camp at nearby Bradmore.[30] In addition to this apparent normality, the patriotic socialists were also heavily involved in support for the war. In February 1916 the Clarion supporters set up a 'Welcome Home for Tommies' scheme. Many of the socialists involved in this kind of activity would have also supported the writer of a letter headed 'Pacifist Piffle' which the Clarion printed in June 1916. After complaining about the 'poisonous piffle saturating some BSP branches' the author went on:

> The Nottingham branch is unfortunately one of these and one has to listen to the usual nonsense about this being a capitalist war; that England and her

allies are every bit as vile in warfare as Germany and her allies; and that the duty of every horny-handed (incidentally wooden-headed) socialist working man is to stop the war by any and every means.[31]

Throughout the war years sentiments of this kind continued to represent the views of many who had been active members of one or another of the socialist organisations. Some like Arthur Hayday who had been an SDF councillor in West Ham, and at the beginning of the war was a BSP member as well as president of the Nottingham Trades Council, felt so strongly that they were prepared to sit on Tribunals and play their part in judging those socialists who claimed to be conscientious objectors.

Those who opposed the war did their best to sustain and support each other. In May 1916 ILP members came together for a very enjoyable evening which had been arranged for 'the double purpose of showing our appreciation of the young members of the branch who come under the Military Service Act and to secure some help for the family of Mr Maclean of Glasgow.' No one, according to the *Labour Leader*

> not in the know, would for one moment dream that possibly within a week many of the young men present would be guests of His Majesty because they refused to be traitors to the great cause of humanity.[32]

Throughout 1916 the ILP waged their own propaganda war. Fenner Brockway spoke in May on 'War and the Way Out'; in August Clement Bundock addressed large crowds on 'What is the way to Peace?' Over the summer the branch was able to sell 100 copies of E.D. Morel's book, *The Truth About The War*. Gradually, it seems, the local socialists were able to raise serious questions about the war in the minds of Nottingham's workers.

Throughout this period the standard of living of the town's working class was improved slightly although inefficient food distribution remained a major problem. Arthur Richardson, who had been elected Liberal MP for Rotherham in February 1917, described scenes in Nottingham during the course of a House of Commons debate. He claimed that when a queue of women and children, after standing for hours, were told that there was no margarine, a near riot broke out. Richardson added:

> I was at a big Nottingham meeting yesterday and a big trade union meeting the week before. These men are saying that if this thing goes on they will down tools and take the positions of their wives and children. Ministers would do well to listen to these men; they might realize the danger if this question is not dealt with.[33]

The unrest which Richardson is referring to here reached its climax in 1917. In January the Trades Council passed a resolution protesting against the 'enormous and entirely unjustifiable increase in the price of the people's foodstuff'.[34] Later in the year the Commission of Enquiry into Industrial Unrest, after visiting Nottingham, reported that:

> The nerves of the men and their families are racked by hard workshop conditions, low and unfair wages in some cases deficient housing accommodation, war sorrows and bereavements, excessive prices of food, the vagaries of the Recruiting Officer and withal by a feeling that their privileges as members of certain trade unions had been given up only to better the position of others.[35]

In December the Mayor, Sheriff, the Town Clerk and Mr J.W. McCraith JP, the Chairman of the War Economy Committee, were given a rowdy reception when they attended a Trades Council meeting as a deputation to urge economy in the consumption of food. Why, Trades Council delegates wanted to know, was food being preferentially distributed, 'to the advantage of the better off classes'?[36]

Anger over living conditions and determined opposition to conscription were the two features which prevented total adherence to the war by Nottingham's labour leaders. Certainly the declaration of war had blurred any class perspective, but as the conflict continued it became more obvious that there was a real difference between the interests of employers and workers. This recognition led many new recruits into the socialist ranks, and even in traditional organisations like the Trades Council patriotism began to wane. In 1918 the Labour Party annual conference was held in Nottingham, and the changing mood was captured by Beatrice Webb:

> There are about 40 of the leading labour men in this hotel. But this crowd is sharply divided into members of the EC of the Labour Party and those who are primarily members of the NAC of the ILP ... there is no overt hostility, they all greet each other with good mannered intimacy, cloaking their differences in banter and chaff ... the leaders of the labour movement are distinctly uneasy about the spirit of revolt among the rank and file which openly proclaims its sympathy with lurid doings in Petrograd ... the whole body of delegates seem determined that the social order shall be different after the war and for the first time they are keen on the International.[37]

The general move to the left was not just amongst labour leaders, but also amongst the rank and file. Speaking in Nottingham in January 1918, Robert Smillie stated that:

This mining country of Nottingham may be taken as one of the most backward in Great Britain. From the advanced labour and political points of view, it has always been considered reactionary and the home of liberal-labourism as opposed to independence. It is now showing a wonderful movement of a revolutionary character.[38]

Smillie went on to explain that he had addressed three mass meetings in the area during the past week. On the previous night he had spoken to over 2,000 people. Some of the audience were railway workers but the men were chiefly miners:

At these meetings every reference to an early settlement of the war by negotiation, every reference to the building up of the International ... every statement that liberalism and conservatism, the old political parties, should be thrown aside and all classes of the democracy unite together in the building up of a people's party ... was cheered to the echo.[39]

Smillie made the point that only a few months before he would not have been allowed to make these speeches in Nottingham. Quite clearly an important change was under way in many of the attitudes of ordinary workers.

The First World War wrought enormous changes on the labour movement. Hundreds of thousands of working men were either killed or maimed, and those who returned faced an industrial economy quite unlike that of the pre-war period. Dilution and the use of technology aimed at de-skilling had been introduced into most production processes, thus destroying the craft preserve of many skilled workers. Initially this had caused fragmentation of different sections of the working class, but by 1918 they were united in their determination to restore pre-war working conditions and agreements. They believed quite sincerely that the strength of their union organisations would enable them to achieve this, not realising that the basis of that strength had been undermined by the changes introduced.

Those who had been gripped by patriotic fervour in 1914 were disillusioned by the horrors of war and angered by the poverty many working people had had to endure. Their suffering, they felt, should be repaid by the creation of a new and better society. For the socialists there was little doubt about the basis on which this new world should be built, but they were a small and divided minority and the traditional labour movement organisations were more concerned with recreating the old world of pre-1914 than with any visionary ideas for a new society. Thus, the Nottingham Trades Council immediately set about the establishment of Conciliation Boards once peace was announced, whilst the socialists totally opposed joining with the employers in this fashion. George Watts, one of the town's leading left-wingers, advised that

> the capitalist system would break down after the war and the employers were, therefore, trying to delude the workmen to join in bolstering their inefficient system.[40]

Sadly the promise which the socialist movement had shown in the period 1895 to 1914 had been destroyed by the deep divisions created by the war, and although small sections had manged to play an active role in the erosion of patriotism they had not managed to capture any significant section of the working class for socialism.

REFERENCES

[1] Nottingham Trades Council, *Annual Report*, 1914.

[2] Royden Harrison, 'The War Emergency Workers' Committee 1914–20' in Asa Briggs and John Saville (eds), *Essays in Labour History 1886–1923*, 1971, pp.211-59. Ross McKibben, *The Evolution of the Labour Party 1910-1924*, 1974, passim.

[3] Nottingham Trades Council, *Annual Report*, 1915.

[4] G.D.H. Cole, *Labour in Wartime*, 1915, p.61.

[5] Ibid., pp.1-2.

[6] Cyril Goddard, tape-recorded interview, 9 January 1969.

[7] Letter, Nottingham Labour Party to Rt Hon Herbert Samuel MP, 20 October 1914.

[8] Letter, Nottingham Trades Council to Board of Trade, 2 October 1914.

[9] *Board of Trade Gazette*, 14 December 1914, p.438.

[10] *Report and Accounts*, Lace Makers' Society, 30 June 1916.

[11] *Board of Trade Gazette*, November 1916, p.403.

[12] S. Chapman, *Jesse Boot of Boots the Chemists*, 1973, pp.96-102.

[13] Ibid., p.100.

[14] *Nottingham Daily Express*, 11 December 1915.

[15] *Nottingham Journal and Express*, 18 December 1918.

[16] Nottingham Trades Council, *Annual Report*, 1916.

[17] *Nottingham Daily Express*, 9 June 1916.

[18] Ibid., 29 May 1915.

[19] Ibid., 31 December 1915.

[20] Minutes, Nottingham Trades Council, 6 August 1914.

[21] Ibid., 14 June and 25 October 1916.

[22] *Nottingham Daily Express*, 27 May 1916.

[23] *Labour Leader*, 14 December 1916.

[24] Minutes, Nottinghamshire Miners' Association, 30 June 1917.

[25] James Hinton, *The First Shop Stewards Movement*, 1973, p.198.

[26] *Nottingham Daily Express*, 7 May 1917.

[27] Ibid., 17 May 1917.

[28] See, *Clarion*, 14 May and 4 June 1915.

[29] Nottingham Trades Council, *Annual Report*, 1915.

[30] See for instance, *Clarion*, 4 June and 17 September 1915.
[31] *Clarion*, 22 June 1916.
[32] *Labour Leader*, 11 May 1916.
[33] Ibid., 27 December 1917.
[34] Minutes, Nottingham Trades Council, 27 January 1917.
[35] *Commission of Enquiry into Industrial Unrest*, June 1917, pp.35-6.
[36] Minutes, Nottingham Trades Council, 19 December 1917.
[37] Beatrice Webb, Diary, 21 January 1918.
[38] P.H. Kellogg and A. Gleason, *British Labour and the War*, 1919, p.36.
[39] Ibid.
[40] *Labour Leader*, 25 April 1918.

PART THREE

Struggles and Setbacks:
The Inter-War Years
1918 to 1939

CHAPTER ELEVEN

Labour Socialism, 1918 to 1925

The traumas of the First World War brought many individuals in the labour movement towards the acceptance of some form of socialism. The Labour Party was, of course, central to this process, although the arguments surrounding the draft constitution in 1918 indicate how vague many were as to the nature of the socialism they hoped for. The Labour Party annual conference, held in Nottingham during January 1918, referred back the first draft of the constitution, but the recall conference a month later accepted a document which had been significantly altered in order to convince the unions that they could always out-vote the 'bourgeois' socialists.[1] This provision was crucial in convincing the Lib-Lab trade union leaders of the credibility of the new party. It was against this background that the 1918 Annual Report of the Nottingham Trades Council called on all trade unionists to 'associate themselves with the people's party'.

Many of the individuals associated with these changes have been conveniently described by Stuart Macintyre as 'Labour Socialists'.[2] Their theoretical understanding of the political process was more sophisticated than that of the earlier generation of labourist activists, although concepts they embraced were as ambiguous as those of the Lib-Labs. In the fight to win and hold political power these contradictions revealed themselves again and again as Labour Socialists like Hayday, the Labour MP for West Nottingham, fought to win the political allegiance of trade unionists, the majority of whom were clearly not socialists.

When the 1918 general election campaign began in earnest the socialists redoubled their efforts to inculcate an anti-capitalist understanding among ordinary working-class voters. The Nottingham hustings excited the *Labour Leader* to remark that 'Even Nottingham, the despair of Labour politicians, is waking up.'[3] According to the ILP the election campaign had bridged the gulf of 'war differences' between the right and left wings of the local movement so that both were working whole-heartedly for the return of Labour candidates. Three candidates were selected to fight for Labour at the 1918 election, Arthur Hayday, Tom Proctor and Henry Mills. Both Proctor and Hayday were nominees of trade unions, Proctor for the ASE and Hayday, the Trades Council president, for the General Workers. Arthur Hayday, returned as Nottingham's first Labour MP, was the only successful candidate and his personal following amongst the town's trade unionists undoubtedly played a large part in his success.

Hayday also went out of his way to represent himself as a candidate with broad political appeal. Early in his campaign he nicely balanced the assertion that 'thousands of men had had to go through the flame, and they were not going back to the state of things before the war' with the claim that the 'shopkeeper, business people, and upper middle-class citizens need not fear but that even-handed justice would be given them if he was returned.'[4] Although Hayday also claimed that 'his sympathies would be mainly with the workers', his patriotic role in the war won him the support of middle-class voters and of the *Nottingham Guardian*, which pointed out that throughout the war 'Arthur Hayday played a conspicuously patriotic part. On the Tribunals no one was more prompt in unmasking any shirker who masqueraded as a "conchie" ...'[5] Hayday had often made it clear that he was not a 'peace at any price man' and it seems likely that some voters may have supported him because of his patriotic record, particularly when it is remembered that Richardson, the Liberal candidate, was suspected of food profiteering.

The success of Labour Party candidates in the 1918 general election was based on working-class disillusionment with the Liberals. This was not just a result of the horrors of war, but also a response to the economic and social conditions of post-war society. The 1918 election promise of a 'Land fit for Heroes' quickly rang hollow, and as the unemployment figures continued to rise the trade union movement focused its attention on demanding better working and living conditions. Both the lace and hosiery industries suffered severe unemployment from 1918 onwards, and in the 1920s the Lace Makers' Society campaigned for shorter working hours and the abolition of overtime 'to give the honest trade unionist a chance'.

The effect of unemployment on trade unionism was double-edged, since it had both an intimidating and demoralising effect upon workers, whilst at the same time increasing the employers' power to depress wage levels still further. Faced with the challenge of unemployment, the unions seemed paralysed. Little effort was made to organise the out-of-work and the youthful Communist Party and the National Unemployed Workers' Movement were left to organise the unemployed with little or no support from the official leadership, which seemed possessed by a fear that it would lose mass support by association with 'extremists'. The difficulties and complications generated by unemployment in the 1920s produced debilitating inter-union disputes and seriously divided socialist activists. In 1924 the Lace Workers' Society accused the Workers' Union of poaching its members. Eventually, after a TUC disputes committee had heard the Workers' Union attacked for 'scab hunting tactics', they ordered the return of the members in question. This instruction was ignored, producing a bitterness which continued to divide and weaken the local labour movement.[6]

As unemployment tended to weaken the trade union movement, the employers went on the offensive. Trade unionists were victimised and workers were sacked. In 1919 the Nottingham Trades Council found itself fighting on behalf of 600 workers laid-off by the Ordnance factory, 1,000 hosiery finishers on strike, as well as railwaymen involved in a national dispute. The 1919 rail strike aroused intense emotions, and the Trades Council, influenced by its president Halls, also the Nottingham NUR organiser, resolved:

> That this Trades Council, representing 80,000 organised workers in Nottingham and District, having considered the whole of the facts relative to the Railway dispute, hereby pledges itself to do all in its power through its separate and constituent organisations to support the NUR and ASLEF both by action and financially to bring the strike to a successful issue. And, if necessary, will take such steps as will bring about a stoppage of the whole of the industries in this area.[7]

The local press reported the closure of many pits because there were no trains, and also the arrival of 600 troops in 27 military transports. Meanwhile the Automobile Association advertised for motorists to carry mail and Boots the chemists recruited volunteer drivers. At an enthusiastic meeting in the Corn Exchange, Etough, the local railwaymen's leader, claimed that they were 'fighting for the principles of trade unionism. The whole foundation of trade unionism was at stake.' Wallis, the chairman of the strike committee, 'strongly advised removing Geddes [Sir Eric Geddes, Minister of Transport] from his position and allowing the men to work the railways themselves'. Bowles, leader of the local Labour Party, maintained that 'the fight was an exhibition of the strength of trade unionism; it was up to the men to back up their Executive. There would be a revolution and it would take place at election time.'[8]

During the strike A.M. Thompson, the *Clarion* writer, wrote to Robert

Blatchford: 'I suppose you agree with me that the temper of the workers is dangerous. I seem to feel the ground trembling beneath my feet.'[9] Certainly it is interesting to speculate on the outcome, if the strike had continued. Industrial action, as J.H. Thomas makes clear in his autobiography, was taken strictly in defence of existing wage levels. The government, however, sought to brand the dispute as a political strike. All army leave was cancelled and troops called out; 25,000 lorries were requisitioned, volunteers were called for. The National Union of Railwaymen was singularly ill-prepared financially for the strike, for only £3,000 was immediately available, and there was considerable difficulty in realising additional ready cash. The co-operative movement was especially important in helping the union over its early difficulties, and before the strike ended the support of the greater part of the trade union movement had been actively secured. What was particularly notable was the work of the Labour Research Department in the organisation of the national publicity for the NUR.

Just over a month after the strike had ended with a victory for the railwaymen (on 5 October) there came further signs that the mood of the Nottingham working class was developing a new self confidence. Walter Halls, the Trades Council president, had been elected a Labour councillor at a by-election in February. Now, in November 1919, seven Labour candidates were returned in the municipal elections, winning five new seats. These victories must have been particularly encouraging since the Conservatives who controlled the City Council had not only refused to allow the Labour Party permission to hold open-air meetings, but had also supported the Liberal candidate in one ward in an effort to keep Labour out. The Labour Party's success was firmly based on the trade unions, all of the successful candidates being union nominees. Not surprisingly, the local establishment was deeply upset. The *Nottingham Guardian* put it all down to the fact that a new electorate had 'yet to be educated in municipal affairs'.[10] Gibson, the late chairman of the Council's housing committee, went even further and announced that 'if the Government of the country got into the hands of men of the type returned, a state bordering on revolution would arise.'[11]

The local election had been fought around a number of issues, the most important of which was housing. The Trades Council had protested at its October meeting at the vetoing by the City Council of housing schemes, before going on to record its belief that 'such action is direct evidence of the desire to perpetuate the present evils of overcrowding.'[12] In the same month the *Nottingham Tribune*, a newly-established monthly newspaper supported by the Labour Party, listed seven slum areas which 'want reducing to rubble';

> Red Lion Street, Carter Gate, Poplar Street, Barker Gate, Sneinton Market, the Meadows Platts and Glasshouse Street, in these seven districts are 'herded' 12,500 luckless individuals. Add to these hovelled areas the other inhabited pig-sties scattered nearly all over the city and the figures of improperly, unhealthily housed people in Nottingham number 23,500, or more than 1/12th of the city. They 'live' in 7,000 houses, in any one of which the average reader would hesitate to house a pig or a dog.[13]

On the basis of the Conservatives' own estimate 2,200 houses in the town were unfit for habitation and inevitably housing was an important part of the Labour Party political campaign.

Confrontation such as the national rail strike, combined with terrible social conditions and mass unemployment, produced a political atmosphere which was favourable to Labour Party growth. One of the defeated Conservative candidates complained that during his canvass many people had told him that ' they had received instructions from the trade unions to vote Labour.'[14] In the atmosphere generated by the rail strike this seems very likely and it helps to underline Ross McKibben's assertion that voting Labour in this period implied allegiance to certain working-class traditions and not necessarily to any political ideology.[15] This period saw a revival of socialist groups' activity; throughout 1919 and 1920, for example, the ILP held many propaganda meetings, and attendance figures broke all previous records.[16]

Despite these positive signs the local labour movement suffered a serious setback in the municipal elections of November 1920. Three candidates nominated by the ILP, and nine candidates representing trade unions, were all defeated. The local press interpreted this defeat as evidence that the working class population of Nottingham was 'sound at heart'.[17] Close examination of the results, however, makes clear that two major factors had combined to help check the Labour Party's progress. First of these is evidence of continuing Lib-Lab sentiment. At a meeting in Denman Street, Staton, the Labour candidate in Wollaton Ward, was persistently heckled by Nalty, a member of the Trades Council. 'Why', asked the heckler 'had Staton been putting up posters advising voters not to vote for an employer?' Nalty went on to point out that Bowles, the leader of the local Labour Party, was a large employer of labour. Councillor James, a checkweighman at the local colliery, replied that it was inconsistent of 'Messrs Nalty and Darby, as members of the Trades

Council, to support a Liberal candidate.' To this Nalty replied that he would vote for whom he liked before going on to insist that a letter condemning Darby for chairing a Liberal meeting 'was concocted not by the Trades Council Executive but by the officials'.[18] Against this background Staton's failure in a ward with a large population of miners must be taken as an indication of continuing Lib-Lab influence, as was the case of Fraser, the Labour candidate in St Albans Ward. Fraser was a working miner and his defeat by 675 votes in a straight fight with the Liberals in a ward heavily dominated by colliers was a great disappointment for the Labour Party.

The other major factor which helped to defeat the Labour candidates in 1920, and which led the *Nottingham Guardian* to hope they would have to postpone 'the realisation of their dreams indefinitely' was the alliance between the Liberal and Conservative Parties. The best example of this occurred in Bridge Ward, where Major Bradwell, standing as an 'Independent' candidate, was helped by both major party machines. In other wards an obvious alliance could also be seen at work, with Liberals not opposing Conservatives in certain wards and vice versa. This Liberal and Conservative Party co-operation was a major feature of Nottingham politics after the war. Initially its nature was somewhat clandestine, but during a Forest Ward by-election in January 1920 it was made explicit when Huntsman, the leader of the town's Liberals, went so far as to appear on the platform of the Conservative candidate in order to claim that it would be 'a great public disadvantage if the Socialist Party got a majority on the City Council'.[19]

Electoral defeats, such as that suffered by the Nottingham labour movement in November 1920, played a large role in strengthening the position of 'respectable' and liberal elements acceptable to the establishment. During the 1921 municipal election campaign, Alderman Sir Bernard Wright, leader of the Nottingham Conservatives, summarised this attitude:

> It had been put to him that it was a mistake to oppose a moderate man of the Labour Party. The moderate men were, however, associated with men of immoderate and dangerous views. The remedy was perfectly simple, if one of them would have the courage to go on a platform and say he dissociated himself from the nationalisation of industries, and if they would pick their seats with care then all he could say was that Unionists would be the first to welcome Labour on the City Council.[20]

Clearly it was of importance to the establishment to foster divisions within the labour movement, and to encourage the traditional Lib-Lab element.

Perhaps this became more crucial as the left-wing became more articulate and determined in their commitment to socialist ideology.

In 1922 the ILP national conference was held in Nottingham, and the local branch took the opportunity to produce a souvenir brochure which recalled the Luddite riots in Nottingham and reproduced John Burns's 1884 election address. The class approach which underlay this was basic to the ILP and informed all of its electoral campaigns. During the 1922 local elections Mahoney, a founder member of the Communist Party, told a meeting in support of Marriott, an ILP candidate for Byron Ward, that:

> It is only by sending real workers and men of your own class to represent you on the City Council that you will get a fair deal ... many of their opponents claimed to represent Labour simply because they had once been working men themselves ... anyway, it was all rot, they only made that plea to capture the votes of working class men.[21]

At the same meeting Askew of the NMA alleged that certain people were 'doing their best to capture the prominent members of the trade unions. If they succeeded it would go a long way to smashing the NMA.' The insinuation was clear, and there is evidence that Askew's fears were well founded. In the Meadows Ward, Tomlinson, a working miner, stood as an 'Independent' candidate with Liberal and Conservative support. Tomlinson was duly elected, defeating Frank Varley, the vice-president of the NMA. He bluntly announced his position: 'there had been enough of strikes. Better conditions between men and masters were wanted and the only way to achieve that was by working together.'[22]

The 1922 general election stretched the resources of the Labour Party to the limit. In East Nottingham Jones, who had fought the by-election in June, was not re-nominated and the election was a straightforward contest between the Liberals and Conservatives. In South Nottingham, Henry Mills, who had fought the 1918 general election as an Independent Labour candidate, campaigned again but this time as an official Labour Party nominee. In 1918 he had polled 25.6 per cent of the votes cast; this time, however, although his total vote increased, in percentage terms, it dropped to 23 per cent. In Nottingham West Arthur Hayday easily held his seat in a constituency which contained most of the 9.4 per cent of Nottingham's electorate employed as colliers. Nevertheless, Hayday's share of the vote fell from 56.8 to 49 per cent.[23] These signs of a decline in Labour Party support were welcomed by the political opposition, but their anticipation of a total Labour Party collapse was to prove unjustified. Certainly there was a general swing towards Conservatism in

1922 but the Nottingham results were as much due to local factors as to any general decline in Labour support.

In South Nottingham, for instance, Cavendish-Bentinck was an extremely strong and popular Conservative candidate. After publishing in 1918 a study called *Tory Democracy* in which he argued that Conservatives should 'resist the plutocracy' through which 'imperial finances' supported by a 'servile press' and the sale of honours were planning to turn the British Empire into a 'bagman's paradise', he had left the Conservative Party to become, between 1918 and 1922, an unofficial Labour sympathiser. During the 1921 coal strike he led a labour movement delegation to protest to the Home Secretary at the imprisonment of miners who had been involved in brushes with the police. Hayday's result in West Nottingham was, in contrast, achieved against two unknown candidates who seem to have been imported specifically for the election. Since the 1918 election had been a straight Labour-Liberal fight with a very low poll, Hayday's 1922 victory represents a standstill of Labour support rather than the dramatic collapse claimed by the local Nottingham press.

This view is underlined by the political contests of 1923. At the November local elections, despite the fact that Conservatives and Liberals once again 'made common cause', the Labour Party was able to retrieve its lost ground, making three gains. Speaking at the Constitutional Club after the event, the Conservative leader told the audience that he wanted to thank the Liberals for their co-operation and

> express appreciation of the patriotic view the Liberal party had taken of the position. Next November they would have the full weight and help of the Conservative Party absolutely at their disposal against the Socialist Party.[24]

Walker, one of the victorious Conservative candidates, went further and claimed that 'there were no bigger lying scamps than the Socialists and they had to fight in future not with the gloves off but with sharpened swords.'[25] A month later the 1923 general election saw the Labour Party retaining the West Nottingham constituency. Hayday, in a straight fight with the Conservatives, slightly increased his majority and his percentage share of the vote increased to 62.7 per cent. In South Nottingham Mills ran as a Labour candidate for the third time. On this occasion in a three-cornered fight his vote increased slightly, rising to 24.8 per cent of the votes cast; this served to underline the fact that the Nottingham Labour Party was a permanent feature on the political scene.[26]

The minority Labour government which was formed as a result of the 1923 general election soon ran into trouble and its collapse, late in 1924, helped to convince many socialists, as well as the communists, that their revulsion against the compromises and evasions of parliamentary politics was not misplaced. To such men and women many of the older leaders of the trade unions who dominated the Labour Party looked dangerously insular, smug and bureaucratic. As early as November 1919 the *Socialist*, writing of Nottingham commented:

> Inside the Labour Party are men and women who claim to be revolutionaries ... women like Mrs Bloor, men like Walter Halls are lost in the Labour Party. They cannot be reformers and revolutionaries at one and the same time. They have publicly stated that they are in favour of workers' control of industry, why then remain in a Party that opposes it? On with the revolution – that's the only thing that counts.[27]

Given the strength of feeling against the 'Labour Socialists' it is not surprising that the Nottingham branch of the Communist Party, formed in August 1920, selected Tom Mann to contest East Nottingham in the 1924 general election.

As might be expected, Tom Mann's candidature created some concern amongst the establishment, especially as this was the election in which the Zinoviev letter scandal played such an important part. Desperate to ensure his defeat, the *Nottingham Journal* ran a headline:

ZINOVIEV THE TERRORIST – HIS CONTACT WITH TOM MANN.

The same newspaper on another occasion printed an attack on Mann under the heading:

ENGLAND'S PERIL; AMAZING PLOT REVEALED.

There is little doubt that W.H. Coultate, the local ILP chairman and Labour candidate for Central Nottingham, was right to claim:

> Instead of dealing with the real issues the Conservatives curdle the blood of mild old ladies at afternoon tea parties with stories of the nationalisation of women and Bolshevik atrocities.[28]

The Communist campaign certainly started a great many alarm bells ringing and, despite the scare-mongering of the local press, it generated a great deal of enthusiasm.

The Nottingham Trades Council had begun the general election campaign by appealing to the town's workers to work and vote for the Labour candidates. Asked 'What about Tom Mann?' by one delegate, the chairman replied that since Mann was an official candidate financed by the AEU he was included in the recommendation.[29] Tom Mann's candidature and the speeches he made throughout the campaign

certainly alarmed Conservatives and Liberals alike. It also disturbed the
official Labour Party as is evidenced by the nervous anxiety with which
Arthur Hayday tried to distance himself from the Communists,
anxiously insisting that he 'could not for the life of him understand how
the Tories had the audacity to associate the British Labour Party with
the Internationale'.[30] When the results were announced Hayday's
majority was still intact, although it had been reduced by about 2,000.
Tom Mann had polled 2,606 and W.H. Coultate, a local ILP activist,
had polled 6,852 votes. These figures indicated a degree of latent support
for militant policies and the *Nottingham Journal* expressed its concern:

> However 2,606 electors, many of them undoubtedly poor, could have voted
> for a real revolutionary with a record such as Mr Tom Mann's, passes our
> comprehension.[31]

The concern with Tom Mann's vote also extended to the local Labour
Party which in September 1924 had already written to national
headquarters to protest at the exclusion of Communists from panels of
approved nominees, a practice which they considered dangerous because
of its potential to split the Labour vote.

In the period under discussion the defeat of militant socialism is best
symbolised in the failure of the Triple Alliance. On 15 April 1921 the
miners had to strike alone and the failure of the railwaymen and
transport workers to support them on 'Black Friday' was seen as an
appalling defeat. The collapse of what some subsequently called the
'Cripple Alliance' generated a deep sense of shame amongst militants,
summed up in Nottingham by a Broxtowe Labour Party resolution
which deeply regretted and deplored the fact that the Triple Alliance had
'failed to act and do all in its power to support the miners in their fight for
a decent standard of living'.[32] For the Nottinghamshire Miners'
Association the lock-out was a tragedy. The union plunged deeply into
debt and total lock-out payments equalled £153,416 18s 11d. The Trades
Council had raised £181 17s 5d for the miners' children appeal, but
despite collections of this kind a great deal of hardship was inflicted on
the mining community. Four of the Nottingham pits voted against a
return to work (Gedling, Bestwood, Wollaton and Sherwood) and the
Communists were later able to build on the bitterness generated by this
experience.

The Trades Council *Annual Report* for 1921 summarized the period
as one in which 'strife and struggle have been forced on the workers by
their employers, as the capitalist class attempted to cheapen labour in
order that profits might be maintained.'[33] The evidence of a whole series of
disputes points to the truth of this assertion. By July 1922, for instance,

the *Communist* was reporting that on the Nottinghamshire coalfield the

> boss is daily snapping his fingers at the Minimum Wage Act and men are
> coming home with a sum that looks more like a tap room collection on a
> Thursday night than a wage ... there seems to be a tacit agreement between
> the boss and the Trade Union official to crush or starve any rebel or rebels
> who dare to grumble at their sorry plight. Less than 50 per cent are financial
> members of the trade union.[34]

In the lace industry the situation was little better and the union's minute
book was lamenting the fact that when a man has been unemployed for
the best part of a year, as many lacemakers had, he not only became
broken in spirit

> but physically also, and ultimately sick, even to disability to follow any kind
> of employment whatever.[35]

Clearly there was plenty of ground on which the socialists could build,
yet they failed to capture the hearts and minds of the working class.

Part of the failure of the socialists was the result of deep and bitter
divisions within their own movement. Part was their failure to make
proper contact with the mainstream of the labour movement. The
Nottingham Communist Party was, for example, largely composed of
unemployed people, and in consequence they were isolated from sections
of workers. This is underlined by a total lack of evidence of successful
factory groups and a heavy concentration on organising the unemployed.
The difficulty for such working-class Marxists lay in their often
ambiguous relationship with the rest of the local working-class
community. On the one hand they were often at the centre of the
immediate struggle, whilst at the same time they were frequently
estranged from their fellow workers by their contact with the wider world
of economics, history, philosophy and literature. Even left-wing members
of the ILP, like the miners George Goddall of Hucknall, or Herbert
Booth, who after an elementary education had later studied at Ruskin
College or the Central Labour College, were at once representatives of
their community and strangers within it. This remained a problem facing
the members of the Communist Party, and in the years after the war it
combined with what Stuart Macintyre calls 'an over simplified and
dogmatic Marxism'[36] to create within the early Communist Party an
atmosphere uncongenial for all but the most committed militants. The
consequent failure of the socialists to win working-class support left the
stage clear for the Labour Socialists.

1925 was a year full of ironies. In May the Trades Council minutes
report that the Certificated Teachers had withdrawn from the Council
because of its advice to trade unionists to vote Labour. Only a day or

two previously the Trades Council float at the May Day demonstration had featured a rowing boat crashing into the rocks of capitalism manned by workers bearing the motto:

WE ARE ALL IN THE SAME BOAT, WHY NOT PULL TOGETHER?

Needless to say, the oarsmen were all busy pulling in different directions, indicating the disarray of the local labour movement.[37] Tragically, the disunity symbolised here was endemic, although it is worth quoting. Dan Mahoney's observation was that the imprisonment of 12 communists for sedition in October 1925, and the propaganda of the left around this imprisonment, succeeded in building an almost united front. Mahoney recalled a huge meeting held in the Albert Hall to protest at the imprisonment of leading members of the Communist Party, with speakers from every shade of opinion on the left; Sir Ben Turner, Dick Mee, Oswald Mosley. Alderman Bowles was in the chair and on the platform were Labour councillors, representatives from the Labour Party and Trades Council executives and Co-op representatives.

The unity displayed by this action was desperately sought by many in the local labour movement. In December 1924 the Communist Dick Mee moved a Trades Council resolution protesting at the debarring of Communists from taking part in the work of the Labour Party. 73 delegates voted for the resolution, whilst only one vote against was recorded.[38] Similarly, within Nottingham's Labour Party branches, militants sought not only the inclusion of Communist members but also a more extreme political programme. The 1925 municipal elections gave vent to these feelings and, following the election of three labour candidates, Alderman Bowles told the celebratory meeting that there were 'only two parties in the City, one that believed in private ownership and the other which believed in the government of Nottingham for the citizens of Nottingham'. The NUR organiser went on to ask the gathering to remember that 'it was socialism they were out for; he was glad to see that some of the people who had only been described as "Labour" hitherto now wanted to nail their colours to Socialism and join the ILP.'[39] Significantly, claimed Halls, one of the defeated councillors was Tomlinson, the Conservative miner who had won Meadows Ward three years before.

The Nottingham labour movement was no exception to the electoral weakness and lack of self-confidence of the Labour Party between 1918 and 1925, and this was apparent in local socialists' lack of success in their efforts to replace all-pervading community values with a distinctive class consciousness. The efforts of individuals like the ILP stalwarts Jack

Charlesworth and Arthur Statham fell for the most part on very stony ground. Orthodox Labour candidates fared little better and the Trades Council report for 1922 laments the fact that five Trades Council members had been unsuccessful Labour candidates in 1920, and another two in 1921, and comments 'without doubt the cause of these defeats was the coalition of the capitalist parties.'[40] This analysis contained a good deal of truth. Throughout the early 1920s a string of Labour defeats were engineered by a Conservative-Liberal alliance designed to keep the Labour Party out at all costs. During 1919 Labour had won eight seats whilst in 1920 they won none.

In 16 Nottingham wards no Liberal opposed a Conservative in 1919, 1920 or 1921. Only two Liberal-Conservative clashes occurred in the 12 wards contested in 1922, and in 1923 none of the ten contested wards saw a Liberal-Conservative contest. Of the 80 possible ward contests from 1919 to 1923 in only two cases had the old-established parties fought each other. As one successful Liberal councillor put it in 1921, the older parties were 'banding together to fight a common danger in the Socialists and their revolutionary doctrines'.[41] The *Nottingham Guardian* was unambiguous – the municipal elections were 'a straight fight between the local coalition on the one hand and the more recent aspirants for power'.[42]

Labour's lack of progress was due in no small measure to a climate of opinion created and sustained by a growing battery of opinion-forming machinery. Newspapers, radio, the cinema, the church and the education system were all busy at work trying to persuade the labour movement's own leadership as well as the rank and file to endorse the same set of assumptions as the ruling class. As a consequence, sections of the Labour leadership were often caught up in a web of controlling influences exerted by constant informal contact with members of the ruling class. One example of this process was Appleton, the ex-general secretary of the Lace Makers, who in 1920 was described by the *Socialist* both as 'Fakir Appleton' and 'the bosses' handrag'. A more historic case is that of George Spencer, the NMA leader who, during the course of a long career became an active Freemason, led the breakaway Nottinghamshire and District Miners' Industrial Union, and after a good deal of gambling on the Stock Exchange aided with the advice of the employers, managed to leave an estate of something like £20,000.[43]

Such successes as the Labour Party had in this period were based on their ability to appeal to the working class on grounds of social and economic injustice. The election addresses of many Nottingham Labour Party candidates such as Mrs Wallis in 1923 stressed the need to fight for a better social order. On unemployment she promised to address the 'terrible plight of thousands of unemployed men and women in the city', and on housing she claimed that over 3,000 were on the waiting list, though 'the Conservative majority on the Council stopped the Corporation from going on with its housing schemes, preferring to hand over the job to their friends the jerry-builders, with a present of a subsidy of £100 per house.'[44]

Social conditions and resentments of this kind strengthened the determination of Labour activists and were central to the Labour Party success of 1924. Ramsay MacDonald formed the first Labour Cabinet in January 1924 and there is little doubt that the Labour victory caused a number of far-sighted establishment figures to appreciate that it was now feasible and necessary to develop the Labour Party as a constitutional alternative to the Conservatives. As the trade unions consolidated their control of the Labour Party, the Labour left in the ILP and the Plebs League was forced into retreat. The weakness of the socialists lay in their inability to construct a wider alliance, and the contraction of an independent working-class intellectual culture made their task increasingly difficult. In the last analysis, despite their impatience with the excessive caution of leaders like Hayday, and their emphasis on proletarian identity, they remained ideologically weak and constrained by many of the same ideas as the Labour Socialists. The struggle within the Labour Party centred on specific issues like the demand for direct action, support for Poplarism and the affiliation of the Communist Party. In this argument the left suffered the disadvantage of being seen as a threat to unity and was accused of rocking a fragile boat, letting the side down, not playing the game.[45] Against this background it is hardly surprising that the Labour Party leaders in Nottingham, as elsewhere, did not feel strengthened by the militancy of their followers but rather connived to deflect and neutralise pressure for militant action.

As the socialists became more and more isolated, individual trade union politicians became increasingly important as the locus of power within the Labour Party shifted towards the trade unions. In Nottingham the figures of Hayday, Anderson and Edlin of the General Workers, and Spencer and Goodall of the NMA took over the leadership of the working-class movement. The growth of national collective bargaining and the increased complexity of industrial negotiations all helped to strengthen the hand of the full-time officials. Subsequently, when trade union leaders of this kind stood as sponsored candidates in general and local elections they were able to exert a strong pull on their members' loyalty. This was, perhaps, seen best in mining seats like Broxtowe, where Spencer was able to gain support by cataloguing the industrial grievances of the colliers. In the 1923 general election campaign Spencer consistently denounced the iniquities of the Compensation Act from his unrivalled personal knowledge of its provisions, and at least one of his opponents specifically attributed Spencer's success to his astute handling of this issue.[46]

As this group of trade union leaders tightened their grip on the Nottingham labour movement tensions between the Labour Socialists and those to the left of them seem to have increased in inverse proportion to the declining economic fortunes of the town. By April 1926 the unemployed figure stood at 6,143, whilst a further 1,447 were either on short-time or 'stood-off'. The figure for those in receipt of poor relief was also high. During April they numbered 13,335 and in May (the month of the General Strike) they shot up to 59,384, so that only the figures for London, Liverpool, Glasgow and Wigan were higher.[47] The social consequences of the deteriorating economic situation represented by these statistics must have been extremely worrying for all sections of the labour movement. The events of the General Strike were to make the situation much worse, and in a very real sense May 1926 represented the turning point in the struggle to defend working-class living standards by industrial action. It also marked the beginning of a new phase in which Labour Socialists, motivated by a mood of profound pessimism, redoubled their efforts to purge the movement of the militants and to eschew conflict of all kinds.

REFERENCES

[1] Ralph Miliband, *Parliamentary Socialism*, 1979 edn, pp.60-1.

[2] Stuart Macintyre, *A Proletarian Science: Marxism in Britain 1917-1933*, 1980, pp.47-65.

[3] *Labour Leader*, 12 December 1918.

[4] *Nottingham Journal*, 12 December 1918.

[5] *Nottingham Guardian*, 14 December 1918.

[6] Minutes, Amalgamated Society of Lace Makers, 5 April 1925, and Reports and Accounts, Amalgamated Society of Lace Makers, 30 June 1924.

[7] Minutes, Nottingham Trades Council, 1 October 1919.

[8] *Nottingham Guardian*, 3 November 1919.

[9] Letter, A.M. Thompson to Robert Blatchford, 16 November 1919.

[10] *Nottingham Guardian*, 3 November 1919.

[11] Ibid.

[12] Minutes, Nottingham Trades Council, 1 October 1919.

[13] *Nottingham Tribune*, 1 October 1920.

[14] *Nottingham Guardian*, 4 November 1919.

[15] Ross McKibben, *The Evolution of the Labour Party 1910-1924*, 1974, pp.236-47.

[16] See reports in the *Labour Leader*, 31 July 1919 and 19 February 1920.

[17] *Nottingham Guardian*, 2 November 1920.

[18] Ibid., 1 November 1920.

[19] *Nottingham Journal*, 10 January 1920.

[20] *Nottingham Guardian*, 2 November 1921.

[21] Ibid., 31 October 1922.

[22] Ibid., 2 November 1922.

[23] Election Result:

> A. Hayday (Labour)10,787
> G. Powell (Conservative) 6,050
> A.L. Rea (Liberal) 5,163
> Majority 4,737.

[24] *Nottingham Guardian*, 1 November 1923.

[25] Ibid.

[26] Election Results:

> H. Cavendish-Bentinck (Conservative)10,724
> H. Mills (Labour) 5,176
> V.D. Duval (Liberal) 4,966
> Majority 5,548

[27] *The Socialist*, 13 November 1919.

[28] *Nottingham Journal*, 25 October 1924.

[29] Ibid., 16 October 1924.

[30] Ibid., 28 October 1924.

[31] Ibid., 31 October 1924.

[32] Minutes, Broxtowe Divisional Labour Party, 16 April 1921.

[33] Nottingham Trades Council, *Annual Report*, 1921.

[34] *The Communist*, 15 July 1922.

[35] By mid-1922 there were 475 members of the Lace Makers' Society out of benefit owing to their inability to pay union contributions. Minutes, Amalgamated Society of Lace Makers, 3 June 1922.

[36] Macintyre, op. cit., p.94.

[37] Minutes, Nottingham Trades Council, 6 May 1925.

[38] Ibid., 10 December 1925.

[39] *Nottingham Guardian*, 3 November 1925.

[40] Nottingham Trades Council, *Annual Report*, 1922.

[41] *Nottingham Guardian*, 2 November 1921.

[42] Ibid.

[43] Joyce Bellamy and John Saville, *Dictionary of Labour Biography*, Vol. 1, 1972, pp.304-7.

[44] Mrs Wallis, 'Election Address', 1923.

[45] Miliband, op. cit., p.32.

[46] *Hucknall Dispatch*, 13 December 1923.

[47] *Labour Research*, Vol. 15, No. 7, July 1926.

CHAPTER TWELVE

The General Strike and its Consequences

A major confrontation between capital and labour loomed darkly on the horizon from 1925 onwards. Conflict within the mining industry led the government to establish a Royal Commission in 1925, but even as it continued to sit special conferences of national and local representatives of the governmental machine were held in December 1925 and January 1926, to consider ways of defeating the miners, and thus the entire trade union movement.

In March 1926 the Commission reported. Most importantly, it rejected the miners' demand for nationalisation and proposed an immediate reduction in wages. On 9 April the Miners' Federation rejected the essence of the Royal Commission's recommendations and issued instructions to its district Federations that the working day must not be lengthened, the principle of the minimum wage must be adhered to, and that no cut in wages should be accepted. Significantly, George Spencer, the Nottinghamshire leader, spoke strongly against this recommendation, arguing that the Commission's report 'contained elements of usefulness if only they could be applied'.[1] Later in the month Frank Hodges, the secretary of the Miners' International, told a Nottingham meeting that the miners would be prepared to accept longer hours in preference to lower wages and it seems likely that the appearance in the town of this well-known moderate was not unconnected with the general attitude of the leadership of the Nottinghamshire Miners' Association.

On 29 April a special conference of trade union executives met to consider the position. In the face of the mineowners' refusal to agree a compromise solution the conference was forced to draw up proposals for co-ordinated action. In response the Cabinet adopted the Emergency Powers Act on 1 May, troop movements followed and a call for volunteers was issued by the government-backed Organisation for the Maintenance of Supplies (OMS). The conference of trade union executives had issued a deadline by the end of which they hoped the

mineowners would accede to their demands. In the intervening days the
TUC did everything in its power to achieve a compromise solution, but
all approaches were rejected. Finally, following the refusal of print
workers at the *Daily Mail* to print a vitriolic attack on the trade union
movement, the government broke off negotiations and at midnight on 3
May 1926 the General Strike began.

In Nottingham the government's decision to establish strike-breaking
machinery on a divisional basis was quickly implemented. Captain H.
Douglas-King MP had been appointed Commissioner for the north
Midlands region, based in Nottingham. His object was to maintain all
essential services and on 3 May, immediately prior to the strike, he issued
a statement that 'the public can be assured that all preliminary steps have
been taken to ensure the maintenance of supplies of necessities.'[2] A great
deal of work had gone into setting up this strike-breaking machinery.
There were people in every district prepared to open offices and enlist
volunteers as soon as they received the signal. The north Midlands were
divided into eight districts, each with a chairman and road, coal, postage,
haulage, food and finance officer. The social background of these officials
was plain from the fact that three more of Captain Douglas-King's staff
were recruited from the military, whilst the rest came from the business
community.

The town's capitalists and bureacrats had also been busy setting up a
local organisation for the maintenance of supplies. On the eve of the
strike a volunteer recruiting office was opened and advertisements calling
for volunteers placed in the local press. According to one report there
were about 5,000 volunteers in Nottingham. This estimate is almost
certainly inflated, however, since at a meeting of the organisation on 30
April it was stated that in some parts of the county doors had been
slammed in the faces of the organisation's canvassers.[3] At the same
meeting the claim was made that the organisation was established in 118
parishes out of 260 in the Nottingham area. How strong these groups
were is uncertain. Captain H.C. Sherbrooke DSO and Mr H.D.
Cherry-Downes both felt that many people had refused to sign on with
the organisation because they feared victimisation. Captain Turner
reported that the OMS headquarters were disgusted that so little had
been done in Nottingham. He made the point that a poster campaign in
West Bridgford had had absolutely no effect, and Cherry-Downes
advanced the view that the unions had passed round the word that people
should have nothing to do with the OMS.[4]

The activities of the OMS were paralleled by the Volunteer Service
Committee under the local leadership of Major Stuart Hartshorn CBE.

This committee was active in recruiting special constables and more than 1,000 were sworn in during the strike. Amongst these was Sir Ernest Jardine, a local machine manufacturer, who personally marched 130 of his staff to the Guildhall where they were sworn in. Jardine's friend, A.W. Kirkaldy, president of the Chamber of Commerce, was appointed Officer Commanding in charge of one of the volunteer companies and the Chamber's leading role in the strike-breaking force is further evidenced by the appointment of its secretary as one of the six superintendents of the volunteer forces.[5]

When the strike started the Chamber of Commerce placed its transport unreservedly at the disposal of the Civil Commissioner. During the strike the transport department, the only one of its kind in the country, maintained a regular service to and from London. Its vehicles were in use carrying food but also lace, hosiery, tobacco, medical supplies, made-up goods and other products of the Nottingham factories. The Chamber took over a warehouse in the Lace Market which it used as a clearing house whilst maintaining a daily service to London, Birmingham, Liverpool and Manchester. The business-dominated City Council was also fully prepared to back strike-breaking. Leading members like Alderman Sir Bernard Wright and Alderman Sir Albert Ball were appointed to take such steps as they considered necessary to deal with the strike. Perhaps remembering the manner in which the town's workers had fired the Castle in the Reform Bill riots of 1831, their first decision was to close the Castle to the public. Many of the town's aldermen and councillors were intimately connected with Nottingham's industrial life and it is not surprising that they regarded the strike as a fundamental threat to their position.

In contrast with the speed and relative efficiency with which the local representatives of capital organised themselves, the Nottingham labour movement's reponse was slow and hesitant. Much of this disorganisation was the result of ineffective and confused national leadership. Although the Trades Council had helped form a local Council of Action in September 1925, this organisation could not be utilised because of the lack of guidance from the General Council of the TUC.[6] As soon as the strike commenced the Trades Council established a strike committee, composed of two representatives of each of the unions involved in the dispute, together with the whole of the Trades Council executive. Whilst the strike continued this committee sat every day, as did the sub-committees which it appointed to deal with the question of permits, publicity meetings and outside pickets.

The rank-and-file response to the call for a General Strike in Nottingham was almost unanimous. The TUC's official report on the strike records the fact that Nottingham was amongst those towns where the response was 'unexpectedly and amazingly fine'.[7] The strike call was answered first by the transport workers and those working in heavy industry. On the first day of the strike, the local evening newspaper managed to produce an edition which carried a story detailing 'great activity' outside the offices of the TGWU and the NUGMW where workers not yet called out were anxiously enquiring if they should cease work. Jack Charlesworth, a hosiery worker and active member of the ILP, remembered the mood well:

> I remember at Weldon's [a hosiery factory] ordinary people said: 'How is it that we are not on strike?' People who had never been interested in politics or industrial questions or even rates on the shop floor, they said, 'Why are we not involved?' to such an extent that the Union had to go to the TUC to whom we weren't affiliated, to ask if they wanted us to strike. I well remember the reply from the TUC. They said, 'We regard you as the second line of defence along with other industries' … people were really dissatisfied with this.[8]

Meanwhile, huge meetings of transport workers and railwaymen were held in various parts of the town and the atmosphere was summed up at a joint meeting of the three rail unions when W. Halls the NUR organiser, after appealing for order and discipline, went on.

> We knew this day was bound to come sooner or later and we ought to be glad. It is a day we have hoped for and prayed for and looked forward to … we ought to be delighted.[9]

The deep-rooted divisions within the Nottingham socialist groupings were temporarily cast aside in the face of intransigent employers and government. The day before the commencement of the General Strike, several thousand workers assembled on the Forest to celebrate May Day. Alderman Herbert Bowles, leader of the local Labour Party, assured those present that at midnight the local labour movement would stand wholeheartedly with the miners. Arthur Hayday went further and declared that the trouble represented the breakdown of modern capitalism, whilst the president of the Trades Council told the crowd that unless the government capitulated the whole trade union movement would oppose them.[10] Throughout the day feelings ran high in anticipation of the announcement of the strike, and demonstrations and meetings in support of the miners continued. When the final announcement was made at the ILP evening rally and dance, the whole of the hall 'went absolutely mad … they formed chains singing the

"Internationale" and the "Red Flag" as they marched round and round.'[11]

Despite the confusion of the pre-strike period the Trades Council acted quickly to support the strike. Fortunately the skeleton of the railwaymen's 1919 strike committee was still in existence and the Council was able to utilise its skill and experience.[12] The respectable Labour Socialist members of the Trades Council were hesitant to take up a militant position. This is shown by the resignation on 3 May of the secretary, George Thundercliffe, and his replacement by Wallis of the NUR. Many Labour Party activists did, however, play an important role in maintaining the solidarity of the local labour movement. Turney and Ashworth of the Tramways Committee encouraged tram drivers and conductors to join the strike; William Green, a member of the Building Trades Strike Co-ordinating Committee, took personal responsibility for calling out City Council workmen. But at the same time Labour councillors were calling on workers to be peaceful and not to congregate in large numbers.[13]

The second day of the strike saw militant action in Nottingham. Both bus and tram services stopped and the few private buses which ventured into the town were attacked and overturned. During one outburst of anger the private car of a local bus proprietor was attacked. Dan Mahoney, a local activist, claimed that the proprietor had provoked the attack by his provocative and defiant attitude; he had attempted to run his bus fleet with non-union labour, but was foiled by pickets who removed the carburettors from the buses. Later in the day some 2,000 strikers toured the Queen's Drive area demanding that work should stop at a number of factories.

Mahoney's account recalls that the workers

in their excitement and undisciplined way ... decided to have everybody out, so workers marched or rushed from factory to factory and persuaded thousands of non-unionists to come out.

One eye-witness of these scenes remembered:

Queen's Drive was undergoing a re-surfacing and immediately in front of our house was a steam roller, a tar-making machine, a lorry and various tools and implements. I remember seeing a huge mob of men surging from the direction of the station. They were headed by a man who had a pole on which was tied a huge red sock ... a great shout went up and they proceeded to overturn the steam roller, the tar-making machine and smashing such things as the picks, shovels and buckets.[14]

Later the strikers rushed the Nottingham Brewery Company, the police were called and scuffles and fights broke out. They also visited the Midland Timber Company and the works of Messrs Jardine, but these were protected by a strong force of police and the strikers were unsuccessful in their attempt to call out the workers of these firms. Despite these disappointments the strikers were able to halt a lorry owned by Skinner and Rock and successfully removed its cargo of beer and groceries before the police arrived.

The role played by the police in maintaining 'public order' was an issue of great contention. Superintendent Downs has left a useful account of the tactics of both strikers and police:

> Thousands of people gravitated to the Old Market Square and the City Centre to see what would happen. Small incidents like a dog fight would cause hundreds of people to run to see what was going on. This was harmless curiosity, but it was not long before mischief-makers began to make their presence felt. They would leave the city centre in small groups, which grew larger as they went along and suddenly arrive at some works or brewery and demonstrate, threatening what would happen if they did not close down. Some more serious than others declared their intention to stop trains or burn timber yards.

There were numerous calls to the police and police vans or 'Black Marias' were much in evidence. Downs wrote:

> Police experience shows that the militant and disorderly element are in the front of the demonstration followed by sympathisers and curious sight-seers. A cowardly few are usually in the rear and content themselves by throwing stones and other missiles over the heads of the crowd ... about 2 p.m. on the Tuesday a friendly licensee brought some serious information to the effect that he had overheard a gang of rough men planning to hold a meeting on the pavement of Long Row, facing the Old Market Square ... when the meeting was in full swing these men, under cover of the crowd which was sure to collect, intended to loot the shops. In the short time available the police took prompt measures. Inspector Hunt with 40 of the toughest policemen was sent into Norfolk Place. Their job was to deal with looters and violent persons ... Inspector Gregory in charge of the 16 mounted police was moved to a veterinary surgeon's yard in St James Street. The only police on view were the ordinary uniformed patrols and plain clothes men near the proposed scene and seated alongside the driver of a police van was Superintendent G.W. Downs ... sure enough, about 2.30 p.m. the meeting started and as the crowd gathered Superintendent Downs played his trump card. He sent a pre-arranged signal to Inspector Gregory, who brought his mounted men out of St James Street and trotted through Granby Street, Friar Lane and then

past the crowd on Long Row. The whole crowd then saw the fine figure of Inspector Gregory riding at the head of his men at a smart trot up Market Street towards the Guildhall ... the crowd broke away and ran after the mounted police, leaving Long Row empty ... Gregory increased the pace and when in Sherwood Street suddenly turned towards Talbot Street on to Canning Circus and down the Ropewalk back to his base ... Superintendent Downs rode back on the police van, highly satisfied with his successful manoeuvre.[15]

Later that evening Downs was involved in a major fight at the Palais-de-Danse. Superintendent Downs believed that

the gang who had been causing so much trouble had forced their way in and created a great disturbance, intending to break up the function there ... they fought with great determination and both sides had a good innings. Some arrests were made, including the ringleader.

One of the workers who was involved, however, sees this violent disturbance rather differently:

Let me tell you, the fight began inside on the dance floor where the upper classes were enjoying themselves so they did not like us on their dance floor, they started something which they got the worst of. We were an angry, starved lot of miners and then the police arrived and began striking out at everybody within reach of their batons.[16]

The forces opposed to the striking workers did not take kindly to this kind of activity. The local evening paper ran an editorial on 4 May which spelt out the attitude of the establishment:

We now wish to record our protest against the use of the General Strike as a weapon with which to settle a sectional dispute ... we imagine there is very little enthusiasm for a General Strike amongst the vast majority of workers.[17]

The writer of this editorial was not very well informed, because on the following morning his own paper's print workers walked off the job. Nottingham's other newspaper was also hit by the strike. During the dispute it managed to produce a duplicated sheet containing national news items, a summary of parliamentary debates and the cricket scores. The owners of the local press were outraged at this interference and on resuming publication published a long editorial calling for 'the unqualified support of every man and women who values the English birthright of personal liberty and freedom of the press'.[18]

According to Kenneth Adam, the BBCs Nottingham relay station 5NG decided to ignore instructions from London which were frequently contradictory, and to provide instead 'a full and fair' service. Everard

Guilford, a lecturer in history at the University College, was the hero of the hour when he authorised the decision to broadcast the resolution of the Mansfield miners to 'keep the Fascisti [i.e. troops] out of the town by all and any means'. Later, when the strikers overturned a pirate bus in the city centre, one of the staff gave a brief but chilling eye-witness account. Raids on factories and assaults on places of entertainment were reported. When the public houses began to close down due to lack of supplies, Guilford pointed out that a day or two before a crowd had rushed the premises of a local brewery to bring the draymen out. Subsequently, the Civil Commissioner broadcast the message 'Beer is *not* a food. This is official.'[19]

The strikers' answer to the lack of easily-available and reliable news was to produce their own official strike bulletin. Mahoney makes the point that the central strike committee had plenty to deal with: 'Daily papers were coming out by comrade duplicator. The railwaymen had direct contact with London, motor-cyclists and pedal-cyclists despatch riders were everywhere.'[20] Using these methods of news-gathering the strike bulletin was first produced on 6 May. The bulletin was issued twice daily during the dispute and Issue Number 1 warned workers to ignore 'any government or anti-strike propaganda publications, obviously inspired to mislead the public and to attempt to break the General Strike.' This strike sheet was produced at the ILP hall which was quickly turned into the strikers' main communication centre and strike headquarters. From this hall for the next nine days the men and women leading the strike would challenge the assumptions of the town's ruling group.

Supporters of the establishment did their best to organise a private transport system by using volunteers' private cars. Miss Kentish Wright was able to claim that she had saved hundreds of women and girls long walks to work by the private service she organised, morning and evening, from Basford, Bulwell, Daybrook, Sherwood and Netherfield into the centre of the town. Meanwhile the strike among railwaymen continued almost completely solid. On 10 May the LMS claimed it was running 32 trains and the LNER 31. The official strike bulletin, however, claimed that 'The much vaunted service is being maintained by the same engine, train driver and guard, who work about 16 hours a day each.'[21] Dan Mahoney recalls one railway union bulletin which read: 'Train left Grimsby, two wagons going badly, arrived at Alford, changed engines, arrived Louth still going badly, 21 miles in $8\frac{1}{2}$ hours – this is a sample of student volunteers.'[22]

Violent disturbances were almost certainly provoked by blacklegging activity of one sort or another. Early in the strike a crowd of about 500 went to Player's tobacco factory to encourage the workers to join the strike. They were met by a force of police with drawn batons and a serious fight broke out. Several of the strikers were felled, stones were thrown and one arrest was made. When tried, this man, a 22 year-old miner, was found guilty of committing an act likely to cause disaffection and sentenced to six months' imprisonment. The forces of law and order were pitted against all those committed to the strike and many arrests took place. Four brewery workers attempting to dissuade men crossing picket lines were charged with committing an act likely to impede or restrict transport. They were found guilty and fined £2 each.

Billy Lees, a member of the Communist Party and the Trades Council executive, and Thomas Kilworth, active with the unemployed and a candidate in the municipal elections, were both arrested for giving seditious speeches. Kilworth, it was alleged, had encouraged the miners to maintain their action, advising them:

> I would say to the miners, stick out, fight for your rights and I hope that when the National Strike comes in about two years we shall have the good old red flag flying over Buckingham Palace. And when we have got our new town hall we shall have it flying over there, with Councillor Billy Green as Mayor ... next Sunday I am taking a crowd outside the prison to sing the 'Red Flag'.[23]

Instead of leading the chorus outside the prison, however, Kilworth found himself a prisoner inside the jail and so did Lees after a speech, notes of which were taken by Inspector Castle. Castle alleged that Lees had said:

> I am a member of the local strike committee. One of our trade union leaders, there is no need to mention his name, says the Chief Constable wants law and order. Well, during the last two or three days he has shown how he wants law and order. He will have among you two or three plain clothes men and if there are groups of people some of whom are expressing their views, one or two are pointed out. Down comes the van full of coppers, you are struck with a lump of wood, thrown into the van and away to the police station. But you wait until our comrades have to take a more active part in holding up transport. It will give the Chief Constable the chance to come amongst you and show how pretty he is.[24]

After remarks about the *British Gazette* and the bad position in London he is alleged to have continued:

> There is a person named ... who comes as a delegate to the Trades Council. Well, he is on duty in the signal box at present, so there you are. Wait 'till he comes again, I'll do my best to out him, I'll play ...

Despite the fact that Lees had three witnesses willing to speak for him, he was convicted and sent to prison for three months.

Of the local leadership Lees stands out as being the most determined militant and he is remembered by other members of the Communist Party as being one of the few individuals who really understood the full potential of the situation. But behind the scenes many of the national leadership had been wavering from the beginning. At a meeting of the TUC General Council on 11 May Arthur Hayday argued that the miners were not

> trade unionists in the general sense. They were ignorant of the position. They lived in villages and they thought in the mass. They did not realise that we could not keep people out much longer. They would never understand that all there would be left to sacrifice in a few days would be the broken-hearted best of our members.[25]

On 12 May representatives of the General Council of the TUC went to Downing Street to tell the Prime Minister that they had decided to call the strike off. At 1 p.m. the news was broadcast by the BBC, and later in the day newspapers came out with enormous banner headlines:

'GREAT STRIKE TERMINATED'; 'STRIKE OVER'; 'NO MORE VOLUNTEERS WANTED'.

Amongst the ruling class congratulations were the order of the day but the striking workers struggled to understand what was happening.

In Nottingham the news was met with stunned dismay. The local paper was able to resume printing and an editorial went right to the heart of recent events: 'Unless a General Strike has a revolutionary aim it is bound to be futile.'[26] As the truth of this statement was being realised by the strikers, the different elements in the town's ruling group hurried to congratulate each other. The local press congratulated the government on standing firm and Sir Charles Starmer, the managing director of the *Nottingham Journal* received a letter of thanks for his efforts during the strike from Asquith of the Westminster Press. The proprietor-editor of a blackleg news-sheet also received letters of appreciation from Sir John Turney and the Chamber of Commerce. The Lord Mayor's appeal for thanksgiving contributions to the local police fund was soon answered with £500 from Boots, £250 from Shipstone's Brewery and £150 from the Raleigh Cycle Company.[27]

Meanwhile, the Nottingham strikers remained shocked. Jack Charlesworth remembered the capitulation:

> I heard it on the radio. It was a most pitiful story ... where they went with the

caps and took their cloth cap off, and this, of course, is how the commentator at the time reported it. They really apologised and wanted to get the country back on its feet … it was a shocking statement.[28]

Cyril Goddard remembered 'utter dismay and disbelief' and George Hamilton had memories of 'real gloom cast over everything after the nine days'. The strike was a tragic defeat for the workers of the town, and the repercussions of the failure were to scar the local labour movement so deeply that the marks remained for many years.

Once the General Strike had been called off the Nottingham employers were quick to push home their advantage. In West Bridgford, a middle-class suburb, more than 50 per cent of the transport workers employed by the Council had their jobs filled by blackleg labour. Four members of the United Builders who had struck work at the Raleigh Cycle Company were not re-employed despite letters to Sir Harold Bowden, the company chairman, from the Trades Council. 17 of the motormen employed by Shipstone's Brewery were not allowed back. Only 80 per cent of the workers at Cammell Laird were re-engaged and the City transport department attempted to get returning workers to sign a document promising that they would not 'at any time withdraw service except after seven days' written notice to the manager'.[29] Notices posted by Blackburn and Sons, Stevens and Williamson and the Standard Company stated that shortage of work would mean staff 'alterations', and notices issued by Erricsons stated that it would not be possible to re-start all the workers at once.

In the weeks after the strike the Trades Council continued to help those who had been victimised. By October they had managed to raise £600 for the miners' distress fund. The cost to the dignity and self-respect of the labour movement was extremely high. Everywhere militants were black-listed. The signing of the new tramway agreement meant that many lost their record of service, or were dropped to a lower grade. The LNER stated they would need less staff and that those who worked during the strike would be given preference. Many of the miners, too, were victimised. Cyril Goddard remembers:

Oh yes, any amount in the pit, my God, yes! Poor old Jack Smith, he was a fine lad. They wouldn't have him at any price … he was a fine good supporter of Cook but they broke his heart. Any amount didn't get their jobs back … I remember an old miner who told me after the strike the owner said to them: 'Yes, you've been on strike for so many months now, I'm going to make you eat grass' and he did make them eat grass as well.[30]

George Hamilton remembers six or seven committee men from Bulwell pit being sacked after the strike, and he himself was sacked in 1929: 'They'd had their eyes on me for years. I could have told you the names of those who would go.'[31]

Those who had provided the leadership during the General Strike were forced into a defensive position in the months following defeat. They faced a programme of victimisation and harassment from employers and also came under criticism and attack from within the labour movement. These strains soon showed within the Nottingham Trades Council. In June 1926 an attempt by Daniel Mahoney to persuade the Council to establish a Workers' Defence League was heavily defeated by those who felt any involvement with the left was a danger to be avoided. At the August 1926 meeting the full Council voted, by 41 to 14, to ignore the executive's recommendation not to be represented at a Minority Movement conference. Billy Lees was sent as representative, an action which incurred the wrath of Arthur Hayday who threatened that his union might disaffiliate in response. The main problem appears to have been the close involvement of Communist Party members in both the Minority Movement and the Trades Council. The Lace Makers had already broken away from the Council, convinced that it was composed chiefly of Communists.[32] Similarly the local Labour Party refused to endorse the Trades Council's nomination for the municipal elections, Billy Lees, because of his membership of the Communist Party.[33]

The attempt to purge the labour movement of its militant members, conducted from outside and inside the movement, was one of the most serious consequences of the failure of the General Strike. The witch-hunt that followed was to undermine solidarity and confidence. In January 1927 Arthur Hayday informed the Trades Council that the GMWU would withdraw its affiliation; in February the Labour Party made enquiries into the political affiliations of delegates; in March the TUC threatened the disaffiliation of Nottingham Trades Council if it continued to support the Minority Movement.[34] These skirmishes in the struggle for leadership illustrate the gradual processs by which the demand for direct action was first of all weakened, and then supplemented by a policy of trade union collaboration with employers and the State. Solidarity was eroded as the rank and file, demoralised by the surrender of the leadership, was forced into confusion, apathy and bitterness.

The period following the General Strike saw a hardening of the divisions between left and right. The Trades Council was dominated by the left and, in January 1928, a leading Communist Party member, Bill Lees, was elected vice-president, and two other Communists were elected to the political committee of the Council. Meanwhile the Labour Party and the trade unions moved increasingly to the right. These divisions led the Trades Council early in 1928 to pass a resolution which 'condemned the compromising actions of the Borough Labour Party'. The ILP also suffered from disunity and in June 1927, Coultate, the branch chairman, offered his resignation, explaining that he

> Hadn't the confidence of the Executive of the branch. Policy of the branch being influenced by 'certain' members, to its detriment. Constant hostile attacks in branch meetings.[35]

The ILP branch certainly avoided too close a relationship with the Communist Party, but there is evidence to suggest that the branch was moving towards the left throughout 1928.

At the end of 1928 it was clear that the Conservative government would introduce a 'not genuinely seeking work' clause into the unemployed scheme, a policy that was challenged by the militants on the left through street campaigns and Hunger Marches. It received little attention from the right. Despite the fact that the TUC refused support for the National Unemployed Workers' Movement (NUWM), the Nottingham Trades Council supported the 1929 Hunger March, providing food and bedding as well as political backing.

By 1930 a Labour government was in office and those actively trying to help the unemployed faced opposition from within the trade union and Labour Party bureaucracy. The determination of the dominant section in the labour movement anxious to isolate the militants soon crystallised into a series of crude attacks on the most active and courageous leaders of the unemployed, attacks which were to contininue throughout the 1930s. The attitude of those opposed to the NUWM was well summed up at the 1930 Trades Union Congress, held in Nottingham. Mr John Beard, in a truly remarkable presidential address, dismissed 'Socialism in our time', the programme of the ILP, with a sneer and asserted 'expediency must be our guide', and boldly announced that 'the figure of 2,000,000 unemployed does not appal me.'[36]

By 1931 the Nottingham Trades Council and Borough Labour Party had established a Joint Consultative Committee which reflected the links established at national level between the TUC and Labour Party bureaucracy. This axis quickly found itself assailed by a group of militants who were determined to use direct action to force a change of political attitude. The Trades Council report for 1931 detailed a year in which 'lower wages, growing unemployment, greater insecurity of employment and the general lowering of standards has produced a feeling of embittered bewilderment in the minds of working people.'[37]

Later activities of the Trades Council were to show that they were determined to attempt militant action around the various issues generated by unemployment, even if the labour movement at a national level was inclined to be passive.

In January 1931 the executive of the Trades Council rejected a letter from the Nottingham Unemployed Workers' Committee, asking for Trades Council affiliation. Later in the month the Communist Dan Mahoney successfully moved to refer back this decision at a full Council meeting. Five months later the Trades Council decided, by 50 votes to 10, to set up its own unemployed section and to call an open meeting for those out of work. Later it was reported that about 250 unemployed had attended an open air meeting and that 81 had applied for individual membership.[38] By August the Bulwell unemployed section had merged with the organisation established by the Trades Council, and in September it was reported that at another open meeting, 'every available seat and standing place was occupied, the platform invaded and 650 application forms filled in.'[39] As 1931 drew to a close the Trades Council Unemployed Section had 1,100 members, of whom 300 were women. At a full Council meeting held on 16 September 1931, in the middle of the general election campaign, a resolution was passed calling on 'all workers, as time and opportunity serve, to resist the proposals of the Government' and declared the determination of the Trades Council 'to support and work for the policy of the TUC and the National Labour Party'.[40] This resolution neatly underlines the ambivalent attitude of many of the town's trade unionists, since even at this early stage of the depression it was already clear that neither the TUC nor the Labour Party had any clear policy.

The militant policies of the left in Nottingham led to several public disturbances in October 1931 which resulted in legal action. Donald Iving, the Communist Party organiser, was detained in Lincoln prison for eight days and bound over for one year in the sum of £25 and one surety of £25. The Conservative alderman who presided over the bench informed the court that Iving was 'a danger to society', and that at a meeting in the Market Square on 23 October Iving had said:

Now I put it to you, there are 336 policemen in this City against 32,000 of our lads. We can win by numbers alone. Admitted they are trained and if it was 300 policemen against 300 of our lads I would give way but against 32,000 they have no chance ...[41]

Rioting followed this speech and windows of the car belonging to Holford-

Knight, the National Labour candidate for South Nottingham, were smashed.

Iving's arrest did not intimidate the NUM and militant agitation continued. Such incidents gave ammunition to the right wing, which was able to marginalise the major issues of the day. The failure of the General Strike had produced a trade union morale which resisted militant activity. This position enabled the government to contain the labour movement and to win acceptance of a political programme based on economic 'necessities'. Many were uneasy with this, and in November 1931 the Broxtowe Labour Party branch argued that they should refuse to comply with central government instructions if it meant administering government cuts.[42] That the labour movement failed to resist the national government, despite the commitment of militants at the local level, reveals the extent to which the movement had been divided and demoralised by the outcome of the General Strike.

REFERENCES

[1] Quoted by A.R. Griffin, *The Miners of Nottinghamshire 1914-1944*, 1962, p.151.

[2] *Nottingham Guardian*, 3 May 1926.

[3] *Nottingham Journal*, 30 April 1926.

[4] Ibid.

[5] *History of the Nottingham Chamber of Commerce 1860-1960*, p.88.

[6] See Minutes, Nottingham Trades Council, 2 December 1925.

[7] Raymond Postgate *et al., A Workers' History of the Strike*, 1927, p.30.

[8] Jack Charlesworth, tape-recorded interview, 12 January 1969.

[9] *Nottingham Guardian*, 4 May 1926.

[10] Ibid., 3 May 1926.

[11] Frederick Perkins, tape-recorded interview, 24 February 1977.

[12] Daniel Mahoney, duplicated reminiscences in the possession of the author.

[13] Handwritten notes on the General Strike, by ex-Police Superintendent Downs, in the possession of the author.

[14] Private correspondence from Peter Leyden, in the possession of the author.

[15] Handwritten notes, Superintendent Downs.

[16] Private correspondence from A. Sharpe, in the possession of the author.

[17] *Nottingham Guardian*, 4 May 1926.

[18] *Nottingham Evening Post*, 10 May 1926.

[19] Kenneth Adam, Letter in the *Listener*, May 1976.

[20] Daniel Mahoney, reminiscences.

[21] *Nottingham Strike Bulletin No. 2*, May 1926.

[22] Daniel Mahoney, reminiscences.

[23] *Nottingham Guardian*, 18 May 1926.

[24] *Nottingham Evening Post*, 12 May 1926.

[25] *Nottingham Guardian*, 13 May 1926.

[26] Ibid., 18 May 1926.

[27] Ibid.

[28] Jack Charlesworth, tape-recorded interview, 12 January 1969.

[29] Minutes, Nottingham Trades Council, 26 May 1926.

[30] Cyril Goddard, tape-recorded interview, 9 January 1969.

[31] George Hamilton, tape-recorded interview, 19 January 1969.

[32] Minutes, Lace Makers' Society, 5 January 1924.

[33] Minutes, Nottingham Trades Council, 28 August 1926.

[34] Ibid., 30 March 1927.

[35] Minutes, Independent Labour Party, 15 June 1927.

[36] *Nottingham Journal*, 2 September 1930.

[37] Nottingham Trades Council, *Annual Report*, 1930.

[38] Minutes, Nottingham Trades Council, 18 July 1931.

[39] Ibid., 2 September 1931.

[40] Ibid., 16 September 1931.

[41] *Nottingham Evening Post*, 2 November 1931

[42] Minutes, Broxtowe Divisional Labour Party, 28 November 1931.

CHAPTER THIRTEEN

Old Boars Rear Their Heads: Splits and Divisions 1926 to 1939

With the collapse of the General Strike the miners remained locked out, although in Nottinghamshire local traditions and the influence of George Spencer and his associates ensured a weakening of the miners' solidarity much earlier than in other parts of the country. In the Nottingham area a gradual drift back to work had begun to worry the militants soon after the General Strike ended. At a national conference in July 1926, William Carter, one of the NMA agents, had reported that apart from safety-men there were only 500 men in the county actually at work, although 'outcropping' was a serious problem. At the subsequent August conference it was claimed that there had been a steep rise in the numbers working outcrop. Carter put the figure at 1,700, with some pits being run by what were called 'free colliers'.[1] Meanwhile, in early August the coalowners had written to the NMA in an attempt to drive a wedge between the militants and the waverers, by suggesting that a local agreement might be reached. In early September Carter had to report that 7,000 to 8,000 men were back at work in Nottinghamshire; in addition, approximately 1,500 were engaged in outcropping. By the end of September 16,000 to 17,000 had returned to work according to Carter, but the NMA Council meeting on 1 October estimated the figure at twice that number.[2]

George Spencer, general secretary of the NMA and the Member of Parliament for Broxtowe, then become involved in negotiations with the coalowners about the right of remaining union members to return to their old jobs. Later, after a stormy meeting of the MFGB at which A.J. Cook had said, 'Mr Spencer is a blackleg of the worst order: a conscious blackleg,'[3] the council of the NMA at a meeting on 16 October suspended Spencer until the council itself was reconstituted. These events led to a meeting at the Victoria Hotel, Nottingham, at which Spencer, with the help of the coalowners, set up the Nottinghamshire and District

Miners' Industrial Union. In order to help establish the new organisation the employers quickly agreed to deduct trade union contributions at source, whilst shortly afterwards they presented Spencer with £10,000, to which they later added a further £2,500, with which to start a pension fund.[4]

Against the background of these events Spencer began to be sharply criticised by the local labour movement. Early in July the Broxtowe Divisional Labour Party considered a letter from members at Selston which suggested that 'Mr Spencer is not a fit and proper person to represent this Division.'[5] Later in the same month there was a further discussion about the role being played by Spencer, coupled with a call for the resignation of the divisional secretary. In the heated exchange which followed the secretary alleged that this attempt to remove him 'was part of the disruptive tactics of the supporters of Communism and left-wingers',[6] and it is significant that the left-right split was carried over into what might have been thought to be a straightforward issue.

A month later the argument surfaced again. This time the divisional secretary of the Labour Party explained that he had cancelled a meeting previously arranged after having received a telephone message from headquarters. It seems that a resolution expressing no confidence in Spencer would have been on the agenda then and the secretary had been told that the meeting could not take place until all the local Labour Parties affiliated to the division were 'properly constituted'. A major row ensued,[7] but in spite of these efforts to dampen down the criticism of Spencer the argument continued, and it was not until late in 1926 that a resolution 'that the resignation of Spencer be called for' was finally passed.[8]

Spencer did not resign his parliamentary seat until just before the general election of 1929, but at a Labour Party selection conference in August 1926 Seymour Cocks was nominated to fight the Broxtowe seat. This selection was made in spite of a letter from Labour Party members at Greasley expressing the view that 'Seymour Cocks is not a fit and proper candidate for a mining constituency.'[9] In any event the internal disputes within the Divisional Labour Party seem to have continued, and at a meeting in early October a new secretary was elected although his predecessor refused for a time to hand over the minute books. Late in October, at another meeting, speaker after speaker spoke against Spencer and the role he was playing and during the course of the discussion it was argued that 'the gaining, by Spencer, of the admiration of the owners is sufficient to indicate his betrayal of the workers'.[10]

Meanwhile, the consequences of these developments within the NMA were beginning to have repercussions amongst the rest of the Nottingham labour movement. At the annual general meeting of the Southern Division of the Labour Party in 1927 it was requested that Joe Cobley be expelled for joining the Spencer Union. After a long and heated discussion it was agreed that no action be taken, although many delegates obviously felt strongly that the Labour Party should purge itself of Spencer supporters.[11] Further to the left, feelings were even stronger. Laura Johnson, a member of the Communist Party remembers going to see Spencer with a neighbour who was about to be evicted:

> I'd got Barry [her infant son] with me ... we kept him nice even though we were badly off. Spencer said 'Oh, what a lovely litle boy' and he picked him up and went to kiss him. I said 'Oh you must not do that!' Spencer said 'Why not?' I said 'It would upset my husband.' Spencer said 'Why, is he a big believer in hygiene?' I said 'He is where rats are about.' ... I mean I was bitter, my husband had been victimised.[12]

The bitterness being expressed here was partly generated by the sense of despair felt by militants as they witnessed the gradual erosion of the ethics of group solidarity. Apathy and demoralisation became the characteristics of large numbers of the rank-and-file miners and many seem to have played safe by becoming members of both the Spencer Union and the NMA.[13] In these circumstances Spencer's Industrial Union enjoyed a good deal of initial success.

The difficulties in combating Spencerism were compounded by the fragmentation of the local labour movement. In June 1927 a meeting of the Nottingham Trades Council heard about the gravity of the situation from a delegation of the Radford Colliery Lodge of the NMA. They reported that although there were still 320 paying members of the NMA at the pit, 30 others had joined Spencer, with the consequence that the owners had given notice to the entire checkweighman's committee, all of whom were members of the NMA.[14] Faced with intimidation and victimisation from employers many men deserted to Spencer reducing the membership of the NMA from 27,000 in 1926 to 13,500 in 1927.[15] The split between left and right within Nottingham's labour movement debilitated them, and prevented any strong resistance to the tightening grip of right-wing reformists committed to a political programme of gradualism.

By 1928 the NMA had been very considerably weakened. In September it affiliated only 1,560 members to the Nottingham Trades Council and there is no doubt that it was continually losing members to the Spencer union. By now Spencerism had become the main preoccupation of the Trades Council, and throughout 1928 there was a lot of activity intended to resolve the difficulties caused by the company union. In February the TUC General Council met in Nottingham where it received a delegation of local trade unionists calling for action on the Nottinghamshire mining problem. Later, in response to a Communist Party resolution, the Trades Council set up a joint mining committee to try to defeat Spencerism, but despite the efforts of a panel of speakers which this committee set up, the ideology of which Spencerism was the industrial expression retained a very strong grip. Foremost of the voices raised in the Trades Council against Spencerism was that of Ernest Cant, who had been elected to the Council's political committee in January 1928. Cant had been one of the 'Communist Twelve' sent to prison in 1925 for sedition. Now he was in Nottingham as the Communist Party's full-time organiser. In May 1928 Cant was appointed to the Joint Mining Committee which had been set up together with representatives from the Borough Labour Party, the ILP, Trades Council and local Co-op. In late May this Committee issued 1,000 vouchers for 2s 6d redeemable at the Co-op to victimised miners, and all the members of the Committee were active in trying to counteract Spencerism. During one campaign in 1928 the Communist Party held over 50 meetings and distributed over 25,000 leaflets attacking company unionism.

Despite its concern at the threat constituted by the existence of the Spencer union, the trade union establishment was extremely anxious about the activity of the Communists amongst the Nottinghamshire miners and Citrine, the General Secretary of the TUC, wrote to ask the Trades Council for a full report on the statements which the Communists, Cant and Lees, had been making about the Nottinghamshire coalfield and the TUC's failure to deal with its problems.[16] At this point, however, the trade union leadership seems to have been out of step with the views of the rank and file, as was made clear in September when the Broxtowe Labour Party passed a resolution expressing its sincere sympathy with Arthur Cook, the militant miners' leader. Cook was ill at this time and the Broxtowe Labour Party wished him well and hoped that he would 'speedily resume his fight against Spencerism, Mondism and Capitalism'.[17] The ILP was also deeply concerned at the rise of Spencerism in the Nottingham coalfield. Gilbert Hall, the Nottingham delegate, told the 1928 Norwich conference of the ILP that he had 'listened to Shinwell with anxious interest because he had expected to get some message for the miners in the Notts area'. After criticising the ILP for its lack of action to oppose Spencer, Hall concluded by claiming that the miners were 'facing a set of conditions grinding them down to the lowest point'.[18] A month later, however, after

Nottinghamshire Miners' Association

Affiliated to the Mine Workers' Federation of Great Britain

December, 1936.

FELLOW CITIZENS,

Trades Unions functioning in a legitimate manner make a valuable contribution towards the management of the present social order, and are accepted by all broad-minded people as the instrument of collective expression for the workers generally.

The miners of Nottinghamshire have been denied the right of collective bargaining for a period of ten years, as the result of the coal-owners' action in fostering a form of " company unionism " which precludes the operation of " Free Trades Unions." The effect of this is that the miners in this county have no means of discussing matters which adversely affect them only through channels which will never give them satisfaction.

At Harworth Colliery, on November 4th, 1936, a ballot vote was taken, under public supervision on the public highway, to ascertain the views of the men as to which organisation they desired to be attached to—The Miners' Federation or the Spencer Union.

1,175 voted for the Notts. Miners' Association and the M.F.G.B. whilst only 145 voted for the Spencer or the Company Union.

The management of the colliery totally ignored the wishes of the men, and endeavoured to impose membership of Spencer's Union as a condition of employment, and asked many of the men to sign a form authorising contributions to be deducted from wages.

A very large number of the men rightly refused to sign away their freedom, and consequently were not allowed to work ! we consider they were locked out and we advised the rest of the men to give notice to terminate contracts, which has been done. The Miners' Federation endorsing this action and giving full financial support.

This effort to re-establish the right to choose their own union must be appreciated by all freedom lovers, we are therefore appealing for you to show your appreciation in a practical manner by sending as large a contribution as possible to augment the funds so very generously created by the miners from every part of the British coalfield.

Contributions to the Harworth " Fight for Freedom Fund " will be gratefully received by the Financial Secretary of the Notts. Miners' Association.

Signed,

Miners' Offices.
Nottingham Road,
Old Basford,
Nottingham.

VAL. COLEMAN, *General Secretary*.

ALD. W. BAYLISS, J.P., *Financial Secretary*.

Anti-Spencer leaflet issued by the NMA

a discussion on organisation and propaganda work, the Trades Council
Action Committee found it necessary to agree, on Ernest Cant's
prompting, that 'irrespective of the view of the TUC, the Joint Mining
Committee should carry out the work for which it was originally
formed.'[19] Despite the TUC opposition an organising campaign was
subsequently undertaken by the Trades Council using Cant, Nally,
Button, Askew, Key and Hewing as the major speakers.

The ending of company unionism in the Nottinghamshire coalfield
came in the years 1936-37. The catalyst was the long and bitter dispute
at the Harworth colliery, a pit which was remote from the rest of the
Nottinghamshire coalfield and would have been part of the Yorkshire
coalfied had it not been for the vagaries of county boundaries. There
were a series of incidents, beginning in 1936, in which the management
behaved in a notably arbitrary fashion, and by October 1936 it was
already becoming clear that the Harworth situation was crucial in the
struggle against Spencerism. A ballot of Harworth miners, supervised by
a Nottinghamshire magistrate, produced 1,175 votes in favour of the
NMA and the Miners' Federation and 145 for Spencer's Industrial
Union (it was estimated that about 88 per cent of those employed at the
pit voted in the ballot). Spencer's union was, of course, the only
organisation recognised by management for bargaining purposes.

The struggle at Harworth was one of the classical battles in the history
of trade unionism in the mining industry. There was considerable police
intimidation of the families of striking miners, heavy police guards for
miners who continued working and many arrests. The police presence in
the village became notorious, and the National Council for Civil
Liberties, established only three years earlier, sent its general secretary,
Ronald Kidd, to investigate the situation. His report published in March
1937 recorded the 'high-handed action of the police' in many instances.[20]

The threat of a national coal strike forced the intervention of the
government, and the outcome, after lengthy negotiations, was dictated
more by Spencer than by the Miners' Federation. The NMA absorbed
the Spencer union and Nottinghamshire coalowners recognised its right
to represent the county's miners. That the amalgamation of the NMA
and the Industrial Union was not an outright victory for the former was
recognised in the Communist Party pamphlet *Notts United*:

> This agreement, it is true, is a compromise, but if we examine it soberly and
> refuse to allow ourselves to be led away by talk of 'sell-outs' and 'betrayals', it
> is obvious that it represents a tremendous step forward.[21]

It was only the coming of war and the establishment of the National

Union of Mineworkers in 1945, following a conference in Nottingham in 1944, which began to establish something more than a surface unity. Spencerism had deep roots in the county and the Nottinghamshire coalfield has continued to show the marks of the long conflict between the supporters of the Industrial Union and those who followed the national union. Spencer himself retired in 1945, having shown his political position to the end by opposing both the formation of one union for mineworkers and the nationalisation of the mines. Asked to explain Spencerism, Ernest Cant claimed that:

> It was based on fear of unemployment. If you didn't join 'em, you got the bloody sack ... it was a very big influence, it was very dangerous, very bad, it was splitting the miners nationally ... we had to get him out. Spencer asked for compensation for loss of office and we were blackmailed into it ... a lot of Puritans fought against it, but what could you do? I mean, we got him out of it and got them back into the national union.[22]

The heroes of the Harworth struggle were the whole village community on strike, and especially the branch chairman of the NMA, Mick Kane, who after work was resumed at the pit came up for trial with ten other miners and a miner's wife, and in his case received a two year sentence that caused alarm and indignation throughout the labour movement; after considerable agitation the Home Secretary granted considerable remissions to the twelve prisoners, and Kane himself was released in August 1938.[23]

Any explanation of why Spencerism took root in Nottinghamshire must take a number of factors into account. A.R. and C.P. Griffin have explained the role played by historical and economic factors which helped to ensure that Nottinghamshire miners often enjoyed better wages and conditions of employment than those current elsewhere in the country.[24] Equally important is an understanding of the careerism of George Spencer and the extent to which the political ideology which he represented and espoused, that of pre-First World War Lib-Labism, was acknowledged and adopted by Nottinghamshire miners. A further consideration must be a recognition of the traditions of collaboration advanced by Nottinghamshire mineowners since the late nineteenth century.

The organised labour movement did not respond submissively but was active in its attempts to undermine Spencer. The problem was their failure to carry the rank and file with them, and were increasingly distanced by the activities of the right wing. Such problems were not just experienced in the fight against Spencerism, but were also present in the other campaigns mounted in the 1930s, especially against rising unemployment.

Militants in Nottingham had sought to organise the unemployed throughout the 1920s, but it was not until 1929 that a branch of the National Unemployed Workers' Committee Movement was founded. This group demanded direct action from the labour movement at a time when the Labour Party was seriously embarrassed, first by the failure of the 1929 Labour government to deal effectively with what MacDonald called the 'economic blizzard', and secondly by the political events which led in 1931 to the forming of the 'National Government'. This last move created confusion and bitterness amongst supporters of the Labour Party as is indicated by a Trades Council resolution which called on all workers 'as time and opportunity serve, to resist the proposals of the Government'.[25] At the same time, however, the Trades Council committed itself to work for the policies of the Labour Party and the TUC, both of which at this time were equally confused and divided about policy.

As the unemployment figures continued to mount, there developed within the British labour movement a serious breach between those supporting direct action and others advocating palliative measures of one kind or another. At both the 1931 and 1932 TUC conferences the unemployed delegates, organised by the National Unemployed Workers' Movement, were separated from TUC delegates by the police, which infuriated the militants and helped to increase the pressure on the General Council. As a consequence the TUC leadership felt that the time had come to re-establish unemployed associations and this decision helped to sharpen the conflict in the localities. Throughout 1932 the struggle in Nottingham centred on a scheme to offer the unemployed work in special workshops and to introduce a programme of recreational and social functions. As the year continued the argument tipped first one way and then the other. In May the Trades Council was organising successful 'official' propaganda work in the Arnold area, whilst in June left-wing pressure resulted in a decision to convene a special conference to set up a Council of Action on the unemployed question. In August two members of the executive of the Trades Council reported on 'informal meetings' which they had attended with Canon Gordon who was seeking Trades Council support for a scheme to assist the unemployed. Despite strong criticism for having taken part in these conversations, the delegates concerned were successful in persuading the Trades Council to co-operate. This victory for the moderate element amongst the delegates was strengthened later in the month when, against the background of a balance sheet which showed an Unemployed Workers' Section income from subscriptions over a six-month period of £45 5s 6d, it was decided to abandon the Council of Action in favour of a simple, if pious, call on the TUC nationally to take 'whatever action was needed'.[26]

By December 1932 the arguments surrounding unemployment had become so acute that after a long debate about the Nottingham scheme for the unemployed, the Communist Daniel Mahoney announced that his patience had run out and he resigned from the Council's Unemployed Committee. The labour movement was divided, nationally and locally, on the usefulness of the Hunger March as a form of direct action. In Nottingham it would appear that those who favoured direct action managed to retain control of the Trades Council. Daniel Mahoney was elected vice-president of the Council in March 1933. This success followed a stand made by the delegates representing the Sheet Metal Workers who opposed the continued participation in the Nottingham scheme for unemployed workers. By July the left had won this particular argument and the Trades Council withdrew its support for the scheme. Despite the fact that the left-wing was in ascendency the official policy of the Trades Council remained weak and ineffectual. The Unemployed Section had 2,500 members in 1933, and in August they mounted a campaign to press the local authority to introduce a forty-hour week and to improve the system of employing men on relief work, but such action was limited by the lack of bargaining power of the unemployed.

That direct action made sense to many unemployed men and women, is indicated by numerous marches and demonstrations staged in Nottingham. In January 1934, 200 unemployed whose allowances had been reduced or disallowed under determinations of the newly established Unemployed Assistance Board (UAB), took part in a protest meeting outside the Employment Exchange.[27] In February a much bigger demonstration sang the 'Red Flag' in the Market Square whilst calling for Alderman Bowles and Alderman Green. Both men were long-established Labour Party stalwarts, but their record on employment issues did not guarantee them a good reception when they eventually appeared and agreed to meet a deputation.

Meanwhile, hundreds of the demonstrators moved from the Square to the office of the UAB chanting, 'We want Betterton, dead or alive.' This group managed to stop the traffic whilst they sang the 'Internationale', and later Mr Bentley, the area oficer of the UAB, agreed to see a deputation.

A member of this deputation was Mrs Laura Johnson, a keen Communist and the wife of an unemployed Hucknall miner. She was active throughout the 1930s, representing individual claimants before the Court of Referees and frequently becoming involved in direct action:

> We women went to the office of the area organiser of relief. They had a new man from Cardiff, we'd had warning of what a devil he was, so we decided to go and see him. We went to this place on Huntingdon Street and we raided his ofice. We went in a group ... he jumped up but his telephone hadn't been fixed properly, so he got the wires round his legs whilst trying to get from behind the counter. I turned round and locked the door, but the police had been sent for. Quite a struggle developed. He'd got hold of me trying to take the key out of the door. Julie Ellis jumped on his back and Mrs Ellis was tugging his arm. I think he thought he'd come to a proper old hell hole ... he wasn't there a month before he asked for a transfer.[28]

Next day Mrs Johnson visited the office again to find that all the doors had been removed. Asked what had happened to them the official in charge replied 'You should know! They've taken them away so that you can't fasten yourself in.'

To make this demonstration a success the NUWM had put in a great deal of work. Harold Davies, the organiser, remembers:

> The area organiser of the UAB could never be found. We could never get at him for a bit of bedclothes, or shoes for the kids, or winter relief. We got a whisper that he was in Huntingdon Street, so we dressed Jack Watkins up. He had an Oxford accent, he went in and found the office. Then we got Di Lee to hold a meeting on the Square, to fetch the attention of the police. Next, we got six women to walk in and lock the door. They were there an hour with a placard hanging out of the window, saying 'WE REFUSE TO STARVE'. We had a student running on a motorbike back and forth from Huntingdon Street to the meeting in the Square, to tell how things were going on. It was an hour before anything happened. The women put it to him from the point of view of the women and kids. The police chucked 'em out in the end.[29]

The NUWM's strategy was to create as much public attention and embarrassment as possible. In 1935 Harold Davies helped to organise a gate-crash of a UAB official dinner and the NUWM continually organised mass attendance at the Labour Exchange to produce chaos and muddle by their demand for work.[30] When the newly-built Nottingham Labour Exchange was opened by the Minister of Labour, the NUWM attempted to occupy the building but were prevented by the police.[31]

By 22 January 1936, 16,466 men and women were registered as unemployed at the Nottingham Employment Exchange. The human misery that these bare statistics represent is vividly recalled by Harold Davies:

> Lots of unemployment, 16,000 at a rough estimate, conditions of living were very bad. One lavatory for about four houses. Milk Square, Radford Independent Street, Broad Marsh, Narrow Marsh ... they used to call it 'Queen of the Midlands'! Carlton Street, there was a butcher – Evans, his name was; if you showed him your unemployment card he'd give you a three-penn'oth wrap-up, bits of stewing meat and two links of sausage. In the old market you had Lievers, the bacon people. They'd give you six pennyworth of bits of bacon ... it was all right talking about the 'Queen of the Midlands'![32]

Faced with conditions like these, it was difficult for the right-wing of the labour movement to justify its antipathy to calls for direct action. In October 1936 the Nottingham Trades Council was moved to pass a resolution 'That the Trades Council support of hunger marches be conditional upon the sanction of the General Council of the TUC.'[33] Faced with the appalling human costs of mass unemployment even the moderates were moved to agree that some form of action was necessary.

Several Hunger Marches passed through Nottingham during the course of the 1930s, and their numbers were swelled by members from the Nottingham branch of the NUWM. Di Lee, Harold Davies, Frank Treble, Arthur West, Arthur Hutchinson and Ernie Spray were ranked amongst the Nottingham men who marched to London several times to protest against unemployment. It is significant that these men were members of either the ILP or the Communist Party, for the Labour Party showed little enthusiasm for the Hunger Marches. Arthur Statham, who ran the town's left-wing bookshop, described the Labour Party's relationship with the unemployed as 'distant ... oh, very distant', whilst Cyril Goddard was more explicit:

> NUWM the Labour Party didn't recognise, but when Wilkinson came through with the Jarrows they couldn't do enough for them ... they was a respectable crowd. I remember in November Di Lee had come down organising a march. The municipal elections was on and I took Di to practically every school in Nottingham, to ask the chairmen of the Labour Party election meetings to give Di a five minute speech and they all refused ... yes, not a word.[34]

The opposition of the Labour Party to the NUWM was based on stubborn anti-Communism, but the national leadership of the TUC did not attempt to implement an alternative programme, but rather exerted increasingly rigid control over local Trades Councils and Labour Party branches to ensure that they remained distant from the NUWM.

At the 1937 TUC conference these tensions came to the fore as the official attitude came under increasing attack. Every Trades Council representative who spoke at the conference condemned the General Council's policy of opposition to the NUWM, and it was finally voted down. This defeat allowed Trades Councils throughout the country to offer genuine support to the Hunger Marches, as was the case in Nottingham. A resolution was passed which informed the national TUC that when considering support for 'unofficial' marches the Nottingham labour movement 'would take such action as seemed desirable under the special circumstances'.[35] This change of heart was linked both to the changing political climate as the British economy geared itself towards the possibility of war, and also to the gradual lowering of the high unemployment levels.

The years following the General Strike, saw victimisation and intimidation by employers of those in work, and unemployment for many thousands of others. In Nottinghamshire the mood of fear, defeat and lethargy was emphasised by the demoralising experience of Spencer unionism. Divisions within the labour movement had existed well before the 1926 strike, but there can be little doubt that they were sharpened and made more intense by the experience of industrial and political defeat. The left viewed the General Strike as an example of future action, whilst the right's response was 'never again'. Whilst the movement was so severely split it was impossible to provide any united response to the economic pressures of the 1930s, yet these were years in which unity was desperately required. As Alan Clinton has indicated, Trades Councils in this period were changing from 'constituents of a movement relying on local initiative to humble instruments of a professional union leadership', and this transformation further hampered any effective challenge to the government.[36]

The fear with which the Labour Party and TUC leadership viewed the Communist Party and all activists on the left led to bans on any involvement with them or bodies on which they were active. Such divisiveness had tragic consequences for the labour movement, both nationally and locally. At a personal level the mounting suicides reported in the local press, the fight against the bailiffs and the struggle to make ends meet were human experiences which were etched on the consciousness of activists. In terms of the wider labour movement the lack of leadership on the issue of unemployment produced a weakened and demoralised rank and file. The only political vigour shown in these years was that of the NUWM, as is indicated by a song used on Hunger

Marches and remembered by Harold Davies:

Now the unemployed are on the march,
Marching to London Town.
Marching forward to Victory.
Give us your help, boys!
We're fighting the battle for you!

Men and women in their homes are starving.
We're the standard bearers on the road,
Marching forward to Victory.
We're fighting the battle for you!

Millions of workers are starving in revolt.
With our flag of red we'll blaze the trail,
Marching forward to Victory.
We're fighting the battle for you!

Victory is certain for our cause.
We call to arms the workers of this land.
Marching forward to Victory.
We're fighting the battle for you![37]

REFERENCES

[1] A.R. Griffin, *The Miners of Nottinghamshire 1914–1944*, 1962, p.171.
[2] Ibid., p.176.
[3] Miners' Federation of Great Britain, Minute Book, pp.899-901.
[4] A.R. Griffin, op. cit., pp.207-11.
[5] Minutes, Broxtowe Divisional Labour Party, 3 July 1926.
[6] Ibid., 29 August 1926.
[7] Ibid., 23 September 1926.
[8] Ibid., 23 October 1926.
[9] Ibid., 28 April 1926.
[10] Ibid., 23 October 1926.
[11] Minutes, Southern Divisional Labour Party, 14 March 1927.
[12] Laura Johnson, tape-recorded interview, 13 September 1973.
[13] Arthur Horner, *Incorrigible Rebel*, 1960, p.138.
[14] Minutes, Nottingham Trades Council, 29 June 1927.
[15] A.R. Griffin, op. cit., p.210.
[16] Minutes, Nottingham Trades Council, 16 May 1928.
[17] Minutes, Broxtowe Divisional Labour Party, 22 September 1928.
[18] Independent Labour Party, Conference Report, 1928.
[19] Minutes, Nottingham Trades Council, 8 September 1928.

[20] *The Harworth Colliery Strike: A Report to the Executive Committee of the National Council for Civil Liberties*, pamphlet March 1937.

[21] *Notts United*, pamphlet, June 1937.

[22] Ernest Cant, tape-recorded interview, 9 January 1969.

[23] See the Communist Party pamphlet *Free the Harworth Prisoners*, August 1937.

[24] A.R. and C.P. Griffin, 'The Non-Political Trade Union Movement', in Asa Briggs and John Saville (eds), *Essays in Labour History 1918-1939*, 1977.

[25] Minutes, Nottingham Trades Council, 16 September 1931.

[26] Ibid., 31 August 1932.

[27] *Nottingham Journal*, 19 January 1935.

[28] Laura Johnson, tape-recorded interview, 13 September 1973.

[29] Harold Davies, tape-recorded interview, 19 January 1977.

[30] Harold Davies, *Ten Lean Years*, manuscript account in the possession of Mr Davies.

[31] Ibid.

[32] Harold Davies, tape-recorded interview, 19 January 1977.

[33] Minutes, Nottingham Trades Council, 21 October 1936.

[34] Cyril Goddard, tape-recorded interview, 9 January 1969.

[35] Minutes, Nottingham Trades Council, 16 February 1938.

[36] Alan Clinton, *Trades Councils in Britain 1900-1940*, 1977, p.112.

[37] Harold Davies, *Ten Lean Years*, manuscript account.

CHAPTER FOURTEEN

Labour Party Politics and Electoral Fortunes, 1926 to 1931

Shortly after the end of the General Strike the Trades Council decided to open a general recruiting campaign in a joint effort with the Labour Party. It was decided that the objectives of the campaign would be 100 per cent trade union membership, to protest at the government's decision to increase working hours and to urge all workers to organise politically as well as industrially. This campaign had some success and in November 1926 the Trades Council minutes record 'splendid victories' in the municipal elections. The Labour Party had contested all 16 wards with a varied group of candidates comprising four trade union officials, two railwaymen, a haulage contractor, a casemaker, an insurance agent, marine dealer, dairyman, draper, lace manufacturer, dentist, builder's labourer and a housewife.

Predictably, the *Nottingham Guardian* dismissed 'Labour's untried crew, eager to venture on an uncharted sea' and called on the electors to save the city from a 'spendthrift socialist régime'.[1] Ignoring dire warnings of this kind many working-class voters supported the Labour candidates and the Labour Party registered five gains, four from the Conservatives and one from the Liberal Party whilst at the same time retaining three other seats. This result meant that the Conservatives lost overall control of the Council and it is significant that the Labour vote exceeded that of the combined Conservative/Liberal candidates by nearly 1,000. Labour was particularly proud that Mrs Hyatt had become the first woman socialist to be elected. Bulwell, too, had abandoned the Liberals and moved to Labour and had the Tories and Liberals not made common cause in some wards there is little doubt that the Labour Party would have made even bigger gains.

Casting round for an explanation of these disastrous Conservative results, the *Nottingham Guardian* made the point that the loss of Bridge and Meadows Wards had not been unexpected since the miners in these two areas 'vented their feelings over the strike fiasco by voting against the party in power'. In Castle Ward where Wesson the Labour candidate had won by eight votes, explanations were not so easy to come by, although the local Conservatives comforted themselves with the thought that Wesson was 'a Labour man of the moderate type and it is to be hoped that he may exercise a restraining influence on some of his more turbulent colleagues.'[2] In fact, the local establishment was worrying itself quite unnecessarily. The Labour Party was fully reconciled to constitutional gradualism and an influx of middle-class ex-Liberals, like Ashworth and Shaw, two lace manufacturers, as well as Seymour Cocks and Holford-Knight, two well-known barristers who were now Labour candidates for Nottingham constituencies, helped to ensure that the militant and Marxist elements were kept well under control.

Despite the very mild reforms being advocated by the Nottingham Labour Socialists the local press continued to talk in blood-curdling terms of the dangers of a Labour victory. Just before the 1927 municipal elections the *Nottingham Guardian* came out with large headlines which warned:

THE MENACE IN NOTTINGHAM
NOTTINGHAM'S PERIL.[3]

In the event the Labour candidates made two net gains, winning three wards but losing one. At the celebration meeting in the Mechanics' Hall a packed audience expressed 'great jubilation'. After the unsuccessful candidates had blamed the weather and apathy among working-class voters for their defeat Bowles, the Labour leader, went on to claim:

> Labourism ought to have been strong enough to have carried Labour supporters through the rain ... women Labour supporters ought not to have waited for their husbands to come home, they ought to have voted on their own in the morning.[4]

In fact, just over half of those eligible to vote had turned out and the Labour gains put them within striking distance of the Conservatives who held 21 seats to Labour's 18 and the Liberals' 7.

The electoral progress of the Labour Party continued, and in the autumn of 1928 Labour took control of the City Council, holding 22 seats to the Conservatives' 18 and the Liberals' 7. Encouraged by these victories the Labour Party seems to have redoubled political propaganda work. At the end of January 1929, for instance, Arthur Hayday and Mrs E. Barton, the prospective Labour/Co-operative candidate for Central Nottingham, spoke at a crowded meeting in Noel Street baths when the community singing of labour songs alternated with speeches. A couple of days later, 250 Labour supporters and young co-operators were at a fund-raising dance and concert at the ILP hall. The ILP continued its own propaganda work and during the course of 1929 it established a Guild of Youth, organised a special week of propaganda work with Mrs Jean Mann and set up a panel of five regular speakers for its programme of street corner meetings. In May the ILP branch won first prize in the May Day competition with a dray which portrayed 'Family Allowances'. That this propaganda strengthened the convictions of many Labour Socialists is without doubt, and it is significant that the Central Nottingham delegate to the 1929 national conference of the Labour Party moved the reference back of the policy document *Labour and the Nation* on the grounds that 'there is too much Liberalism and not enough Socialism in it.'

The Trades Council also seems to have stepped up its political work in this period. At the January 1929 meetings a contribution was made to the St Ann's Ward Labour Party funds. At a second January meeting the Council, after an approach from the Friends of Soviet Russia, agreed to write to the appropriate department to protest at governmental hostility to the Soviet Union. Later, on 1 May, the political purposes committee of the Trades Council issued a manifesto which called on all workers to vote for Labour Party candidates in the forthcoming general election, and subsequently a major effort was made by the Nottingham labour movement which was better organised and more determined than at any previous election.

The 1929 general election campaign was fought by the Conservatives around the slogan 'Safety First'. In Nottingham, despite a Conservative campaign designed to persuade people of the need to protect the lace industry, the Labour and Liberal Parties won three of the four Nottingham constituencies. Of the two Labour victories, the defeat of the popular Conservative MP Cavendish-Bentinck in South Nottingham was the most significant. In 1927 Cavendish-Bentinck had voted with Labour against the Trades Disputes Act and his personal appeal had enabled him to hold on to the seat for nearly three decades. The Labour candidate who dislodged him was G.W. Holford-Knight, a London barrister who had been a very keen supporter of the Workers' Educational Association. In a three-cornered fight with an 80.4 per cent turnout he won 42.9 per cent of the vote, and had a majority of 548.[5] In West Nottingham Arthur Hayday easily held his seat, beating Conservative and Liberal opposition to increase his majority, whilst in the Central Division the Labour/Co-operative candidate managed to beat the Liberal into third place. In East Nottingham, however, the Labour nominee came bottom of the poll, although even here the 9,787 Labour votes represented 28 per cent of the poll and were only 1,332 less than those registered by the Conservative, who came second to Norman Birkett, the Liberal candidate.[6]

The 1929 general election was a high point in the political fortunes of the Nottingham Labour Party. In the years which followed unemployment, the demoralisation of the rank and file within the trade union movement and a loss of political direction within the Labour Party, all combined to produce a move away from the Labour Party. At the national level, Stanley Baldwin, the Conservative leader, taunted the Labour government in the House of Commons with the charge: 'The enthusiasm is running out of your Party all over the country, because you have lost faith in Socialism.'[7] This reflection was certainly true and public dissatisfaction with the performance of the Labour Party mounted as they sanctioned wage reductions and the introduction of the means test for the unemployed. When economic pressures led MacDonald to form a National Government with the Conservatives in 1931, socialists within the labour movement were totally exasperated. Significantly, when the National Government sought public approval in the general election of October 1931 the Labour Party suffered a defeat which was the most catastrophic in its history.

All four Nottingham seats went to the National Government. Throughout the town and county the votes recorded for the Labour Party dropped dramatically. In South Nottingham the Labour vote fell by 4,217 and in West Nottingham Hayday saw his vote drop by 3,630. Many on the left felt betrayed, especially since Holford-Knight supported the strategy adopted by MacDonald and agreed to stand by the National Government. In September 1931 the Nottingham South Labour Party called a special meeting and gave Holford-Knight ten minutes to state his reasons for supporting the 'National Government'. In his speech which followed, Holford-Knight bitterly attacked the trade union movement, which led Alderman Halls to state that he was

> surprised at a man like Holford-Knight making an attack on the Trade Unions – the very people who had helped him in his present position ... if this was his appreciation it was time we did part company.[8]

The local elections which followed closely after the general election reflected the national trends. Labour experienced a 'crushing defeat' and were left with 15 seats against the Conservatives' 25, while the Liberals held 7 and there was one Independent. At a Labour Party meeting which followed their defeat Bowles, the local leader, explained the defeat in the following terms:

> It is a repetition of last Thursday. It was not unexpected. The times are against us and the pendulum which has now swung away from us will swing our way before we are very much older.[9]

The task of repairing the damage done to the Party by the 1931 split required a great deal more work than was anticipated by Bowles. Many members resigned in protest, as did Thomas Lynch, brother of Councillor J. Lynch, who in 1932 could not remain a member of a Party which sanctioned the means test; instead he decided to stand as an unofficial candidate in St Albans Ward.

The formation of the National Government, and the defection of prominent Labour personalities, was responsible for the public and bitter expression of the deep divisions within the labour movement. Thomas Lynch attacked the traditional elements by claiming that

> 90 per cent of the Socialist leaders of the City were businessmen misleading the masses and obtaining their money by a system which they denounced from the platform.[10]

Certainly there were several prominent manufacturers in the local Party, including Alderman Shaw a lace manufacturer and Ashworth a hosiery businessman. Significantly these men had been involved in the labour movement over many years and their integrity had never been questioned. The 1931 split in the Labour Party changed this spirit of tolerance and unity which had been maintained despite ideological differences.

At the 1932 local election the disunity and lack of trust was exhibited by the fact that candidates from the ILP, and the Communist Party stood against Labour Party nominees. In 1933 this trend continued within the ILP opposed official Labour candidates in three wards, the 'Progressive Labour' group stood candidates in two wards, and the Communist Party fielded James Wright, an asphalter, in Wollaton Ward. These socialists polled very few votes; in three wards the total vote for the ILP was 468 whilst in two wards contested by 'Progressive Labour' the vote was 579. In total the vote gained by candidates to the left of the official Labour Party amounted to a miserable 1,122.[11]

Despite these poor results for the left, the official Labour Party's fortunes seem to be reviving and they managed to regain two seats and now held 19 seats as against 25 held by the Conservatives. It is probable

USE THE CITY COUNCIL IN THE FIGHT FOR SOCIALISM.

All Power to the Workers !

CAPITALISM is breaking down—and it cannot be made to work successfully any more in Nottingham than anywhere else. That is why we have great Unemployment, increasing Poverty and Slums, the Means Test, the P.A.C. and the rapid preparations for War.

THE I.L.P. CANDIDATES (Marshall for Manvers Ward, Statham for St. Ann's, and Levy for Byron) declare that the domination of the owning and monied class must be broken, and **Workers' Power** for the **Building of Socialism** must be substituted.

This change cannot be entirely effected by **Voting alone,** but important work towards it can be done on City Councils, providing the workers send there **Determined Socialists** who intend to **put Socialism and the Needs of the People first on all issues,** and who will all the time **refuse to compromise with the Capitalists on the Council** It is not the job of Socialists to help the Capitalists to administer capitalism.

FOR THE UNEMPLOYED. We demand that the workers' contribution to Unemployment Insurance shall be abolished, and the **entire cost** of the **full maintenance** of the Unemployed shall be a **National Charge** to be met by **Direct Taxation of the Rich.**

The Iniquitous Laws and Regulations, such as the Means Test, the Anomolies Act, Test Work, etc., which now press so harshly on the Unemployed, should be **immediately** abolished.

HOUSING. We believe that large scale building of good and healthy houses for the workers should be undertaken by direct labour under public control; and that the Government should provide the necessary financial grants **free of interest.**

All working class rents should immediately be reduced to a level that the workers can afford to pay Ten per cent of the workers' income should be the maximum, as in Soviet Russia This means that a man with, say fifty shillings a week, would pay five shillings rent, and so on proportionately. One way towards making this practicable would be by **De-rating all Working-class Houses.** Re-rate the de-rated rich and de-rate the over-rated poor. Another would be by instituting a **Means Test for Moneylenders of** Council Loans, with the object of ensuring that **no interest be paid unless it could be shown to be necessary** (as it might be in the case of widows and others with no other source of income)

CHILDREN. Believing it to be wrong to pay £10,000 for useless War Memorials while there are **Children without proper boots, clothing and nourishment,** we demand **Free boots, clothing, milk and food for all necessitous children.**

WHILE URGING THE ABOVE immediate needs, the I.L.P. Candidates stand by **A FULL SOCIALIST PROGRAMME AS THE ONLY SOLUTION OF THE WORKERS' PROBLEMS.**

Hear our Plans and Programme at our Meetings. **QUESTION our SPEAKERS & HELPERS,** and come to our

BIG RALLY in the Victoria Baths on Sunday. Oct. 29th at 7 p.m., when the Candidates will be supported by prominent I.L.P. Speakers.

VOTE FOR MARSHALL IN MANVERS WARD !
VOTE FOR STATHAM IN ST. ANN'S WARD !
VOTE FOR LEVY IN BYRON WARD !

1932 ILP election address following the split between the ILP and the Labour Party

that the strong stance taken by right-wingers like Arthur Hayday was partially responsible for this shift. During the campaign Hayday was forced to answer strong questions on the means test. In reply he forcibly made the point: 'Damn their charity – I want to be powerful enough to demand our rights!'

The political split in the local movement was deepened in 1934 by a series of attacks on Bowles, the leader of the Labour Party, by Alderman Sir Albert Ball, one of the leading Conservatives. In these attacks Ball accused Bowles of being fond of 'hobnobbing' with local Conservative businessmen. This charge was seized on by the 'Progressive Labour' supporters, and Cobley and Lynch, the two leading members of this group, ridiculed the claim that Labour Party members were socialists.[12] Angered by this charge, disaffected individuals did their best to wreck the 1934 municipal election campaign of Lynch and his colleagues and meetings in Meadows Ward had to be abandoned. Conservative Party election meetings were also disrupted by unemployed militants who accused the Conservative candidates of a mean-spirited approach to the unemployed. This feeling was probably a good deal more widespread than appeared on the surface and it may well help to explain the four seats which the Labour Party gained in 1934 (three from the Conservative and one from the Liberals).[13]

The 1934 municipal election results point to the fact that the Labour Party was slowly winning back much of its traditional support. The mood amongst Labour Party activists as the decade continued gradually became more hopeful and optimistic. The 1934 local elections resulted in widespread Labour gains throughout England and Wales. In Nottingham even defeated candidates like Mr H. Lloyd announced that they were 'by no means down-hearted but full of vim for the next contest'.[14] Fund-raising continued with the Central Division's programme including regular Sunday evening meetings in the Labour Institute on Alfred Street Central. The meetings opened with community singing and *Nottingham Forward*, the Labour Party's local newspaper, announced that 'a very attractive syllabus of speakers had been arranged.'[15]

The optimistic mood of Nottingham Labour Party members continued into 1935, a year in which the local election campaign merged with a rumbustious general election contest. In the municipal struggle the Labour candidates gained two further seats, pushing the Labour Party total to 29, compared with 32 held by the Conservatives. Two weeks later, in the general election, Hayday regained his West Nottingham seat with a majority of 2,710. The Nottingham Central and Nottingham East seats were both held by the Conservatives, and in South Nottingham the

'National Labour' candidate defeated an official Labour nominee and a Liberal. Despite these disappointments, however, the Labour Party, in a steady, unspectacular way, with a gradually rising membership and a clear programme, was beginning to win back lost ground. In the 1935 general election, Labour won 154 seats, a gain of more than 100 since 1931. Told of his victory, Hayday gave as the main reasons for his success 'unemployment, the Means Test and the re-armament policy of the Government'. His Conservative opponent had a simpler explanation, simply claiming 'It was the miners' vote.'[16] There was truth in both explanations. Certainly, many miners, bitter and disillusioned with the experience of Spencerism, must have voted Labour, but of equal importance was the fact that other workers were also returning to the fold. In Wollaton Ward the 1936 annual general meeting reported nearly 500 members and in the same period Maddison, the secretary of the Labour League of Youth, speaking to the Trades Council, claimed 250 members in the town.[17]

On the face of it, political developments in 1936 contradict this analysis. After an anti-Labour press campaign which ended with the assertion that the town's 'Constitutionalists were determined to keep them out', the Labour Party suffered a major reverse in the November local elections. At the after-poll meeting in the Mechanics' Hall Labour supporters were initially reported as being 'on a wave of enthusiasm'. This rapidly subsided as each successive defeat was announced, until by the end of the evening, when it was clear that the Labour Party had suffered a net loss of one seat, a deep gloom settled on the Party activists.[18] Looking for an explanation, Coffey, the candidate in Trent Ward, claimed that 'the poorest of the poor have not played the game. They have voted against us,' whilst Arbon, the defeated candidate in Bridge Ward, complained of 'a filthy campaign — I refused to shake hands with my opponent.'[19] In fact, many of the results had been extremely close. Labour's total vote of 24,404 was more than the 23,313 registered for the Conservatives and when this fact is put alongside the Trades Council report that 'not for many years has the Council been able to report such a great addition to its affiliated membership as can be recorded for 1935-36,' [20] it is obvious that the earlier mood of optimism was fully justified.

The same points can be made about the 1937 local election results in the town. The Labour Party made gains from the Conservatives in Bridge and St Ann's Wards, but as they lost seats in Byron, Meadows and Trent Wards they again finished the campaign with a net loss of one. At the Labour Party meeting which followed the poll Bowles was given a rough reception and ran into 'considerable opposition from a small section of the audience, much of his speech being drowned by interjections'.[21] Despite this, close examination of the results reveals that the Labour Party had held its own in terms of the total vote. On this occasion 21,580 voters had supported Labour candidates against 19,799 for the Conservatives and 2,490 for the Liberals. Throughout 1938 the position remained similar in party political terms; both Labour and Conservative retained the same number of Council seats although in the November elections each party lost and gained one seat. The Labour Party fought vigorous campaigns and its overall vote increased steadily. The 1938 candidates issued an election leaflet which advocated the building of houses at low rents for the lowest paid, the introduction of nursery schools, free school milk, antenatal clinics, a maternity home and a tuberculosis sanitorium. To help the unemployed the Labour Party advocated the abolition of local authority overtime and the introduction of a maximum 2d tram fare.[22]

On the basis of the quickening recovery of the industrial and political wings of the movement it seems likely that the 1939 local elections would have seen significant Labour gains. Fred Perkins, an ILP activist, supported this view. Reflecting on the progress of the Nottingham Labour Party in the 1930s he remembered:

> They lost support at first, but they still got the class voter ... then Nottingham began to change. The slums of Nottingham were always Tory, but then people were moved out to Aspley and Arnold and as their circumstances changed, possibly they got jobs, they became Labour, not politically but in class terms, working class.[23]

In fact, because of the outbreak of the Second World War the 1939 elections never took place. Instead the Nottingham Labour Party had to wait until 1945 to come finally into its own. In the interval a metamorphosis in the thinking of millions of ordinary people took place so that even the Nottingham newspapers which had argued against the Labour Party for three decades registered no real surprise at the capture of all four Nottingham parliamentary constituencies in the 1945 general election and the subsequent achievement by Labour in the local elections of an overall majority of ten which gave them real power for the first time.[24] Undoubtedly the change from the despair invoked by the compromises of the Labour Party in the early 1930s to the positive representation of working-class interests by 1939, could not have taken place without those left-wing militants who throughout these years had worked so hard to achieve a change in working-class political consciousness.

This process of change was not an easy one, and it is a just criticism that the militants failed to develop, at either a national or a local level, a theory of socialism with which to oppose the right wing. This failure led to bitterness and recrimination which was often expressed as attacks on individual 'betrayers', rather than political attacks on the ideology and theory which such individuals represented. These mistakes should not be under-estimated, for they were in large part responsible for the divisions within the movement. Nevertheless the strength of the contribution of the militants lay in their deep commitment to socialist ideals and their determination to see them put into effect. They campaigned to make changes within the Labour Party and the trade union movement and to obtain a wider adherence to the politics they espoused.

REFERENCES

[1] *Nottingham Guardian*, 30 October 1926.
[2] Ibid., 3 November 1926.
[3] Ibid., 31 October 1927.
[4] Ibid., 2 November 1927.
[5] Election results: South Nottingham, 1929 general election:

G.W. Holford-Knight	Labour	14,800
Lord Henry Cavendish-Bentinck	Conservative	14,252
C.L. Hale	Liberal	5,445
majority 548		

[6] Election results: East Nottingham, 1929 general election:

W.N. Birkett	Liberal	14,049
L.H. Gluckstein	Conservative	11,110
J.H. Baum	Labour	9,787
majority 2,939		

[7] Robert Graves and Alan Hodge, *The Long Weekend*, 1941, p.254.
[8] Nottingham Southern Divisional Labour Party, Minutes, 13 September 1931.
[9] *Nottingham Evening Post*, 2 November 1931.
[10] Ibid., 21 October 1932.
[11] In Broxtowe Ward the 'Progressive' candidate polled 163; in Meadows Ward, J. Lynch 'Progressive Labour' 462; in Byron Ward, T. Lynch polled 54 votes. The ILP won 41 votes in Byron Ward, 391 votes in Manvers, and 36 votes in St Ann's. In Wollaton Ward a Communist Party candidate polled 75 votes.
[12] *Nottingham Evening Post*, 27 October 1934.
[13] In Meadows Ward the 'Progressive Labour' candidate polled 366 votes. This was enough to lose the Labour Party an additional seat.
[14] *Nottingham Forward*, November 1934.
[15] Ibid.
[16] *Nottingham Evening Post*, 15 November 1935.
[17] Minutes, Nottingham Trades Council, 1 April 1936.
[18] *Nottingham Evening Post*, 2 November 1936.

[19] Ibid.
[20] Nottingham Trades Council, *Annual Report*, 1936.
[21] *Nottingham Evening Post*, 2 November 1937.
[22] St Ann's Ward Labour Party, Election Address, 1938.
[23] Frederick Perkins, tape-recorded interview, 24 February 1977.
[24] *Nottingham Evening Post*, 2 November 1945.

CHAPTER FIFTEEN

Left-Wing Protest, 1931 to 1939

The time and energy of men and women on the left throughout the 1930s was increasingly dominated by international issues connected with the rise of fascism and the threat of war. For such people these issues had a parallel with growing unemployment and the strength of right-wing thinking at home. A reading of Trades Council and Labour Party minutes for the early 1930s makes it clear that, despite the efforts of left-wing theoreticians, these parallels were not generally recognised. In April 1930, for instance, the Nottingham Trades Council passed a resolution calling for Indian self-government, whilst at the same meeting rejecting a request for help from the Nottingham Hunger March reception committee.[1] Similar contradictions can be found in the resolutions passed and the lack of action proposed to back them. Late in 1931, for example, the Broxtowe Labour Party passed a resolution demanding that 'the basis of our propaganda should be the principles of Socialism versus Capitalism.'[2] What form of socialism and how it should be achieved does not appear to have been discussed.

Great frustration and disillusionment was expressed by militants faced with these contradictions. This was best seen in the deteriorating relationship between the ILP and the Labour Party. In January 1931 the Nottingham branch of the ILP had agreed to remain affiliated to the Labour Party, but by August 1931, Arthur Statham, a leading ILP member, had decided to resign his individual membership of the Labour Party because:

> I feel that the Labour Party as at present constituted and controlled, is retarding rather than forwarding that advancement towards socialism in our time to which my political energies have always been devoted.[3]

Later, this individual decision was endorsed by the ILP nationally when it agreed to disaffiliate from the Labour Party. Delighted with this decision, Statham wrote:

> I heartily endorse its decision to withdraw from the Labour Party, whose

record as a working class party has been thoroughly discredited by its reactionary and time-serving policy during its term of government and by its timidity in working for real Socialism.[4]

For socialists like Statham disillusionment with the Labour Party was one thing, but they also recognised the urgent necessity of popularising their own political views in order to provide a credible alternative to right-wing reformism. In the 1931 local election campaign the ILP had argued that:

No party could honestly hold out the promise of remedying the colossal problem of unemployment within the present system. The sooner people realized that there was no hope under existing conditions, of the three million unemployed being absorbed into industry and faced up to the need for reconstructing society on a more equitable basis, the better.[5]

It was this recognition that led the ILP to seek a Joint Council of Action on which all socialist views could be represented, including those of the Labour Party.[6] This aim was never realised, but Statham continued to argue that collaboration with groups like the Communist Party was the only way in which socialists could expand their ideas to a wider audience.[7]

The political consequences of the disaffiliation of the ILP from the Labour Party were made more serious in the context of the formation of the National Government and the debilitating effect of rising unemployment. It seriously weakened the combative spirit of the labour movement at a time when maximum unity and solidarity were called for. Reviewing the events of 1932 the Trades Council executive made the point that 'national events have had their local repercussions' before going on to state that:

Lower wages, growing unemployment, greater insecurity of employment and the general lowering of standards has produced a feeling of embittered bewilderment in the minds of working people and very often a lack of interest in anything more than their immediate well-being.[8]

This point of view was endorsed by many of the militant left wing. Cyril Goddard considered that building a revolutionary alternative to right-wing elements in the Labour Party and trade unions was extremely difficult:

When they've got you down you can't do nothing with them [the working class]. They're too poor, they've not got the spirit ... starvation doesn't make revolutionaries ... little kids with no shoes and stockings on, breeches behind out, pale sickly-looking things, they'd hardly got strength to go to school, poor little devils. Mind you, I will say this – the militants *were* militants.[9]

Goddard's point was that poverty and misery could not create a revolutionary situation. The fear of unemployment and the consequent reduction to a state of poverty already being suffered by the mass of the unemployed had the opposite effect, counteracting any revolutionary impulse. Poverty was widespread in the Nottingham of the 1930s; the Medical Officer of Health's reports for the period demonstrate widespread malnutrition, but notwithstanding a poorly-fed, housed and educated working class, the militants in the town could not hope to fundamentally change the economic and political system in the absence of any real revolutionary thinking and activity by those in control of most working-class organisations.

A great deal of energy was expended in developing an internationalist perspective within the British labour movement. This effort was in part motivated by the need to combat the anti-Communism of the national leadership of the TUC and the Labour Party, although it was also a crucial element in the militants' concept of how socialism was to be achieved. The official leadership of the labour movement stubbornly resisted internationalist approaches as well as demands for united and militant action on domestic issues, as is indicated by their failure to combat Mosley's activities and the rise of fascism in Spain. At the local level, however, an internationalism existed, as can be seen in a firm commitment to the Soviet Union. Soviet films were shown regularly in Nottingham, and the ILP celebrated the fifteenth anniversary of the Russian revolution in November 1932. Many leading activists, such as Alfred Marshall and Arthur Statham, made friendship visits to the USSR, returning home to give public speeches on a system which had proved capable of 'passing the acid test of all theories – it worked'.[10]

Support for the Soviet Union extended to the Nottingham Trades Council which, in January 1932, passed a resolution requesting a withdrawal of the Labour Party ban on the Friends of Soviet Russia society. A commitment to internationalism was also displayed by the Broxtowe Divisional Labour Party who wrote to headquarters in June 1933 urging the immediate launching of an anti-war campaign. In April Broxtowe had passed a resolution protesting at the refusal of the TUC and the Labour Party to discuss proposals with the ILP and the Communist Party for the setting up of a United Front.[11]

In January 1934, the Trades Council agreed to send their president as a representative to a conference of the British Anti-War Movement. Throughout the year the Hosiery Finishers Union, of which Jack Charlesworth, a Communist, had become president in 1930, organised a series of out-door propaganda meetings to discuss international developments, culminating in a mass meeting against fascism in September. In September the Broxtowe Divisional Labour Party passed a strongly-worded protest 'against the present Home Secretary having shares in armament firms'.[12] But not all of the movement shared these concerns, for in October 1934, the National Union of Railwaymen's Nottingham branch disaffiliated from the Trades Council because of its involvement with the Anti-War Movement which was on the Labour Party's list of proscribed organisations.[13]

The fight against fascism was a determined attack on a political ideology considered damaging to both the interests of the working class, and to world peace. It was also considered to be illustrative of the type of united political activity necessary to combat all major social and economic issues of the day. In June 1933, Arthur Statham wrote to the *New Leader* to explain this linkage:

> The ILP has got to show the apathetic masses that it has finished with the old gang whose indecision and procrastination have caused their apathy and has got to tackle the situation by emphasising the need for development of workers' democratic machinery along the lines of workers' councils so that the mass power of the workers can be forged into a weapon capable of being brought effectively against the power of capitalism. The present United Front committees may be regarded as a preliminary to the establishment of Workers' Committees.[14]

Calls for united action, and for joining the Communist Party in a 'United Front' came not only from the ILP, but also from within the Labour Party. In May 1935 the Arnold Ward of the Broxtowe Labour Party protested at the divisional decision to withdraw from 'United Front' activity. The decision was opposed by 23 votes to 7, although a Communist Party appeal for an election pact was allowed to 'lie on the table'.[15]

The major forum for those advocating a 'United Front' during the thirties was the Cosmopolitan Debating Society. The 'Cosmo', as it was affectionately known by generations of left-wingers, provided a platform for all the best speakers in the local movement. Jack Charlesworth remembered it as

> one of the most lively forces in the city. If you didn't get there early, in a room that held 400, you wouldn't get in ... I've seen that place, Sunday after Sunday, packed, people standing all round ... they had the cream of the country ... like Cohen, the free-thinker, Page Arnot, Palme Dutt, Pollitt ...[16]

Arthur Statham, writing to a friend about the possibility of organising an ILP conference, explained 'The Sunday is useless for conference purposes, as we should clash with the Cosmopolitan Debating Society which attracts an audience of upwards of 400 working class thinkers.'[17] Tom Mosley, the Gedling Colliery checkweighman who acted as the 'Cosmo' secretary from 1928 to 1958, maintained that the debating society was an important part of Nottingham's intellectual life, and throughout the 1930s it provided a unique platform for all shades of left opinion. Mosley made the point that on Sunday after Sunday

> The capitalist system was pulverised, broken into pieces and replaced by a saner and more rational mode of production, the only regret of the Cosmoites being that on Monday morning they were back in the same industrial jungle.[18]

The reality of this industrial jungle was the major factor behind the calls for united action which continued to echo throughout the decade. During 1935 many within the Broxtowe Labour Party continued to press with the Communists for the formation of a 'United Front' to include not only the Labour Party but the co-operatives and trade unions, to fight around the need for an Unemployment Bill; a programme of rearmament; resistance to the capitalist attack on the co-operatives; and the building of trade union membership. Although the evidence of this campaign demonstrates that some activists were pressing the need to rearm in the face of the threat posed by the growth of fascism, the possibility of war was not universally acknowledged. The Broxtowe Labour Party had many members with pacifist sympathies. Early in 1936 this group organised a series of meetings around the need for a 'pacifist peace policy and a war against poverty', and in June 1936 the divisional Party censured Seymour Cocks for what were described as 'flamboyant and jingoistic utterances in the House of Commons and elsewhere'.[19]

Despite growing demands for action, the national leadership and its representatives in the localities consistently ignored the rank and file, confining political struggle to constitutional campaigns in the parliamentary arena. Militants argued that after the fiasco of 1931 the Labour Party could only rehabilitate itself via a sustained and vigorous critique of the government's policy, but this was not forthcoming. Instead the leadership, through bans and proscriptions, sought to restrain local initiatives. Whilst militants argued for united action on issues such as unemployment, the TUC insisted that unemployed workers were the responsibility of the appropriate trade union. The response of the right-wing was to suggest the provision of social and sporting facilities for the unemployed, an idea considered fatuous and inappropriate by the militants. For the supporters of united action, such policies were half-hearted and ineffectual, but far worse was the fact that the TUC and Labour Party denounced all 'unofficial' attempts at united action.

The left-wing within the labour movement attempted to fill the vacuum created by the lethargy of the national leadership by propagating internationalism and by actively supporting organisations like the NUWM. The written word was also seen as a major weapon, and in this respect the Left Book Club played a significant role. In June 1937 the Nottingham branch, together with the Trades Council, established a special library for the unemployed.[20] Left-wingers, unlike the national leadership, recognised the need to recruit the working class to the fight for socialism, and propaganda was seen as crucial to this process. It was not only necessary to convert manual workers, but also their wives and daughters and indeed the entire community, if the Labour Party was to capture power with a significant majority; united action and aggressive propaganda and campaigning work were seen as essential in this struggle.

It is easy in retrospect to dismiss the left of the 1930s as a marginal influence given the strength of right-wing thinking amongst the national leadership. This impression is, however, incorrect, for the left played a crucial role in obtaining a recognition of the need for wider membership of the labour movement. This was especially so amongst trade unionists. The Nottingham Trades Council, responding to the influence of the left, commenced a vigorous recruiting campaign in 1934. They held 20 work-gate meetings and 500 personal letters were issued, leading up to a mass meeting on 18 September with a platform occupied by Mitchell, the NUR organiser, Val Coleman of the Nottinghamshire Miners, Carnell of the Paperworkers, Walter Halls from the Co-operative Society and Mrs Eddishaw of the Borough Labour Party.[21] The process of expanding membership was a protracted one, and not all unions were happy with the activities of the Trades Council and certain other trade unions. NUPE, for example, was extremely active under the dynamic leadership of Bryn Roberts, an ex-miner from Wales. Their rapid expansion of membership angered the GMWU who felt that NUPE was 'poaching' their members. Such antagonism illustrates the different political concepts of organisation, for the union hierarchy still retained a determination to preserve sectionalism through exclusivity. This criticism also applies to the more progressive unions like NUPE which attempted to control rank and file activity very closely. Fred Perkins, who had joined NUPE in 1927, discovered this quite quickly:

When they first formed a branch at the City Hospital I joined then. A chap called Bob Berry, he was a socialist, he became organiser. I tried to get the staff at Shakespeare Street Unemployment Office to join. I got about six people to attend a meeting, there was hell to pay because I'd done it ...[22]

The trade union establishment, throughout this period, exerted pressures to oppose the influence of the left. At the end of 1934 the national TUC issued the infamous 'Black Circulars'. The Nottingham Trades Council decided, by 24 votes to 14, that these circulars should not even be read. In April 1935, however, the TUC informed the Nottingham Council that they would be denied attendance at the annual conference of Trades Councils if they failed to implement these circulars. This threat persuaded the Trades Council to recommend that the circular banning communists be implemented, and this was endorsed by 29 votes to 8.[23] This decision meant that the communist vice-president, Mahoney, was forced to resign, a move which led to the resignation of the NUR No. 2 branch and a threat of similar action from the Hosiery Finishers.

The anti-communism of the TUC was not accepted by many sections of the labour movement who recognised the need for a non-sectional unity amongst the different constituents of that movement. Certainly within the Labour Party there was a determination to exclude all communist influence, as is indicated by the extent to which the Nottingham Labour Party hounded a Mr S. Atkin, a Trades Council delegate whom they suspected of being a Communist Party member. They also insisted that a joint committee between themselves and the Trades Council to organise May Day activities must only include delegates who were eligible for individual membership of the Labour Party. Despite this there were also sections of the movement that were appalled by this approach to communists. In 1936 the Broxtowe constituency passed a resolution that they viewed 'with concern the suggestion that action be taken against members of the Socialist League for public association with the ILP and CP and ask if such action be taken, it be likewise taken against Mr Walter Citrine for association with Mr Winston Churchill on the platform.'[24]

Arthur Statham claimed that in the 1930s, although

people were still fairly sectarian ... the united front effort derived a good deal of impact from the movement in France ... it did make headway for quite a few years spearheaded by the Left Book Club.[25]

This impact was perhaps best demonstrated in the activity in the town around the Spanish Civil War. The Labour Party and the Trades Council in Nottingham organised meetings and collections, as well as encouraging members to go to Spain and join the International Brigade. Many members of the Cosmopolitan Debating Society, including Eric Whalley and Bernard Winfield, were killed in action. Those who stayed at home raised funds to provide ambulances and provisions, as well as organising many workplace meetings to discuss the lessons to be learnt from the Spanish experience. In September 1937 the education committee of the local Co-operative Society sponsored the production of *Waiting for Lefty, On Guard for Spain* and *The Fall of the House of Slusher*, whilst the Broxtowe Labour Party organised a day school on the 'Menace of Fascism'.

The labour movement was clearly fragmented throughout the 1930s, and sectional interests produced a deep bitterness between the opposing wings of the movement. The established trade union and Labour Party leadership held firm to traditional methods of organisation despite the fact that they were inappropriate to the needs of a changing economic and political world. In their determination to retain political leadership they condemned any left-wing challenge to their authority, and particularly that posed by the Communists. This hindered the development of a strong, united movement which could challenge capitalism and the class forces whose interests were represented by the maintenance of the status quo. Yet the labour movement retained a militant and articulate section who appealed to the rank and file sufficiently to count many thousands amongst their supporters, and many thousands more who participated in groupings like the NUWM which received its inspiration from those militants, and this was of major importance in ensuring the survival of that movement.

The war was heralded by the wail of air-raid sirens. In a very real sense that mournful cry was representative of a dying decade. The millions of unemployed were quickly absorbed into the army or the war economy. The traumatic experience of war patently had an enormous effect in destroying the apathy and deference which had characterised the labour movement throughout the 1930s, as men and women made a critical assessment of the society that they were fighting for. The protest movements of the 1930s, and the ideas propagated by left-wing militants, were to inform and inspire such men and women, and there can be little doubt that the Labour landslide of 1945 owed much to those who had fought to obtain a militant and united labour movement throughout the difficult years of 1931 to 1939.

REFERENCES

[1] Minutes, Nottingham Trades Council, 16 April 1930.

[2] Minutes, Broxtowe Divisional Labour Party, 1931.

[3] Arthur Statham, unclassified correspondence.

[4] Arthur Statham, 'Election Address', 1931.

[5] Arthur Statham Papers, 31 October 1932.

[6] See Letter, Alfred Marshall (ILP) to Hoper (Secretary of the Nottingham Central Labour Party), 21 December 1932.

[7] See Letters, Arthur Statham to *Daily Worker*, October 1933, and, Arthur Statham to *New Leader*, 26 June 1933.

[8] Nottingham Trades Council, *Annual Report*, 1932.

[9] Cyril Goddard, tape-recorded interview, 12 January 1969.

[10] Arthur Statham Papers, 23 April 1933.

[11] Minutes, Broxtowe Divisional Labour Party, 22 April 1933.

[12] Ibid., 8 September 1934.

[13] Minutes, Nottingham Trades Council, 17 October 1934.

[14] Arthur Statham, letter to *New Leader*, 26 June 1933.

[15] Minutes, Broxtowe Divisional Labour Party, 3 May 1935.

[16] Jack Charlesworth, tape-recorded interview, 12 January 1969.

[17] Letter, Arthur Statham to Hilda Browning, 13 February 1933.

[18] T.M. Mosley, '*Cosmo*' *Memories and Personalities*, p.7.

[19] Minutes, Broxtowe Divisional Labour Party, 6 June 1936.

[20] Minutes, Nottingham Trades Council, 2 June 1937.

[21] Ibid., 18 September 1934.

[22] Frederick Perkins, tape-recorded interview, 24 February 1977.

[23] Minutes, Nottingham Trades Council, 17 April 1935.

[24] Minutes, Broxtowe Divisional Labour Party, 19 December 1936.

[25] Arthur Statham, tape-recorded interview, 11 January 1969.

Conclusion

This study of the Nottingham working class has taken as its starting date the year 1880. The decade which was to follow represented in many areas of social life an important watershed. It witnessed the return to Britain of socialist ideas – virtually absent since the decline of Chartism in the 1850s – and the establishment of small but active socialist organisations. In national terms the development and spread of socialist ideas was notably uneven as between individual towns and different occupations, and nowhere can the force of tradition be more strikingly illustrated than in Nottingham. The exclusiveness of the town's skilled workers had helped greatly to solidify the labourist tradition of political reliance upon the Liberal Party, and policies of conciliation and arbitration were at the heart of industrial relations in all the main Nottingham trades. It was the Nottingham hosiery manufacturer and Liberal politician, A.J. Mundella, who had been among the pioneers of social philosophy which argued for an accommodation between capital and labour; in his role as a political leader during the 1880s Mundella was to exercise a profound effect upon the majority of politically-active workers in the town.

It was, of course, the acceptance of the ideas of class co-operation and collaboration by leading personalities of the Nottingham trade union movement that was crucial in the political and industrial orientation of the organised working people. In the 1880s and 1890s the most important of these was William Bailey, the leading full-time official of the Nottinghamshire Miners' Association, and W.A. Appleton, the general secretary of the Lace Makers' Society. Each of these men played a major role in conserving the political traditions of the Nottingham labour movement. William Bailey, for instance, was vociferous in his antagonism to the concept of independent political representation for the working class, and was a firm supporter of Henry Broadhurst, the Lib-Lab MP for West Nottingham. While these two later argued over the question of the introduction of an eight hour day for miners, Bailey's political affiliation continued to be Lib-Labism.

The adherence to the Liberal Party continued to find strong support amongst the Nottingham working class, especially among the aristocratic lace workers. Towards the end of the nineteenth century, however, economic transformations which undermined the basis of craft exclusiveness wrought changes in the political outlook of many workers. On the one hand certain sections of the lace trade shared their employers' attitude to depression and the dangers of foreign competition, with the consequence that they became increasingly more moderate industrially and more traditional in politics. On the other hand the rise of the semi-skilled worker threatened the exclusiveness of the lace workers' position, with the result that some among them began to shift to the left. Both of these trends can be seen in the career of William Appleton, who became the general secretary of the Lace Makers' Society in 1896. Initially, Appleton remained a committed Liberal. Throughout the 1890s and into the twentieth century he did his best to obstruct the efforts of the early socialists. By 1903, however, in spite of his continued anti-socialism, he had decided to throw in his lot with MacDonald and the Labour Representation Committee. Appleton, like Bailey, remained, however, a moderate Lib-Lab. His boast to MacDonald that the miners and lace makers could between them effectively counter the efforts of the early socialists was probably true. Certainly, the alliance played an important part in slowing the advance of socialism and ensuring that large numbers of Nottingham workers remained firmly wedded to the Liberal Party until after the First World War.

Despite the efforts of Appleton the revival of socialism in Nottingham which began in the 1880s was partly due to the efforts of skilled lace and hosiery workers. The task which faced them was particularly difficult since the labourist attitudes of many miners and lace makers were similar to those of other important groups like the engineers, building workers and railwaymen. The Lib-Lab manoeuvring of Hancock, Bailey's successor as the leader of the NMA, aided and abetted by Appleton, ensured that the ILP had to wait until 1908 before Ernest Gutteridge, its leading activist, could win election as Nottingham's first genuinely socialist councillor. Despite these difficulties, however, the town's early socialists, through the medium of a very active Labour Church and the range of organisations associated with the *Clarion* newspaper, were able to draw into their activity a large number of the town's workers.

Supplementing the demand for independent working-class politics, changes in the industrial structure of the town helped the socialists to make further progress. The decline in importance of lace and hosiery to the Nottingham economy and the growth of light engineering, tobacco and pharmaceuticals, all helped to blur the dividing lines between various working-class strata, while sharpening those between workers and employers. The importance of these developments, however, was somewhat minimised by the particular nature of the Nottingham workforce with its large number of non-unionised, a-political female workers. In the period after the election of Gutteridge in 1908 the socialists made every effort to consolidate their position. Some small gains were made between 1908 and 1914 but when they are set against those registered at nearby Leicester, or in other large towns, it becomes obvious that although the Nottingham movement had its fair share of hard working, committed individuals, the difficulties which faced them were very great.

In electoral terms these difficulties, in the period before the First World War, were compounded by the boundaries of the Nottingham constituencies. These, probably by accident, achieved a mixture of social groups, and as a consequence, a working-class majority was extremely difficult to accomplish. West Nottingham had a sizeable working-class population. It contained nearly all the miners and many lace workers. The Southern Division comprised the old town centre with its business and commercial interests, together with some very poor districts in which railwaymen and lacemakers lived, as well as some miners. East Nottingham contained the heart of the lace trade, including the Lace Market. Two of its wards were substantially working-class but the division was most remarkable for a strong middle-class presence. The Nottingham constituencies then contained a variety of social groups on the electoral roll, and there was no sharp social differentiation between divisions as in some other large cities. Working-class voters were important in all three constituencies, although not in sufficient numbers to predominate. In these circumstances the Nottingham Liberals, not having a double-member constituency like their counterparts in Leicester, seem to have found it difficult to come to terms with the emerging Labour Party. Nevertheless the efforts of the committed Lib-Labs amongst the town's trade unionists avoided any permanent split between Liberalism and Labour until after the First World War.

In many ways the First World War acted as an important transitional stage between the early workers' organisations and the labour movement of the inter-war years. The vast majority of workers supported the war effort and the major upheavals which were witnessed in some other large towns did not materialize in Nottingham. The failure of the engineers in the town to produce an unofficial and articulate rank-and-file movement such as that which developed on the Clyde or in Sheffield was probably a result of a combination of factors. First the extremely strong Lib-Lab tradition must have been important, and second, the light engineering industry, based as it was largely on the making of cycles, had successfully introduced a dilution of labour well before the war broke out. Third, the very high percentage of non-union female labour must have had a weakening effect on the policies of unofficial activists, while the vigorous pro-war stance of Arthur Hayday of the General Workers, the most important trade union official in the town, helped to reinforce the attitudes of those who opposed the militants.

Equally important was the way in which the war, by strengthening the industrial side of the labour movement, altered the balance of power to the disadvantage of the ILP and the other socialist groups. The system of arbitration and governmental control of certain industries encouraged the development of industry-wide pay settlements and this in turn helped to confirm the position of the full-time trade union official, particularly in areas like Nottingham where no militant rank-and-file organisation had developed. In this period individuals like Hayday were able to enhance their status by their involvement in the national recruiting effort and the system of tribunals. Hayday capitalised on his enhanced reputation at the end of the war when he became Nottingham's first Labour Member of Parliament in the 1918 'Coupon Election'.

The years immediately after the First World War were extremely important for the developing Nottingham labour movement. The victory of a significant number of Labour candidates in the 1919 local elections indicated a change of mood among many workers. For a time it seemed that the Council of Action set up in the town might indicate a real change of direction, but in the end the left wing was effectively controlled by the official leadership. In the same period small groups of Nottingham militants came together to found the town's branch of the Communist Party. The Nottingham Communists seem to have been drawn mainly from the ranks of the unemployed and this fact helped significantly to hold back their efforts to create a viable alternative leadership to that of the Labour Party.

In general terms, however, there was no real following in the labour movement for an alternative leadership organised outside the Labour Party. This fact was well demonstrated during the 1926 General Strike when in spite of the fact that the Nottingham Communists were in many key positions of leadership, the local movement found itself outflanked by those whose apprehension made them anxious to deflect the pressure for militant action. The best Nottingham example of this process is seen in the career of George Spencer who, between 1926 and 1937, created and ran the Nottinghamshire Miners' Industrial Union as an alternative to the official union. 'Spencer's Union', as it was known, played an important role in weakening the efforts of local activists to build a united movement with which to face the consequences of the depression and mass unemployment. Nevertheless, the coal owners' support for Spencer caused a bitterness among many local workers which helped to build support for the Labour Party. In the years after the 1931 split the loyalty of Labour candidates to the NMA and their condemnation of Spencerism helped to build working-class support for the Labour Party, enabling it gradually to recapture the allegiance of many workers. The re-establishment of Labour's grip on the working-class vote took time, however, and this was probably because of political disagreements within the wider movement between Left and Right about unemployment, the Spanish Civil War, the United Front and the Popular Front.

In the difficult circumstances of the 1930s it is not surprising that the Labour Party, as the main organised political voice of the Nottingham workers, had to wait until 1945 before it could win a majority on the City Council. Nevertheless, in the period covered by this study, there had been many changes. In 1880 few working men could vote, the word 'socialist' had been almost forgotten and the unions organised barely one worker in twenty. By 1939 a transformation had taken place. Men and women voted equally and every other worker was a trade unionist. The Nottingham pioneers were at the centre of the struggle to achieve these changes. This was the real measure of their contribution to the modern movement.

Index